SOCIAL WELFARE EAST AND WEST

Social Welfare East and West
Britain and Malaysia

Edited by

JOHN DOLING
University of Birmingham, UK

ROZIAH OMAR
University of Malaya, Malaysia

LONDON AND NEW YORK

First published 2000 by Ashgate Publishing

Reissued 2018 by Routledge
2 Park Square, Milton Park, Abingdon, Oxon OX14 4RN
711 Third Avenue, New York, NY 10017, USA

Routledge is an imprint of the Taylor & Francis Group, an informa business

Copyright © John Doling and Roziah Omar 2000

All rights reserved. No part of this book may be reprinted or reproduced or utilised in any form or by any electronic, mechanical, or other means, now known or hereafter invented, including photocopying and recording, or in any information storage or retrieval system, without permission in writing from the publishers.

Notice:
Product or corporate names may be trademarks or registered trademarks, and are used only for identification and explanation without intent to infringe.

Publisher's Note
The publisher has gone to great lengths to ensure the quality of this reprint but points out that some imperfections in the original copies may be apparent.

Disclaimer
The publisher has made every effort to trace copyright holders and welcomes correspondence from those they have been unable to contact.

A Library of Congress record exists under LC control number: 00133998

ISBN 13: 978-1-138-73802-7 (hbk)
ISBN 13: 978-1-138-73799-0 (pbk)
ISBN 13: 978-1-315-18506-4 (ebk)

Contents

List of Tables		vii
Foreword		ix

1	Britain and Malaysia: the development of welfare policies *Ann Davis, John Doling, Zainal Kling*	1
2	Work and social security provision in Britain: seeking a third way *Ann Davis, Sue Wainwright*	23
3	Social security policies in Malaysia *Siti Hajar Abu Bakar, Faizah Yunus*	39
4	For richer and poorer? Pension policy in the United Kingdom *Tony Maltby*	53
5	Formal old age financial security schemes in Malaysia *Mohd. Fauzi Yaacob*	71
6	Managing a mixed economy of social care: community care in Britain *Rosemary Littlechild, Liz Ross*	85
7	Community care in Malaysia *Faizah Yunus, Siti Hajar Abu Bakar*	101
8	Britain's evolving health policies *Mike McBeth*	115
9	Getting well in Malaysia *Roziah Omar*	129
10	Housing policy in Britain *John Doling*	143

11 Public housing policy in Malaysia   157
    Mohd. Razali Agus

12 Crime and penal policy in Britain   173
    Mike Nellis, David Stephenson

13 Imprisonment in Malaysia   187
    Abdul Hadi Zakariah

List of Tables

Table 1.1	Siaroff's four welfare regimes	5
Table 1.2	Social protection measures (1995) and expenditure (1992)	7
Table 1.3	Demographic, economic and welfare indicators	8
Table 2.1	Government expenditure in real terms by function	26
Table 2.2	Benefit expenditure by recipient groups, 1999	27
Table 2.3	Men and women working, 1986 and 1998, full-time and part-time	30
Table 2.4	Unemployment rates, age 16-24, 1991-1997 (GB)	31
Table 2.5	Receipt of occupational pension and average weekly payment	32
Table 3.1	EPF and SOCSO schemes	43
Table 3.2	Malaysia: profile of labour force, 1990-2000	47
Table 4.1	Changes in employment, unemployment and economic inactivity rates, 1979-1997 (percentage points)	62
Table 4.2	Contribution to changes in employment patterns, 1979-1997 (%)	63
Table 7.1	Number of recipients of aid and expenditure by types of disability, 1995-1996	107
Table 7.2	Population size: ethnic groups, age structure: Malaysia, 1995-2000	110
Table 7.3	Malaysia: average household size and rate of household types, by stratum, 1980-1991	111
Table 7.4	Proportion of older people by age group Malaysia, 1990-2030	111
Table 7.5	Social services operating expenditure	113
Table 8.1	Age-standardised mortality rates per 100,000 people by social class, selected causes, men and women aged 35-64, England and Wales, 1976-1992	119
Table 9.1	Selected indicators for health status in Malaysia	130
Table 9.2	Health expenditure in selected Asian countries	133
Table 9.3	Development allocation for health, 1996-2000	134
Table 10.1	Housing tenure, Great Britain (%)	145
Table 11.1	Public low-income housing expenditure, 1971-2000	160

Table 11.2	Squatters by major ethnic groups in Kuala Lumpur, 1970-1992	163
Table 11.3	Sustainable low-income housing in Kuala Lumpur, 1996	165

Foreword

This book is one product of a link, stretching back over the last five-years, between the Department of Anthropology and Sociology, University of Malaya, Kuala Lumpur and the Department of Social Policy and Social Work, The University of Birmingham, UK. Supported in its first three years by British council funding, the link has involved staff visits, exchanges of reading lists and curricula, a workshop, and a number of research and publishing projects. Also, though co-incidentally to the link, the University of Malaya has established the existing Social Administration programme, formerly within Anthropology and Sociology, as a separate department.

Throughout the visits and the discussions the differences between the two countries and their welfare systems figured prominently. Even with the impact of the Asian financial crisis in 1997, the dynamic, bustling economic growth in Malaysia in which at every visit there was something new in the urban landscape to report - the Petronas twin-towers, a rapid transit system, a new capital city at Putrajaya – contrasted with Britain as one of the old industrialised countries that typically had lost much of its industry and in which public infrastructural investment had slowed to a trickle. Malaysia has highly residualised and stigmatised social welfare policies in which only education and to a lesser extent health care have wide support. As a proportion of total government expenditure social welfare spending in Britain exceeds that in Malaysia by a factor of at least two. Yet despite all the differences, the similarities have also become clearer. These go beyond the historical connections between the two countries such as the arrangements set up in Malaya during the colonial period, some of which have survived, even if in modified form. In both countries, governments have pursued low taxation, low spending objectives that impose continuing downward pressure on welfare spending and asserted the merits of privatisation. At the same time, changes to traditional sets of values about the family, and particularly the role of women - in part because of their greater involvement in the labour market - have resulted in similar tensions around who takes on responsibility for those elements of care not provided by the state.

It was such connections that stimulated the writing of this book. As a group of academic researchers, we wanted to write something that not only presented an introduction to the development in both countries of policy in a number of areas of welfare, but also identified current issues and debates. Through this we have been able to provide an understanding of ways in which social welfare provision in two countries, half a world (or at least 12 hours in a jumbo jet) away, may have similarities. Through identification of these differences and similarities we may also be able to learn from one another as well as to contribute to debates in both our countries about how to respond to globalisation and about global social policy.

Accordingly, we arranged ourselves into pairs - one Malaysian, one British - to write reviews of one of each of six areas of social welfare. Along with an opening chapter in which the aim was to identify a number of frameworks and issues that would allow the rest to be put into a context, the twelve chapters, each restricted to around 5000 words, provide a service by service account.

Writing on behalf of our colleagues, we wish to acknowledge the financial support and encouragement given to us by The British Council and our two universities. We owe a particular debt of gratitude to Sue Gilbert whose stirling efforts in formatting and proof correcting has enabled the delivery of the manuscript to the publishers much earlier than would otherwise have been the case.

We wish to dedicate the book to cross country understanding and respect.

John Doling
Roziah Omar
Kuala Lumpur, March 2000.

1 Britain and Malaysia: the development of welfare policies

ANN DAVIS
JOHN DOLING
ZAINAL KLING

Introduction

The aim of this chapter is to assist the understanding of developments in the individual elements - service sectors - of welfare policy, discussed in subsequent chapters. This is achieved, in part, by the presentation of brief, historical accounts of the broad characteristics and evolution of welfare policies in the two countries. These accounts are themselves devices that, through specific example, identify the location of Britain and Malaysia in wider frameworks encompassing all industrialised countries - both east and west. The first of these frameworks - the concept of welfare regimes - starts from the assumption that industrialised countries can be classified according to the particular type of welfare model they have developed. As an approach, it is one that emphasises difference rather than similarity and emphasises the dynamics of the political, the ideological and the cultural in shaping difference. The second framework, in contrast, emphasises the process of globalisation in establishing conditions that are common across countries and may be thought of, though not necessarily so, as leading to some convergence, or greater similarity, of welfare systems.

Whereas these two frameworks constitute distinct approaches, they are not mutually exclusive in the sense that to pursue an interest in how countries might be similar, to have similar pressures on them and to act in similar ways, does not rule out the concurrent exploration of ways in which they are different and make different decisions. In other words, for the purposes of focusing on social welfare in Britain and Malaysia we can - and should - both compare and contrast, exploring ways in which their economic paths have been accompanied by similar forces and similar responses at the same time as noting and defining aspects that set them apart both from one another and from their regional settings.

Out of this approach a number of themes are identified: the nexus of family values and the role of women that can be seen to underlie different welfare approaches in the two countries; developments in labour markets, particularly associated with high levels of unemployment; and, developments in public expenditure constraints. One dimension of the themes, particularly relevant to our study, is that politicians in both countries are increasingly faced with the same challenge: in short, deciding what sort of welfare state is compatible with the objective of enhancing national economic competitiveness.

Welfare regimes

Methodologically consistent with the Weberian notion of ideal types, welfare regimes are caricatures of approaches to welfare, providing one- or two-sided templates against which actual welfare states can be compared and contrasted. They are not descriptions but abstractions; and they are not right or wrong but merely more or less useful for the purpose in hand. Having a relatively long pedigree, this approach received a considerable fillip with the publication by Gosta Esping-Andersen of his work related to a sample of western nations (Esping-Andersen, 1990). The basis of his typology was the nature of class conflict in western, industrialised countries and the resolutions that determined the extent to which access to welfare goods was separated from labour market position. His concept of de-commodification thus included the extent to which welfare states provided socially acceptable standards of living independently of participation in economic activity, on the eligibility criteria and on levels of benefits or provision. It can, therefore, be seen, as Bonoli (1997) points out, to incorporate elements of both the scale and the nature of state intervention. On this basis Esping-Andersen proposed three, distinct regimes. Liberal regimes, of which the US could be viewed as the archetypal case, take a minimalist position, providing welfare as a last resort, in the event of the failure of markets to provide, generally means-tested and to a minimum level. In conservative-corporatist regimes - West Germany being archetypal - there is no great attempt to modify status differentials, welfare being typically delivered through or in relation to occupations; the family and the Church are key elements in welfare provision. Finally, social democratic regimes - here, Sweden is archetypal - are based on broad consensus across social classes, with universalist principles aimed at achieving high levels of de-commodification and equality; here, the state is the first, not the last, resort.

How does this typology help in the identification of the principal characteristics of welfare policies in the new industrialised countries of south and East Asia? In fact, not only has it been recognised that Esping-Andersen's three worlds are insufficient to encompass the full range of regimes in western countries, with the case being made in particular for a fourth category relevant to Mediterranean Europe, the Latin rim (Leibfried, 1993), but also that the eastern industrialised countries - Japan and the newly industrialised societies of south and east Asia - constitute quite a different case to any of them. (Gould, 1993; Jones, 1993; Kwon, 1997).

Whereas from the perspective of the west these economies have sometimes been thought of as examples of rampant capitalism they do not match Esping-Andersen's liberal type in that they are characterised by high levels of central direction and low levels of individual rights (Jones, 1993). The absence of any developed sense of individual rights or equity also rules out a social democratic model, with the nearest model appearing to be the conservative-corporatist. But, such comparisons miss the fundamental point: the Esping-Andersen typology is based on historical resolutions in Europe that have no direct parallels in the very different historical circumstances of south and east Asia (Kwon, 1997). A specific difference is that, unlike European corporatism - that particularly underlay the Bismarkian social programmes in Germany - social policies in the Asian industrialised economies have generally not been introduced against a background of threats from the working class (Kwon, 1997). Rather they can be viewed as a reflection of the perception of what has been necessary in order to ensure economic growth. The political strategy, in other words, was driven, pragmatically, by considerations of what policies, with respect to welfare, were deemed most appropriate for achieving increased national prosperity. This was carried out against the background, in many Asian countries, of Confucianism in which it is the group - the family, the firm and the nation - which takes precedence over the interests of the individual. Such systems are highly structured such that duty is owed upwards and responsibility down, the family is the basic building block of a grand, national corporation which is characterised by authoritarianism, the incorporation and neutralising of opposition, and subservience to the needs of the whole with the result that welfare policy 'has been more strongly shaped by the developmental priorities of politically insulated states than by extra-bureaucratic political forces' (Deyo, 1992, p.304). In general this has meant that the de-commodification of welfare has not been greatly pursued so that social expenditures have been restricted in order that the 'primary goal of national policy' (Ku, 1995, p.360) would not be starved of the necessary resources.

Family, Gender and Welfare Regimes

In his work Esping-Andersen draws attention to the importance of taking 'into account how state activities are interlocked with the market's and the family's role in social provision' (Esping-Andersen, 1990, p.21). Feminist scholars have demonstrated that critical to developing an analysis of the part that the family plays, and is expected by the state to play, in welfare provision is a consideration of the role and needs of women.

In contributing to the development of comparative perspectives, feminists studying welfare regimes (for example, Lewis, 1993; Orloff, 1993; Sainsbury, 1994; Pascall, 1997) have highlighted the limited potential of the Esping-Andersen formulation (including the incorporation of the Asian variant) for analysing the role of the family and of women. They have argued that the class redistribution focus of Esping-Andersen's approach cannot fully accommodate the necessary comparative examination of the contribution of both unpaid and paid labour to welfare states and welfare provision.

From this literature, to date there are two formulations that have attempted to build critically on Esping-Andersen's work. Orloff (1993) has developed a framework that she suggests should be used to compare welfare states in order to accommodate an analysis of the contribution of women and the family. The framework comprises five criteria: the way in which state-market-family relations deliver patterns of social provision; an approach to stratification which embraces the impact of state provision on gender relations, including the treatment of unpaid and paid labour; an examination of social citizenship in order to identify the differential effects of benefits on men and women; differential access to paid work; and, the capacity which exists to form and maintain an autonomous household.

Siaroff's approach (Siaroff, 1994) has taken as its starting point the ways in which OECD welfare states are meeting women's needs. She uses three criteria to measure, on a scale of 1-3, the extent to which each regime meets fully or partly the needs of women: the family orientation of policy; the ease with which women can work on equal terms with men; and, the parent who receives benefits for the children. Her work has generated a cluster of four regimes. Three fit Esping-Andersen's formulation and the fourth 'late female mobilisation welfare states' is used to identify welfare regimes which neither encourage women's work nor support women's caring (see Table 1.1).

Table 1.1 Siaroff's four welfare regimes

Welfare Regime Type	Typical country	Extent of meeting women's needs
Liberalism	USA Australia	2
Conservatism	Germany France	2
Social democratic	Sweden Denmark	3
Late female mobilisation	Japan Spain	0

Source: adapted from Deacon et al. (1997)

The potential contribution of these two approaches to the development of comparative analyses is as frameworks to facilitate the exploration of the ways in which the family, in its various formations, contributes to welfare provision. In focusing on the family in this way the gendered divisions of paid and unpaid labour as well as family responsibilities become key characteristics of welfare regimes.

In considering the current situations of Malaysia and Britain the adoption of such approaches need to be considered with some caution with regard to the context of contrasting historical, social and cultural understandings of family, state and gender. Yet even with this caveat, they may have a potential to provide an initial orientation to the meanings which welfare regimes attach to family life and associated gender relationships. Such an orientation is particularly relevant to societies which in responding to economic and social change are faced with intended and unintended consequences for family formations and values. Of particular relevance here are the ways in which changes in the labour market and in levels of public welfare expenditure impact on women and the family and the relationship between men and women as workers, citizens and family members.

The Foundations of Welfare Policies in the Two Countries

In this section the origins and underlying philosophies of the welfare systems in Britain and Malaysia are presented. Whereas there were common elements, for example deriving from their colonial relationship, it begins by emphasising their different approaches.

It could be argued that in the early post war years Britain's welfare policies developed elements of all three of the Esping-Andersen regimes - a mix of minimalist, means-tested benefits and universal benefits, some benefits tied to occupation, and the nuclear family, with particular welfare roles expected of women, underpinning the system. The Malaysian case, in contrast, can be usefully depicted in relation to a regime type in which the development of welfare has been greatly influenced in ways seen by governments to be functional to the needs of an economy growing rapidly to achieve the status of an advanced industrialised country. In short, it broadly conforms to the model characteristic of the newly industrialised countries of south and East Asia.

The contrast can be seen, even decades later, in data describing the nature and scale of social policies. Britain is representative of a western tradition in which a wide range of social protection measures consumes a large (between a quarter and a half) of all government spending, with Malaysia typical of a lower spending, eastern tradition (Table 1.2). This contrast is maintained in health care spending, but in education spending the positions are reversed: by western standards the Asian economies have invested heavily in the development of human capital as a fundamental part of their strategy to achieve rapid economic growth (Table 1.3). On this view, then, Britain and Malaysia are not at different stages in social welfare development but are representative of fundamentally different approaches.

Table 1.2 Social protection measures (1995) and expenditure (1992)

	Old age, invalidity, death	Sickness and maternity benefit	Work injury	Unemployment	Family	Social protection expend. as % all government expend.
Hong Kong	*	*	*	*	*	-
Japan	*	*	*	*	*	36.7
Malaysia	*		*			5.6
Singapore	*		*			2.0
S. Korea	*		*			8.1
Taiwan	*	*	*			13.8
France	*	*	*	*	*	34.2
Germany	*	*	*	*	*	46.5
Netherlands	*	*	*	*	*	33.6
Portugal	*	*	*	*	*	27.3
Spain	*	*	*	*	*	36.7
Sweden	*	*	*	*	*	46.4
UK	*	*	*	*	*	29.6
USA	*		*			22.2

Source: Encyclopaedia Britannica Yearbook

Britain The Beveridge report and Keynesian economics - products of Liberal Collectivism - were the foundations on which the welfare state was established in post war Britain (Ginsberg, 1992). Beveridge argued that the State should extend its responsibilities in order to offer protection to citizens against social need in all its forms. It was a model much influenced by the way in which the British war time government had mobilised the nation, relying on direct state provision of benefits and services with little emphasis on contributions from voluntary and private commercial organisations (Dunleavy, 1989). From 1946-1948 a range of state agencies was established. Funded from general taxation, they included: a national health service, free at the point of delivery; a state education system for all 5-15 year olds; a national state funded insurance and assistance scheme for those who were old, unemployed, disabled or sick; public housing; and local authority health and welfare provision for children, families and older and disabled adults in need of support and protection.

Social Welfare East and West

Table 1.3 Demographic, economic and welfare indicators

Country	Population (mills) 1995 (1)	Largest city as % total pop.1995 (2)	% urbanisation 1995 (3)	GNP per capita 1993-4 (4)	Unemployment % 1993-4 (5)	Health as % all govt expend. 1992 (6)	Education as % all govt expend 1992 (7)
Hong Kong	6.2	95.0	95.0	17060*	2.0	11.1	17.1
Japan	125.3	21.5	77.6	37560	2.9	1.5	6.3
Malaysia	20.0	6.2	53.7	3160	3.6	5.9	19.6
Singapore	3.0	100.0	100.0	19310	2.7	6.1	22.3
S. Korea	44.8	25.9	81.3	7670	2.8	-	15.5
Taiwan	21.3	-	-	11629	1.6	-	18.8
France	58.1	16.3	72.8	22760	12.4	15.5	7.0
Germany	81.9	7.9	86.6	23630	8.7	16.8	-
Netherlands	15.5	7.2	89.0	20710	7.5	13.6	10.8
Portugal	9.9	19.0	35.6	7890	5.2	9.0	12.4
Spain	39.2	10/3	76.5	14230	16.6	6.3	4.4
Sweden	-	17.6	83.1	24830	8.2	-	9.3
UK	55.5	12.6	89.5	17920	10.2	14.0	3.3
USA	263.0	6.2	76.2	25850	6.1	16.0	1.8

Sources: (1)(4)(5) Encyclopaedia Britannica, Yearbook (1996)
(2)(3) UN Statistical Yearbook (1993)
(6)(7) IMF Government Finance Statistics Yearbook (1996)
* = GDP

The welfare state created in Britain at this time was celebrated by a leading social policy academic as adding a social dimension to civil and political citizenship (Marshall, 1950). Through its commitment to meet basic social needs it provided a guarantee of social rights. As Alcock summarises it: 'The welfare state of the post war period appeared to be the embodiment of social citizenship and to have created the basic framework for a new role for the state as the provider of social services' (Alcock, 1996, p.8).

The welfare state was embedded in, and seen to be contributing to, a Keynesian approach to the management of the economy, an approach which was directed at achieving levels of employment, economic growth and stability that would generate the resources required for welfare state provision. But, it was also embedded in a set of assumptions about gender divisions in which the role of men was as labour in the formal workplace and the role of women was as wife, mother and carer undertaking unpaid labour within the home and nuclear family. Moreover, entitlement of many of the benefits came through the husband rather than by the wife in her own right (Williams, 1989).

With modifications over time, these arrangements attracted widespread political and public support. Through successive Conservative administrations in the 1950s the Welfare State established itself as an essential element of government activity. During the 1960s both Labour and Conservative administrations continued to increase investment in welfare state services. However, though the numbers of people employed in such services grew by a third during that period, the level of investment never rose, as a proportion of Gross Domestic Product, beyond the OECD average.

Malaysia The present-day welfare services in Malaysia are the product of the immediate post-war co-operative efforts by government and various voluntary organisations to relieve hardships and distress. Since there was no traditional system upon which the British Administration in Malaya could rely, to a considerable extent the services were based on the ideas of the British welfare system. Although not much has been written on the early history, it is nevertheless clear that the provision of welfare services was not a universal effort, covering the larger population as characteristic of at least some elements of the British system. Even later, when the Federation of Malaya was established, welfare arrangements continued to be very selective, largely confined to the groups generally categorised as the 'needy', and 'those in need of special help if they were to lead normal, happy lives' (Jones, 1958, p.iii). It did not approach the ideal of the embodiment of social citizenship nor a Keynesian approach to the management of the economy.

From the very beginning, then, social services were regarded as additional burdens on government finances with the problem being of 'how to equate expenditure on development in the six years 1950-1955 with the limited amount of revenue which may be available for the purpose' (Malaya, 1950, p.2). Indeed, the conclusion of the Draft Development Plan was even more pessimistic in the possibility of expanding the general social services in the country even at a minimum level: 'The general conclusion is, therefore, that apart from whatever may be provided by the Colonial Development and Welfare Fund, very little capital will be available for expansion of the social services, unless cuts are made in present recurrent expenditure, or revenue is increased' (Malaya, 1950, p.3).

During the post-merdeka (independence) period - 1957-1970 - the principles underlying social policy were never fully spelled out by the government except to continue with the existing model. Gradually there has developed a greater awareness of the need for human development and for the welfare agency to be more developmental in approach rather than merely distributive. Since then much of public policy has been formulated within the parameters of the New Economic Policy with its two-prong objectives: restructuring society and eradication of poverty. The principle of growth with equitable distribution became the catch phrase of the subsequent five-year development plans. The major challenge was seen as that of achieving a modern society and the attendant complex and stressful results of rapid socio-economic development. Broadly, its goal statement was for a secure and stable society for the nation's progress.

Whereas the overall target of the policy statement is,'towards all levels of society, particular groups - those special groups generally categorised as the weak, the needy and those exposed to moral danger - are clearly identified. Thus the target groups include children, adolescent delinquents, the disabled, those in poverty, women, the elderly, terminally-ill patients, families, ethnic minority groups, drug addicts and disaster victims. The spectrum of people seems to cover the majority of the population yet the coverage is actually quite limited. Moreover, the system of social security in the form of the Employees Provident Fund does not cover a large population of rural dwellers whose income level is far below those of the urban centres who benefit from the EPF. Likewise, the establishment of the National Social Security Organisation (SOCSO) only demands contribution from those in the labour market but not the self-employed who do not have any form of social security safety net in case of experiencing health, income loss or accidental problems. The single major exception has been in the development of an education system in which considerable amounts of the national budget have been devoted to the provision of schools, the state funding of students in universities in the economically advanced countries and the provision of tax relief against school and university costs

Notwithstanding the limits of the formal provisions for welfare - in terms of both the size of the national budget allocation and the coverage of the population - there is an important informal dimension to the Malaysian system. In common with other economies in South and East Asia there are strong and pervasive culturo-religious forces underlying the welfare of the population. In the case of the Chinese community, that constitute the second largest ethnic group, Confucianism has supported the role of the family as the basic organising unit and the responsibility of the individual within the family and group network. For the Malay majority, Islam has provided the basis of welfare support through the church and through the family. Thus, for both groups the extended family system has meant that adult children have taken major responsibility for the well being of their parents in older age, while there is a strong expectation on all adults to contribute economically. In part the contrast with the welfare systems in western countries is therefore to be found in different understandings of the appropriate role of the state, the family and the individual.

Globalisation

Notwithstanding the differences in the ideologies underpinning and in the outcomes resulting from welfare systems in different countries, there is a view, gaining increasing support, that global processes are resulting in some lessening of differences (see Deacon, 1997). The argument is, broadly, that the welfare systems developed up until the mid 1970s (later in some countries) were the products of national economies that were themselves relatively closed. With financial systems heavily regulated by individual, national, central banks, national governments were free to act with considerable autonomy in setting interest rates, inflation targets, taxation rates and so on. Transport costs and market protection enabled them also to impose their own national rules including taxation and social costs on manufacturing capital. The globalisation thesis, already developed in the 1980s but extended in the 1990s, was based on observations that national economies were becoming increasingly open. The deregulation and internationalisation of financial markets and the increasing ability of manufacturing capital to switch production sites from one part of the globe to another transformed this. World-wide markets for standardised products were developing offering opportunities for economies of scale, and a new international division of labour was developing in which many areas of mass production were switched to low wage, low social cost countries (Frobel et al, 1980; Levett, 1983). All this has meant that national governments can no longer act without consideration of the consequences for the flight of capital, whilst also having to recognise challenges that had not been significant in their earlier and longer periods of economic growth. Two of these challenges - labour market and public expenditure developments - are examined in the next section.

New Labour Markets

The new world has also been characterised by new technologies that have not only resulted in over capacity in many manufacturing sectors, but also a replacement of labour with machinery and IT. One result has been a change in the demand for labour. In the earlier post war decades the major European economies experienced labour shortages leading them to encourage the immigration of cheap labour: Turks into Germany, North Africans into France and West Indians and Indians/Pakistanis into the UK. In the countries of South and East Asia there have been similar in-migrations; in the case of Malaysia there has been large-scale migration from Thailand, Indonesia and Bangladesh, in particular. At different levels and different times western economies have, since the 1970s, experienced high rates of de-industrialisation as their traditional industries have closed, contracted or switched their production sites to other countries - in many cases to the newly industrialised economies of south and east Asia. Unemployment has risen to historically high levels - varying from time to time, and from country to country - to as much as 15 per cent or more, and, in parts of some urban areas being as high as 50 per cent or more. Economic changes in Malaysia are also affecting the number of jobs. This is part of a wider, global problem: recent estimates by the ILO indicate that across the world as a whole one billion people are unemployed or underemployed, with the financial difficulties in south and east Asian economies adding a further 10 million in 1998 alone (ILO, 1998).

The higher levels of unemployment pose a series of direct challenges to national governments. Firstly, unemployed groups may place demands on governments for assistance, in money or in kind, to enable them to purchase goods and services - food, clothes, housing and so on - that formerly they purchased out of income. So, there may be immediate demands on the public purse to compensate people for the failures of the labour market. Secondly, some welfare benefits - such as health care and pensions - may be dependent on employment in the sense that contributions are related to incomes. Clearly, where there is no employment and thus no income there may be no contribution. Whether the contribution would normally accrue to a national pot or an individual one, the long-term outcome - insufficient money in the pot to meet later demands - may be the same. A general problem facing national governments, therefore, is how to meet the costs of welfare for the large numbers of people without their own means.

Not only is the total demand for labour insufficient to provide jobs for all those living in industrialised countries who would wish to be economically active, but the nature of the jobs that are available is also changing. Atkinson and Meager (1986) argue that new technical and production systems have forced firms to adopt new labour strategies. These strategies can be summed up as the development of the flexible firm in which the labour force can be divided into core (well-paid, full-time and permanent positions) and peripheral (part-time, contract and temporary) workers. In western economies the tendency has been for core workforces to shrink (leading particularly to male unemployment) and for peripheral workforces to grow (leading particularly to more jobs for women). This changing gender division of labour has potential implications for the nature of welfare policies insofar as these were predicated upon assumptions about who would earn and who would care. In addition, as jobs become more precarious - that is more likely that workers will be in them for shorter periods of time - the more likely it is that they will not be able to contribute regularly to private or public forms of insurance. Flexible labour markets, part of what Beck (1992) has termed the 'risk society', thus both increase the importance to individuals of some form of safety net, but it may make them less able themselves to contribute to the creation of the safety net.

Public Expenditure Constraints

This problem is not simply one of people without incomes from the labour market placing demands on government, but their lack of income also means that national governments cannot derive income tax from them. So, governments may be hit not only by increased demand but also lower tax revenues. In fact this can be seen as part of a more general problem faced by the older industrialised countries: by the early 1970s the development of capitalism had been such that industrialised countries were experiencing increases in welfare expenditures that were rising faster than increases in state income (O'Connor, 1973). The so-called 'fiscal crisis of the state' not only described the increasing difficulty of governments in meeting demands for social expenditure but also the perception of such expenditure as not so much investing in human capital or meeting social commitments as squeezing the productive, private part of the economy. State expenditures, particularly on social goods, came to be seen as a burden on the restructuring of capital necessary for further capital accumulation (Pierson, 1991). This meant that the issue came to go beyond that of how much each country thinks its fiscal position justifies its spending on social goods to the perception of the impact of the nature and amount of social spending on national competitiveness, summarised by the title of one book as 'Can the Welfare State Compete?' (Pfaller et al, 1991).

In fact, not only can western welfare states be seen to have taken a variety of forms - or regime types - but they have also pursued a range of approaches to this issue. Esping-Andersen (1996) has argued that amongst western countries it is possible to 'identify three distinct welfare state responses' (1996, p.10): the Scandinavian; the labour reduction; and the neo liberal routes.

The Scandinavian route describes those social democratic countries, Sweden being the archetypal case, in which the welfare state project was founded on a commitment to both 'maximizing employment and equalizing the status of women' (1996, p.11). Given the decline in manufacturing employment this has been pursued by expanding public sector jobs. But, in recent years the fiscal burden imposed has, with the exception of Norway benefiting from oil revenues, led to increasing levels of unemployment and pressures to trim benefits.

The labour reduction route pursued in many of the countries of mainland Europe - Germany, France, the Netherlands, and Italy - has encouraged early retirement. The productivity gains deriving from reduced numbers in the workforce has however been achieved at the expense of high levels of unemployment amongst the elderly but also the young who find it difficult to break into the labour market. Whereas the incomes of those in work, and their occupational benefits, are maintained this is at the expense of later entry into the formal labour market - delayed by an extensive educational requirement and an increase in black economy and self employment jobs - and earlier exit. In short there is here an 'insider-outsider' divide.

The neo liberal route, adopted in the US, Britain and New Zealand in particular, is characterised by policies designed 'to manage economic decline and domestic unemployment with greater labour market and wage flexibility' (Esping-Anderson, 1996, p.15), achieved by relaxing labour protection, including minimum wage, legislation. This approach has also involved, as (Pfaller et al, 1991, p.252) point out, a commitment to reducing 'onerous burdens of various kinds' on industry and higher income individuals which in turn has created downward pressure on social spending. Whereas, overall, this route has resulted in a widening distribution of income, it has nevertheless, to date, been the most successful in creating jobs. In these countries, therefore, unemployment rates are generally lowest though many of those in work receive low incomes and a reduced social wage.

In Malaysia and the other newly industrialised Asian countries, the economic developments have taken a somewhat different course with crisis coming far later. Throughout the 1970s and 1980s, and indeed much of the 90s, their economies expanded rapidly, in general more so than in the west. Not only did full employment continue longer, but social goods were more limited and governments have been able to maintain a stable basis for capital accumulation. In the last three years, however, this has changed with economic crisis across the Asian region bringing to them policy dilemmas, some similar to those faced earlier in the West.

Searching for New Directions

In this section the responses of the British and Malaysian governments to the new challenges presented by the processes outlined above are considered.

Britain As elsewhere, the growing economic difficulties in Britain in the late 1960s and early 1970s led to a questioning of the size, direction and purpose of social policy and welfare state provision. In 1972, with unemployment affecting 1 million people for the first time since the 1930s, the consequences of the economic problems and decline in Britain's manufacturing industries, was also becoming increasingly visible. The government found itself battling with inflation and increases in world oil prices. This situation fuelled debate about the long-standing consensus around the management of the economy and social welfare. As Deakin summarised it:

> The 1974 Labour government faced major difficulties - a rapidly rising rate of unemployment and inflation on the verge of getting out of control - with the additional anxiety that the tools that had once provided reliable means of addressing these problems had proved fallible (Deakin, 1994, p.53).

In such a climate social welfare was increasingly viewed as part of the problem rather than a solution to the social problems generated by a distressed economic order. These views were expressed from the left as well as the right of the political spectrum, but it was the re-emergence of critiques of the Welfare State from the latter, which, in focusing on the failure of economic policy, opened up questions about purpose and outcomes of thirty years or more of growing state investment in welfare. These provided an opportunity for a new liberalism to emerge and achieve prominence in academic and political debates. Not only did the growing costs of public expenditure interfere with the effective workings of market economies, but also high taxes were reducing profits, crippling investment and driving capital overseas. What was more, the supply of welfare services was said to encourage feckless and dependent citizens with no incentive to work, save and choose how they would meet their social needs. Public sector services were thus viewed as an intolerable financial burden and morally corrupting.

1979 saw Margaret Thatcher returned as prime minister and a major objective set by government to reduce public expenditure because it was seen to be 'at the heart of Britain's present economic difficulties' (Her Majesty's Government, 1979, p.1). A framework for welfare change was set. For nineteen years there were discernible shifts in the way welfare provision was viewed and, in some areas, delivered. Britain experienced a move from a Liberal Collectivist consensus towards a neo liberal position more akin to the United States.

In promoting and responding to these concerns governments stressed the need to eliminate waste and inefficiency from public sector welfare services. The means identified to do this were more targeting of limited resources on those most in need; deregulation of state dominated provision; and exhorting families to be more responsible for providing for the welfare of their members. Three distinct but linked shifts in the manner in which welfare was delivered can be identified. Firstly, a move towards more efficient management of welfare, setting standards and requirements that public funds should be seen to be used to achieve effective outcomes. Secondly, the alteration of the relationship between recipients of welfare and the state. This was achieved through the introduction of market principles to areas of welfare provision, for example introducing internal markets to health and social services, as well as by breaking up previous state monopolies by extending the range of providers of welfare provision beyond state services to the independent and for profit sectors. Thirdly, an attempt to change the basic attitudes of citizens towards the role of state welfare provision. Critical, was seen to be the restoration of a sense of personal responsibility for meeting social need. State welfare provision was increasingly described as engendering dependency and a return to traditional family values was promoted as the way towards independence.

The gender dimension of a third of these has been significant in that it constitutes an increase in the expectations placed particularly on those groups, mainly women, who have traditionally been the (unpaid) carers. Not only has this been happening as the traditional nuclear family as a social unit has been declining relative to other configurations, but also as women have been increasing their participation in the formal (paid) economy. In fact, changes in the labour market over this period have generally been both large and significant for social policy. Britain can be seen as having pursued Esping-Andersen's neo liberal route in aiming for greater labour market flexibility. This has involved a weakening of the rights of trades unions, the abolition of minimum wages and the eroding of redundancy rights. Whatever has been the impact of these changes on developments in capital accumulation, they have not brought unemployment down to levels experienced in the earlier post war period, running throughout the whole of the 80s and 90s in excess of 2 million and sometimes over 3 million. But there has also been a shift away from high paid, permanent jobs particularly in manufacturing and particularly taken by men, toward low paid, part-time and temporary jobs particularly in the services and particularly taken by women.

Yet, despite the political rhetoric of this period, these shifts were not achieved in a context of a cut in public expenditure on welfare provision. Notwithstanding changes to the management, provision and delivery of welfare the levels of public investment on social policy programmes remained, with the exception of housing provision, broadly stable (Glennerster and Hills, 1998). Overall, public expenditure and social policy has been restructured rather than cut, but cut in ways which, to use Mishra's phrase, 'exalts the economic and downgrades the social' (Mishra, 1998, p.485). In practice this has meant that the central objective of securing full employment and full consumption, that characterised the post war welfare state, is giving way, under the onslaught of neo liberal reforms, to the promotion of competitiveness in which social needs are subordinated to the needs of labour flexibility. This shift with its linking of welfare provision to responsibilities on the individual to secure their needs through work has been caricaturised as a shift from 'welfare' to 'workfare' (Jessop, 1996). In some ways it can be seen as a new relationship between the individual, the family and the state which has resonances with that prevalent in the newly industrialised countries of South and East Asia.

Malaysia In the early phase of national development, the general policy was aimed at achieving economic growth whilst, at the same time, raising the socio-economic status of the lower income groups. It was recognised that great poverty existed in rural areas but despite government action over a decade there was very little result that could be called a common prosperity for both rural and urban areas. The industrial policy of import substitution most directly impacted on urban areas. Thus began the large-scale rural-urban drift and the unplanned urbanisation through the build-up of migrant settlements around the fringe of urban centres. They eventually created the pockets of urban poverty which resulted in the growth of a dissatisfied population, finally causing the Kuala Lumpur racial riot of 1959. The riot and ensuing emergency situation forced the government to re-examine the national development policies and to set the stage for a more radical approach to development - the complete recognition of the need not only to alleviate poverty, but more importantly to restructure society so that economic status was not identifiable with ethnic identity.

Slowly, rural life was almost totally transformed into a source of cheap labour for urban-based manufacturing. The economy was further developed through direct foreign investment particularly in the electronic and consumer goods and home appliances. To this extent the development strategies encouraged the emergence of a consumer economy and the commodification of socio-cultural goods and services. The development of export oriented industries received a further boost with increased internal investment. The national car and steel plants were started and supported by an expansion of power generation, telecommunication and transport systems. By the early 1990s Malaysia's success in world markets with growth rates of 7 per cent and more per annum was contributing to an Asian miracle akin to those associated with the four little Tigers.

The market was certainly captivating the policy makers into further and in-depth involvement in the market system. The coming of 'hot money' - the short term investment funds - into the share markets only added to the great confidence of the policy makers that the presence of foreign investors is an attestation of the correctness of development policies and of the country's economic capability and robustness. This turned out to be false confidence when the Thai economic fallout in July 1997 quickly affected the entire region.

In some of the worst affected countries - specifically Korea, Thailand and Indonesia - IMF loan finance has been accepted in order to effect short and long term adjustments particularly in finance sectors. Malaysia, for its part, has acted independently of the IMF and its conditions, but has nevertheless pursued many similar policies. These have included curbs on public expenditure and investments. Also in common with them, real wage increases have slowed (if not fallen) and the demand for labour slumped. In some very general respects, therefore, - in the coming to an end of a sustained period of economic growth and stability - Malaysia faced some problems that bore comparison with those experienced some quarter of a century earlier in western industrialised countries. One of the major differences has been that Malaysia has been able to send some of the foreign workers, who had come to meet the demand for labour in Malaysia's expanding industrial and service sectors, back to their country of origin, thus effectively exporting some of its unemployment.

Conclusions

Over the period from the end of the Second World War to the mid-1970s, then, the general pattern in western industrialised countries was an experience of steady economic growth. Starting later and continuing until the mid-1990s, growth, though rather faster, was a feature of a number of the south east Asian economies. During these periods, governments were able to develop their social policy systems in contexts in which they were able to exercise considerable control over many aspects of their economies. Not only could they influence the main economic variables - interest rates, unemployment, investment, industrial structure - but with the year-on-year increases in wealth these could be directed toward social goals, whilst many of the impacts of social expenditure could be limited to the domestic stage. Thus decisions about whether or not to increase social security payments or expenditure on health care could largely be taken against the backcloth of internal considerations alone. The influences on these internal considerations included ideology and cultural values and norms which, differing from country to country, resulted in welfare systems of varying types or regimes. In many ways those of Britain and Malaysia have been very different. Britain, a relatively high spending, western regime with a mix of safety net and universalist programmes; and

Malaysia reflecting an Asian tradition of low spending, largely minimalist programmes, based on a major role for the family and supporting the needs of economic growth.

The ending of the Golden Ages, however, has given way to new scenarios in which governments, both east and west, have been forced to confront situations where both economic and social policy issues have been increasingly determined externally. As national economies have become less closed not only have governments had to manage their economies against a background of global processes, but those processes have both contributed to the creation of new social problems and ensured that governments have more limited ability to address them.

These different types of strategy with respect to globalisation have had different effects on national labour markets and patterns of work. One significant division is between the low wage, flexible workforce/low unemployment economy currently resulting from the neo liberal route and the high wage/high unemployment economy of the other routes. Whereas, this issue has been central to the strategic deliberations of western governments, it has more recently been thrust upon Asian ones. Thus, the economic difficulties facing Malaysia, and some other Asian economies, over the last three years, have led to challenges for them, similar to those faced in the West: new, that is additional, demands on social expenditure at the same time as considerations of economic restructuring. A fundamental issue is the future of social welfare in the context of globalisation. With financial deregulation, with capital able to re-locate in (for them) more favourable locations, the pursuit of national economic competitiveness may be perceived by governments as incompatible with increased social expenditure.

In the chapters that follow this, each of which outlines developments in a specific area of social welfare in either Britain or Malaysia, the significance of the new challenges - unemployment and public expenditure constraints - as well as the continuation of the distinctiveness of national family values, on the perception of social problems and solutions will be examined.

References

Alcock, P. (1996), *Social Policy in Britain: Themes and Issues*, Macmillan, Basingstoke.

Atkinson, J. and Meager, N. (1986), *New Forms of Work Organisation*, Institute of Manpower Studies, Report No. 12, London.

Beck, U. (1992), *The Risk Society: Towards a New Modernity*, Sage, London.
Bonoli, G. (1997), 'Classifying Welfare States: a Two-dimension Approach', *Journal of Social Policy*, vol. 26, pp.351-372.
Deacon, B. (1997), *Global Social Policy: International Organisations and the Future of Welfare*, Sage, London.
Deakin, N. (1994), *The Politics of Welfare: Continuities and Change*, Harvester Wheatsheaf, Hemel Hempstead.
Deyo, F. (1992), 'The Political Economy of Social Policy Formation: East Asia's Newly Industrialized Countries', in R. Appelbaum and J. Henderson (eds), *States and Development in the Asian Pacific Rim*, Sage Publications, Newbury Park.
Dunleavy, P. (1991), *Democracy, Bureaucracy and Public Choice*, Harvester Wheatsheaf, Hemel Hempstead.
Esping-Andersen, G. (1990), *The Three Worlds of Welfare Capitalism*, Princeton University Press, Princeton.
Esping-Andersen, G. (1996), *Welfare States in Transition: National Adaptations in Global Economies*, Sage, London.
Frobel, F., Heinrichs, J. and Kreye, O. (1980), *The New International Division of Labour*, Cambridge University Press, Cambridge.
Ginsberg, N. (1992), *Divisions of Welfare: A Critical Introduction to Comparative Social Policy*, Sage, London.
Glennerster, H. and Hills, J. (eds) (1998) (2nd ed), *The State of Welfare: the Economics of Social Spending*, Oxford University Press, Oxford.
Gould, A. (1993), *Capitalist Welfare Systems: A Comparison of Japan, Britain and Sweden*, Longman, London.
Her Majesty's Government (1979), *The Government's Expenditure Plans 1980-81, Cmd.7746*, HMSO, London.
ILO (1998), *World Employment Report*, International Labour Office, Geneva.
Jessop, B. (1996), 'Post-Fordism and the State', in B. Greve (ed), *Comparing Welfare Systems: The Scandinavian Model in a Period of Change*, Macmillan, London.
Jones, C. (1993), 'The Pacific Challenge', in C. Jones (ed), *New Perspectives on the Welfare State in Europe*, Routledge, London
Jones, K. (1958), *Social Welfare in Malaya*, D. Moore, Singapore.
Ku, Y-W. (1995), 'The Development of State Welfare in the Asian NICs with Specific Reference to Taiwan', *Social Policy and Administration*, vol. 29, pp.345-364.
Kwon (1997), 'Beyond European Welfare Regimes: Comparative Perspectives on East Asian Welfare Systems', *Journal of Social Policy*, vol. 26, pp.467-484.
Leibfried, S. (1993), 'Towards a European Welfare State', in C. Jones (ed), *New Perspectives on the Welfare State in Europe*, Routledge, London.
Levett, T. (1983), 'The Globalisation of Markets', *Harvard Business Review*, May, pp.92-102.
Lewis, J. (1993), *Women and Social Policies in Europe: Work, Family and the*

State, Elgar.
Malaya (1950), *Draft Development Plan of the Federation of Malaya*, Government Printer, Kuala Lumpur.
Marshall, T. H. (1950), *Citizenship and Social Class*, Cambridge University Press, Cambridge.
Mishra, R. (1998), 'Beyond the Nation State: Social Policy in an Age of Globalization', *Social Policy and Administration*, vol. 32, pp.481-500.
O'Connor, J. (1972), *The Fiscal Crissi of the State*, St Martin's Press, New York.
Office for National Statistics (1998), *Social Trends 28:1998 Edition*, The Stationery Office, London.
Orloff, A. S. (1993), 'Gender and Social Rights of Citizenship: State Policies and Gender Relations in Comparative Research', *American Sociological Review*, vol. 58, pp.303-328.
Pascall, G. (1997), *Social Policy: A New Feminist Analysis*, Routledge, London.
Pfaller, A., Gough, I., and Therborn, G. (1991), *Can the Welfare State Compete?*, Macmillan, London.
Pierson, C. (1991), *Beyond the Welfare State? The New Political Economy of Welfare*, Polity Press, Cambridge.
Siaroff, A. (1994), 'Work, Women and Gender Inequality: A New Typology', in D. Sainsbury (ed) *Gendering Welfare States*, Sage, London.
Williams, F. (1989), *Social Policy: A Critical Introduction*, Polity Press, Cambridge.

2 Work and social security provision in Britain: seeking a third way

ANN DAVIS
SUE WAINWRIGHT

> *"The welfare state now faces a choice of three futures:*
> - *a privatised future with the welfare state becoming a residual safety net for the poorest and most marginalised; or*
> - *the status quo but with more generous and costly benefits; or*
> - *the Government's third way - promoting opportunity instead of dependence, with the welfare state for the broad mass of people, but in new ways to fit the modern world" (Secretary of State for Social Security, 1998, p. 2).*

Introduction

Social security provision is at the core of social welfare programmes in industrialised societies. As these societies respond to, and attempt to manage, economic, social and political change, the purpose and resourcing of state payments to maintain people unable to secure an income through work become matters of contention and debate.

This chapter critically examines the situation in Britain which has led the current government's declaration that they are 'placing work at the heart of social welfare reform'. It does so by, firstly, summarising the economic, social and political contexts which have framed debates about work and social security policy and provision in post war Britain. Secondly, it highlights the ways in which major changes in social security policy and provision made by government during this period have impacted on work and welfare dependency. It moves on to trace the ways in which emerging concerns about work and welfare dependency have influenced social security policy and provision over the last decade. The paper concludes with a consideration of the current and future implications of the five point welfare reform programme introduced by government in 1998 to combat worklessness in 21st century Britain and to that extent has a much narrower focus than the Malaysian governments attempts to establish appropriate social welfare provision for the first time.

Work and welfare in Britain- establishing a second way

In March 1998 the Labour Government published a welfare reform paper for debate and discussion - 'New Ambitions for our Country: A New Contract for Welfare'. This publication marked fifty years of a state social security system in Britain. In the opening sentence of its preface prime minister, Tony Blair compared the opening of debate about change in welfare in the late 1990s with the Beveridge Report - the most radical review and reform of the provision of welfare income support undertaken in Britain during the twentieth century.

The Beveridge Report is a constant reference point for discussions of the past, present and future of social security and employment in Britain. It provided the vision and practical direction for the major post war programme of social legislation which established the British Welfare State. Prior to the introduction of the Beveridge Plan, the income maintenance schemes available to people outside the labour market were based around a mix of trade related initiatives or voluntary and charitable provision, involving very little state support, and where the momentum for change was provided by the labour movement. Breaking with this tradition Beveridge argued that the state should take sustained responsibility for the protection of its citizens who were unable to gain an income through paid work. It was the political acceptance of Beveridge's values and principles that led, in the late 1940s, to the establishment of a significantly more centralised comprehensive system of state welfare in Britain than in most of the rest of Western Europe.

In addressing welfare and work Beveridge argued that the state had a dual role. It should take responsibility for introducing and pursuing economic policies aimed at maintaining full employment. Building on this, it should also make provision for those unable to work as well as those who experienced periods of unemployment by means of a national social security scheme based on contributions as well as assistance. This provision was to be kept to minimal weekly payments in order to encourage individual responsibility to supplement state income as well as seek paid work. Together these measures were to provide a framework for the way in which British governments responded to issues of work and welfare. This framework remained in place for almost thirty years.

The state's role in seeking to maintain full employment to protect its citizens from want, combined from the outset a Keynesian approach by government to economic policy with agencies funded to reskill and build capacity amongst the workforce as well as match unemployed people with work opportunities. The rationale in the 1940s for this approach was that without full employment the whole funding basis for social security provision - the tax and insurance contributions of employers and employed citizens could not be maintained. It is, however, important to note the gendered nature of this approach to citizenship where full employment related to men and unmarried women only (see Lister, 1977, for a fuller discussion of these issues).

The government's management of the economy was seen to visibly falter and fail at the end of the 1960s and beginning of the 1970s. With the numbers of unemployed social security recipients reaching a million in 1972, emphasis on maintaining full employment waned. In its place there was a growing acceptance by government that unemployment was an inevitable outcome of the place occupied by Britain in the new global economic order. Fuelled by two periods of recession in 1980/2 and 1990/2 when official estimates of those unemployment reached over 3 million, government policy in respect to employment shifted. Attempts to secure and maintain full employment were replaced with a broadening range of employment schemes designed to manage a continuing reality of significant levels of unemployment. The management of these programmes have shifted over the last twenty years from direct state provision to the state's funding of a mix of private and public organisation providers.

In surveying the range of available programmes Deacon (1998) has suggested that existing British schemes work in a number of broad areas, involving a mix of work experience, job creation and employment subsidies with advice and support to the unemployed themselves.

All of these measures are directed at achieving more than one objective. In a national and international economic context of changing work opportunities they serve a number of contradictory purposes. For example, the irresolvable tensions between redressing inequality of opportunity within the labour market whilst maintaining a tight hold on social security expenditure; and between attempting to meet employers' immediate requirements for a skilled and affordable workforce and employees' demands for 'real', full time and adequately paid employment rather than temporary work on social security benefit income levels. A great deal of government attention and investment at political and policy making levels, has been focused on designing, promoting and reconfiguring employment schemes and social security responses to those of working age. The dominant government agenda has been to place limits on public expenditure in this area whilst being seen to respond to the needs for income, work experience and training amongst citizens, who find themselves without employment; a much more limited government agenda in relation to employment and welfare than that envisaged by Beveridge.

Table 2.1 Government expenditure in real terms by function

	£billion in 1997 prices		
	1987	1991	1997
Social protection	96	109	131
Health	33	37	44
Education	31	33	36
Defence	30	30	23
Public order and safety	12	15	16
General public services	9	13	15
Housing and community amenities	11	11	6
Recreation, culture and religion	4	5	4
Other	24	26	24
Gross debt interest	30	22	30
Total	280	301	331

Source: Office of National Statistics (1999)

The investment by the state in social security provision was, and remains, substantial. It is the largest area of government expenditure - currently around 35 per cent of total expenditure. The State is not, of course, the sole contributor. It is estimated that three fifths of total expenditure in this area comes from government, a quarter from private sector employers through national insurance contributions and the rest by private individuals through national insurance contributions (Office of National Statistics, 1999).

Table 2.2 Benefit expenditure by recipient groups, 1999

	£million
Family	17,900
Unemployed	5,300
Sick and Disabled	25,400
Elderly	44,500

Source: Social Security Statistics (1999)

The distribution of social security expenditure amongst recipients shows that at any one time one third of the population are in receipt of one or more benefits. Currently almost half of recipients are older people. However, 17 per cent of the people of working age were claiming an income replacement benefit in 1998 (Office of National Statistics, 1999).

These patterns of investment and distribution reflect the political decisions that have been made to use social security benefits in managing the effects of economic recession on the population of working age as well as provide a minimum income for groups wholly or partly excluded from the labour market by virtue of their age, sickness, disability or family responsibilities.

Challenge, change and continuity in social security policy

The strength of Beveridge's approach to welfare and work was the synthesis he achieved in moulding a number of disparate schemes and levels of provision into a cohesive system of social security payments (Secretary of State for Social Security, 1998), and replacing the existing somewhat eclectic mix of public and private provision. The relationship between work and the state's welfare benefit scheme was straightforward. When people were economically active they would be supported by their wages (or that of the family's principal wage earner). The role of the welfare state was limited to supporting them in times of economic inactivity, and to this end the state became involved in defining 'a working life' by the adoption of a state retirement age for men and women. The one exception to this approach was a scheme of family allowances to be paid weekly for the second and subsequent children within a family, regardless of their income. This was a nominal recognition that while earnings would normally be expected to produce an adequate family income, the state should be seen to make a contribution towards the costs of larger families.

The limitations of Beveridge's approach related to the ways in which the welfare benefits scheme treated those who were unable to sustain full time paid employment. Single women were treated as having entitlement to state benefits in their own right. Married women were classified as 'dependants' an approach designed to uphold the view that women should not enter paid work after marriage on anything but an intermittent basis. Women's work in the home as housewives and mothers was viewed by Beveridge as essential for the welfare of the nation as a whole:

> In the next thirty years housewives as mothers have vital work to do in ensuring the adequate continuance of the British race and British ideals in the world (Beveridge, 1942, p.53).

Other groups whose needs were not fully recognised in the Beveridge scheme were those who had no capacity or a fluctuating capacity for work due to disability or long term illness. The needs of those caring for others and unable to maintain full time paid unemployment were also neglected. In the absence of provision being made in the scheme to meet their needs, such groups found themselves having to turn to the means tested assistance scheme for an income.

The political decisions about the scheme's funds effectively undermined the possibility of realising Beveridge's intention that the means-tested assistance scheme would play a relatively minor role in the overall scheme. Means-tested assistance has played an increasingly major role within the scheme in the post war period. In 1979, 7 per cent of dependent children were in families receiving Income Support but by 1996 this had risen to one in four (McKay and Rowlingson, 1999).

The treatment of the state's subsidy towards housing costs were also a limiting factor. While steps were taken by Beveridge to take account of the housing costs of some low income households eligible for assistance benefits, a range of additional local assistance towards housing costs was left in place. Governments in the 1960s and the 1980s sought to rationalise and expand the scope of cover by introducing national schemes of housing cost support (now known as Housing Benefit) delivered through local authorities on behalf of central government.

In the face of the economic, social and political changes which have characterised the post war period, successive governments have taken some steps to make the original Beveridge scheme more responsive and in doing so have added to the complexity of the state's social security scheme. Further complexity has resulted from the way in which governments have sought to restrain public expenditure on social security. Changes tightening eligibility criteria for benefit awards as well as restrictions placed on the scope and time limits of benefit awards are now almost continuous. This is particularly the case in relation to provision for the unemployed where much more restrictive eligibility criteria apply, combined with the need to comply with much more onerous rules relating to their availability for employment and the steps that they have taken to obtain it. Similar restrictions have been introduced for other groups such as the young unemployed whose entitlement has been severely limited in favour of pressure to stay in full time education or undertake vocational training to improve their long term employability. Driven by the desire to reduce costs, pressure has also been exerted on people claiming sickness related benefits where the test of incapacity has been more tightly drawn and associated eligibility criteria made less generous.

Of key importance in this period has been the gendered nature of changes in the labour market which have overturned the assumptions built into Beveridge's approach to welfare and work. Economic change triggered by international and domestic factors has meant that the notion of full time male employment and intermittent female employment after marriage has become increasingly at odds with the economic and social reality of British society. Men's employment security and participation has been decreasing since the 1970s whilst women's participation in the labour market has increased. This is both a reflection of the kind of jobs which have been lost as well as those which have been created. The last two decades has seen employment growth concentrated in part-time, often low paid work in sectors dominated by a female workforce.

At the same time there have been significant social changes in respect to the lives of people with disabilities and long-standing illness. In place of institutional care, successive governments have promoted community care policies designed to offer the majority of people with disabilities and long term illness the opportunity to remain in their own communities and to participate as fully as possible as citizens. This shift in health and welfare policy has combined in the last two decades with unemployment levels which have adversely effected the opportunities available to disabled people in the labour market. The result has been increasing demands on state support to meet the income needs and housing costs of people with disabilities and illness as well as those caring for them. It has also raised issues of discrimination and civil rights in relation to addressing the exclusion from employment opportunities of people with disabilities who wish to be independent of state support (Oliver and Barnes, 1998).

The major government responses to meeting these changes can be traced in legislation in the 1960s and 1970s which expanded the scope of coverage by the state benefit system. A number of benefits outside of both the social insurance and the means-tested social assistance schemes were introduced, designed to provide income for those whose disabilities or caring responsibilities excluded them from paid employment. However, the complexity of the eligibility criteria as well as the low rates of benefits set, meant that the majority of those claiming these new benefits needed to supplement them with means-tested assistance (Berthoud et al, 1993).

Changes at this time also included the introduction of an 'in work' benefit payable by the state for those in full time work with children whose income from work failed to meet a minimum annual level, and supplements to lone parent families at particular risk of poverty.

Table 2.3 Men and women working, 1986 and 1998, full-time and part-time

	1986	1998
Men in work (000)	11,490	14,906
Full time (%)	96.1	91.0
Part time (%)	3.9	9.0
Women in work (000)	9,214	12,042
Full time (%)	55.0	55.1
Part time (%)	45.0	44.9
Total in work (000)	20,704	26,947

Source: Office for National Statistics (1999)

The economic difficulties faced by Britain since the late 1970s marked the end of the expansion of the state social security system. Intensified government concern to manage economic and social change whilst curbing the costs of social security expenditure meant that the 1980s and 1990s were characterised by attempts to manage unemployment through the benefit system. During this period the insurance basis of the state's response to unemployed people virtually collapsed. This has meant that dependency on the state through means-tested assistance has increased in ways which undermine incentives to work and save and become independent of state support.

Young people and older male workers have found themselves particularly vulnerable to unemployment during this period. Government concerns with young people emerged strongly in the recession of the early 1980s when a sharp rise in the numbers of young people coincided with unemployment reaching new heights.

Table 2.4 Unemployment rates, age 16-24, 1991-1997 (GB)

	16-19			20-24		
	Males	Females	All	Males	Females	All
1991	16.4	12.7	29.1	15.2	10.1	25.3
1992	18.6	13.6	32.2	18.9	10.2	29.1
1993	22.0	15.9	37.9	20.3	11.8	32.1
1994	20.9	16.0	36.9	18.3	10.7	29.0
1995	19.6	14.8	34.4	17.0	10.6	27.6
1996	20.2	14.6	34.8	16.2	8.9	25.1
1997	18.2	14.0	32.2	14.0	8.9	22.9

Source: Office for National Statistics (1999)

This situation means that millions of young people have been excluded from entering a state funded system of social insurance. The subsequent dependence of this group on means-tested benefits has created, in the eyes of government, a problem of the state subsidising worklessness amongst a substantial minority of young people lacking the education and skills to secure paid employment. The response to this problem has been changes to the social security benefit provision which have reduced social security protection for young people thereby increasing their dependency on their families. In 1988 the entitlement of young people between the ages of 16 and 18 years to assistance benefit was withdrawn and the rates of assistance benefit payable to young people aged 18-25 years were reduced. More recently government has introduced measures to cut the benefit entitlement for 18-25 year olds needing assistance with housing costs.

At the other end of the age range there has been an increase in unemployment amongst male older workers - aged 50-64 years. This is a group whose work records have earned them rights to social security insurance. The pressure their claims have placed on social security budgets have resulted in governments in the 1990s moving to reduce the scope and generosity of insurance benefits entitlements. A related issue is the failure of state benefit provision to provide an income level for people of retirement age that will protect them from poverty. This has led to demands for a second tier pension to be made available to boost income in old age.

The 1960s and 1970s saw two attempts by government to make more generous state provision available for individuals unable to access private occupational pension schemes. However in the climate of public expenditure constraint in the 1980s and 1990s the government introduced severe cuts in the state pension scheme (Social Security Act 1986) as well as actively promoting private and occupational pension schemes as preferable alternatives to state provision.

Table 2.5 Receipt of occupational pension and average weekly payment

	% pensioners with occupational pension	£pw
1979	43%	49
1989	54%	69
1995	64%	80
1996	65%	91

Source: Department of Social Security (1999)

The result has been an increase in inequality between older people in Britain and a marked associated increase in reliance amongst older people (predominantly women) on means-tested supplements to state retirement pension. While it is clear that certain groups of older people are well provided for through second pensions, personal savings etc. the inequalities of income in later life are typically reflections of an individual's access to the labour market during their working life. Thus those groups most seriously disadvantaged in employment terms through gender, race, disability or family responsibilities for example, are most likely to have experienced poverty during their working lives which will be translated into an impoverished old age. Second pensions have little or no relevance to those groups of people whose income from employment is already insufficient to meet their needs.

Seeking a third way

From the late 1970s there has been a discernible shift in the ways in which discussion of work and welfare provision has been framed politically and academically. Walker and Walker (1997)have argued that a continuity can be traced over eighteen years of Conservative administrations (1979-1997) in framing of the issues in this area as well as the outcomes for those at the receiving end of employment and welfare policies. They suggest that during this period the Government's approach to welfare has been characterised by five related themes.
- the need to cut public expenditure on social welfare;
- the need, through state subsidy, to privatise and extend market principles to areas of welfare provision;
- attempts to replace universal social security benefits with selective means-tested benefits;
- the reduction of taxation to provide incentives and stimulate the growth of private and voluntary welfare provision;
- the centralisation of resource control in social welfare combined with the decentralisation of operational responsibility.

Underlying these themes have been three key assumptions:
- the welfare state creates dependency and this is undermining morally and economically for society as well as the individual;
- non state forms of welfare e.g. the family, self help, non government organisations are superior to state welfare;
- in order to sustain a culture of enterprise in Britain it is necessary to reward those with the highest incomes so that over time the fruits of their enterprise will 'trickle down' to benefit the rest of society (Walker and Walker, 1997).

Government policy and changes to provision in relation to welfare and work reflect these themes and assumptions. From the early 1980s government declared that unemployment was a price 'worth paying' to enable the British economy to become more competitive internationally. As the numbers of citizens unemployed and dependent on state assistance benefits increased government activity was directed at limiting as far as possible the resulting increase in social security expenditure. The evidence of growing poverty and inequality over this period, which was one of the sharpest in the OECD (Atkinson et al, 1996; Hills, 1995) was interpreted by government as evidence of the success of their economic strategy of reducing taxation and stimulating economic enterprise rather than as a social problem which required government intervention to reduce poverty. Indeed, throughout the 1980s government ministers denied that poverty existed in Britain and did not allow the term poverty to be used in official documents (Becker, 1997).

Those citizens of working age who found themselves with the lowest incomes became subject to increasing blame and criticism from government and the media for the part they played in remaining on state benefits. Characterised as a growing 'underclass', young men, lone mothers and members of minority ethnic communities found themselves targeted by politicians and the media as a threat to the social fabric of society because of their unemployment, poverty and receipt of social security benefits. The work of American commentators such as Charles Murray was given credence as both offering an analysis of trends and sounding a warning note to Britain about the dangerous social consequences of allowing such groups to grow with the support from the state and a lack of requirement to work.

As Oppenheim has observed this was a period in which

> At its most reductionist, the New Right defined poverty as 'dependency' which was seen as a behavioural problem caused by the welfare state itself. These ideas have shaped the contours of a debate in which individual explanations of poverty have had much greater prominence than in any other post-war period (Walker and Walker, 1997, p.18-9).

The preoccupation with a growing and excluded underclass has tended to dominate discussion of welfare and work. The solutions sought centred on the possibility of state support being made conditional. That is entitlement being made dependent on individuals providing evidence of seeking work and/or engaging with work experience or training for work. The case that has been made for this is that it acts as a deterrence to those who wish to claim benefit without seriously seeking work. In Britain in the 1990s, it has also been argued that it is a deterrence against abuse of the benefit system. The argument has been advanced that without imposing such conditions those without employment become demotivated to work. A conditional benefit system is therefore seen to be in the long term interests of unemployed people providing them with a positive stimulus. The arguments against this shift emphasise the structural nature of unemployment in the current economic climate, and the absence of work and work opportunities for all individuals of working age. In such a context some argue it is both unjust and ineffective to place pressure on individuals to seek or train for employment.

The 1990s have seen a more conditional approach adopted to the state benefits which are made available for those who are unemployed. Unemployment Benefit available for twelve months to those who were unemployed, had made adequate contributions to the state's insurance scheme and were available for work was replaced in 1996 by a new benefit - Job Seekers Allowance. This benefit is available for six months to unemployed people who have made adequate national insurance contributions and are available to work. Receipt of this benefit is conditional on an individual signing an agreement which details job search activities. For those who do not comply with the agreement, benefit can be withdrawn or an instruction can be issued for them to attend a training scheme or undertake a particular task. In introducing the scheme government estimated a saving of £240 million a year on benefits paid to unemployed people.

Such concerns with savings have also informed the reduction of state assistance to people injured at work and those becoming unemployed because of short term sickness. Within a rising social security budget, fuelled by unemployment levels and the deregulation of the rented housing market which has increased housing benefit expenditure, some groups of people claiming benefit have found themselves losing while others have gained. Claimants of working age, including lone mothers, have been amongst the main losers in the 1980s and 1990s.

'New ways to fit the modern world'?

In promoting its 'third way' for social welfare reform fitting for the 21st Century, the Labour Government has adopted a five point welfare reform programme aimed at promoting work as a means of lifting people from dependency on state welfare. The programme
- introduces direct programmes to help certain groups, i.e. young people, older and long term unemployed people, lone parents and people with disabilities;
- creates individualised, flexible services for people out of work;
- reduces barriers for those groups able and wanting to work;
- integrates benefits and taxation to ensure that work pays;

- ensures that the responsibility of the state to provide support is equally matched with the responsibility of the individual to take it up.

There is a strong sense in which these changes do not represent a significant departure from the direction which has been pursued by Conservative governments in the last two decades. However, there is a discernible shift in emphasis in the provisions made to re-establish work amongst those groups previously excluded from mainstream employment with initiatives aimed specifically at lone parents and people with disabilities.

These reforms can be characterised as a further attempt to adjust and refine the insurance route to welfare incorporating improved incentives to work, and reduce dependence on means-tested assistance. Given the direction in which the benefit system in Britain has been travelling over the past 50 years, this is likely to prove difficult to achieve.

The extent to which the government's programme meets the challenge of worklessness in a modern world remains largely a matter of conjecture in the absence of published economic forecasts. However, earlier work undertaken at the instigation of the current government whilst in opposition provide some useful measures of the likely impact of this strategy. The Commission for Social Justice was set up in the early 1990s to undertake an independent inquiry into social and economic reform in the UK with a view to producing a long-term strategy for national renewal. Taking as a starting point the need to 'transform the welfare state from a safety net in times of trouble to a springboard for economic opportunity' (Commission on Social Justice, 1995, p.1) the Commission identified three goals to be pursued simultaneously in pursuit of this objective;

- to increase employment;
- to ensure a fairer distribution of employment and unemployment;
- to achieve better employment.

It is notable that despite the emphasis in the government's own publication (Secretary of State for Social Security, 1998) on work as the key to its reform programme, no reference is made to these goals. No indication is given as to how the labour market is to be expanded to meet the new demands of the redrawn contract between the state and the individual.

More and better paid employment is also the key to addressing the future funding of social security. To meet the shortfall between contributors and beneficiaries which an ageing population in particular creates, and to safeguard the level at which social insurance benefits are paid, the number of contributors and the level of contributions need to increase. Failure to achieve either of these will necessitate continued and increased subsidy from general taxation to meet costs as well as prolonging reliance on means-tested assistance for those groups unable to be economically active.

In the absence of sustained economic growth and increased capacity at the core rather than the margins of the modern labour market, the reforms at their best seem likely to maximise the potential of those whose needs are easiest to meet. At its worst, the reform package will do little more than create tiers of welfare dependency. At the first level will be the group of people accepted by the state as being unable to provide for themselves and worthy of state support, although the reformers are staggeringly silent on the nature of that support. At the next level will be the group who continue to have a hold, however marginal, on the labour market and perceive themselves as within the reach of these opportunities for self advancement. For those unable to establish themselves in either of the other groups, the outlook is bleak. Deemed unworthy of support and incapable or unwilling to accept the helping hand of the state, poverty, social exclusion and blame, seem inevitable; a situation which resonates with 19th Century Poor Law notions of the deserving and undeserving poor, rather than a strategy responding to the economic and social conditions of the 21st Century.

References

Alcock, P. (1996), *Social Policy in Britain: Themes and Issues*, Macmillan, Basingstoke.
Atkinson, A.B., Rainwater, L. and Smeeding, T. (1996), *Income Distribution in OECD Countries*, OECD, Paris.
Becker, S (1997), *Responding to Poverty*, Longman, London.
Berthoud, R., Lakey, J., and McKay, S. (1993), *The Economic Problems of Disabled People*, Policy Studies Institute, London.
Beveridge, W. (1942), *Report on Social Insurance and Allied Service*, Cmd. 6404, HMSO, London.
Commission on Social Justice (1995), *Social Justice Strategies for National Renewal*, Vintage, London.
Deacon, A. (1998), 'Employment' in: P. Alcock, A. Erskine and M. May (eds), *The Student's Companion to Social Policy*, Blackwell, Oxford.
Deakin, N. (1994), *The Politics of Welfare: Continuities and Change*, Harvester Wheatsheaf, Hemel Hempstead.

Department of Social Security (1998), *Welfare Reform Focus Files*. Department of Social Security, London.
Ditch, J.S. (ed) (1997), *Poverty and Social Security: Issues and Research*, Prentice Hall, Englewood Cliffs.
Ginsberg, N. (1992), *Divisions of Welfare: A Critical Introduction to Comparative Social Policy*, Sage, London.
Glennerster, H and Hills, J. (eds) (1998) (2nd ed), *The State of Welfare: the Economics of Social Spending*, Oxford University Press, Oxford.
Hills, J. (1995), *Joseph Rowntree Inquiry into Income and Wealth*, vols. 1 and 2, Joseph Rowntree Foundation, York.
Lister, R. (1997), *Citizenship: Feminist Perspectives*, Macmillan, Basingtoke.
McKay, S. and Rowlingson, K. (1999), *Social Security in Britain*, Macmillan, Basingstoke.
National Pensioners Convention (1998), *Pensions not Poor Relief*, National Pensioners Convention, London.
Office for National Statistics (1999), *Social Trends 29: 1999* Edition, The Stationery Office, London.
Oliver, M. and Barnes, C. (1998), *Social Policy and Disabled People*, Longman, London.
Secretary of State for Social Security (1998), *New Ambitions for our Country: A New Contract for Welfare*, The Stationery Office, London, Cm 3805.
Social Security Consortium (1998), *Response to the Government's Green Paper*, Child Poverty Action Group, London.
Timmins, N. (1996), *The Five Giants: A Biography of the Welfare State*, Fontana Press, London.
Walker, A. and Walker, C. (eds) (1997), *Britain Divided: The Growth of Social Exclusion in the 1980s and 1990s*, CPAG Publications, London.
Walker, C. (1993), *Managing Poverty: The Limits of Social Assistance*, Routledge, London.

3 Social security policies in Malaysia
SITI HAJAR ABU BAKAR
FAIZAH YUNUS

Introduction

The Employees Provident Fund (EPF), established in 1951, is the legislative foundation stone of the present Malaysian social security system. Whereas its introduction took place within a few years of the setting up of the British social security system, in matters other than timing the two systems are not at all close. Two particular contrasts stand out. First, unlike the British funding of social security through a mix of contributions and taxation, the Malaysian system is based centrally on the principle of personal and employer contribution. Rather than state provided welfare, then, it is more accurate to portray the EPF as a form of mandatory and individualised saving or statutory re-distribution across the life cycle. Second, the EPF started as a mechanism for ensuring an income during retirement. Although it has been widened in scope and extended by the introduction of the Social Security Organisation (SOCSO), it has not progressed as far as providing unemployment benefits for those not working for reasons other than such matters as disability, illness or accident. Social security is perceived, then, more as welfare at the workplace or as ways in which employers, employees and the government facilitate programmes that protect workers and their families during hardship; but neither as compensation for those not in employment nor as initiatives to encourage people to work.

With respect to the second of these contrasts, the case could be made that the non-inclusion of certain types of payment has been fully justified by the particular circumstances of post war Malaysia. These would include the long period of economic growth up to 1997 during which full employment has been generally assured as well as the cultural expectation of family support for all its members and of the responsibility to work. Notwithstanding the historical differences, however, the two systems have also addressed some common issues, such as facilitating the greater entry of women into the labour market. The economic crisis has, in addition, raised concerns about the continuing adequacy of the Malaysian system in the new context of public and private austerity.

In the next section of this chapter, the historical development of the Malaysian social security system will be presented. In this the incremental widening of the coverage of social security both to new groups and new circumstances will be stressed, as will the funding principles. The final section will focus on a number of issues relevant to both the present and the future.

The historical development of social security policy in Malaysia

The British Colonial Period (1850s- 1940s)

In Malaysian society prior to the colonial period there had been widely-practised forms of social security. The custom of providing gifts during the wedding ceremony in order to assist the couple in setting up a family was one form, as was the *Tabung Khairat Kematian* (death alms-giving fund). During the colonial period, when the British established a dependent capitalist economy based on the export of rubber and tin, new forms of social security were developed alongside these traditional forms. They were almost entirely devised and introduced bottom-up by the different ethnic groups, a situation arising from the fact that the welfare of immigrant labourers was not a major concern for many of the European employers. Indeed, the function of the colonial government was conceived as being limited largely to ensuring a smooth flow of labourers to the mines and plantations (ILO, 1962). At this early stage, there was no formal social security organisation formed by the British to take care of the workers, the living conditions of which were often appalling. In these circumstances, the immigrant labourers typically formed their own informal welfare organisations. The Chinese coolies, for instance, made their own arrangements to look after their welfare and security. Since almost all those Chinese who came to Malaya were a member of a triad society, many informal social security organisations were mainly based on their triad clans. These organisations became very powerful. Among the Indians, the *dorai* (Master; term used by many workers on plantations) and the *kangany* (supervisor) were the middlemen in any dispute. In times of trouble these *dorai* and *kangany* were persons who might be approached first, while both often made small loans to labourers.

Post Colonial Dependency Era (1950s-1960s)

Trade unionism played a very significant role in the rise of a formal social security scheme or organisation in Malaysia. Larger and stronger trade unions were organised along primarily industrial and occupational trade principles (Wad, 1997). The unions demanded better wages and better welfare schemes from employers and the government. An important episode took place immediately after World War II when labour protest, strikes and rallies had become everyday events. The peak of the protest was in early 1947 when there was a nationwide strike and demonstrations by rubber plantation workers who demanded better wages. Murders and attacks on European estate managers and pro-management workers increased alarmingly to an extent that the British Military Administration was forced to proclaim a State of Emergency throughout Malaya on 18 June 1948 (Baharuddin, 1994). As a consequence, the colonial government introduced a number of pieces of legislation and guidelines of social security. With these, on 1st October 1951 the Employees Provident Fund (EPF) was established under the Act of Ordinance Employee Provident Fund 1951 for the primary purpose of providing employees with a measure of social security when they retired.

Akin to the provident fund system introduced in Singapore, the Malaysian EPF was an obligatory saving scheme. The EPF is operated through a provident fund scheme. Its principal target groups are the private and non-pensionable public sector employees. Its main objective is to ensure a secure and adequate income maintenance for employees and their dependants during their old age. An employee who was not covered by a pension scheme was obliged to contribute to the EPF. Parallel to its objectives and functions the EPF's mission was built to protect and benefit four groups: contributors; employees; employers; and the nation as a whole.

Interdependent Capitalist Industrialisation Era (1970s and beyond)

The 1970s can be considered as the New Economic Policy (NEP) era; an era of development as an interdependent capitalist and industrialised country. It was a period of rebuilding both economic and social circumstances. This era can be identified as of major historical significance in social security expansion. Three major objectives of NEP were: first, to eradicate poverty; second, to restructure the Malaysian society in order to wipe out the inter-ethnic economic imbalances; and, third, to create national unity. In line with these objectives, the EPF was extended to cover all salaried workers. At the same time, foreign workers and domestic helpers were allowed to contribute if they chose to do so.

Under the Employees Social Security Act of 1969 all industries employing five or more employees were required to contribute to the organisation for their employees. And, all workers employed under a contract service and earning RM2,000 or less a month were covered by the Act. Once covered, they remained covered even if the salary or wages were to exceed RM2,000 per month. This 'once in always in' principle ensures the employee maintains his or her pension rights. However, certain categories of workers, such as those whose employment was of a casual nature and who were employed otherwise than for the purposes of the employer's industry, such as domestic servant, tributer or spouse were exempted from the provisions of the Act (Paguman Singh, 1991).

Another important event was the implementation of the Employees Social Security Organisation (SOCSO) in 1971. This new scheme of social security can be seen as supplementary, yet also complementary, to the EPF. The main objective of SOCSO was to provide certain benefits to employees in cases of invalidity and employment injury including occupational diseases (Row, 1984). It had the effect of extending the social security system beyond its limited focus on retirement pensions.

Since their establishment there have been many changes and improvements to the EPF and SOCSO. Thus in 1994, a new withdrawal package consisting of cash savings, housing and health care was introduced into the EPF. The objective was to enable members to accumulate adequate cash savings to maintain their lives during retirement, whilst owning a house purchased or built using EPF savings and paying for medical bills. Under this scheme each member's fund is divided into three accounts with 60 per cent for retirement, 30 per cent for housing and 10 per cent for medical care.

At the present time, functioning together as a social security or insurance institution, EPF and SOCSO provide a number of schemes to their members and their beneficiaries. Table 3.1 shows the eighteen schemes.

Table 3.1 EPF and SOCSO schemes

EPF schemes	SOCSO Schemes
1. Old Age Pension	1. Invalidity Pension
2. Old Age Benefit For The Armed Forces	2. Workmen's Compensation
3. Teachers Provident Fund (TPF)	3. Sickness and Maternity Benefits
4. Malaysian Estates Staff Provident Fund	4. Employment Injury
5. Housing Withdrawal:	5. Medical Benefits
(i) Low cost housing	6. Temporary Disablement Benefits
(ii) Non-low cost housing	7. Permanent Disablement Benefits
(iii) Reducing/ Redeeming a Housing Mortgage Loan	8. Constant Attendance Allowance
(iv) Buying/ Building A Village House	9. Rehabilitation, Artificial and Other Appliances
	10. Dependants Benefits
	11. Funeral Benefits
	12. Occupational Diseases
	13. Survivors Benefits

Malaysia has adopted contributory benefits as the principal approach in her social security programmes. Under this approach, workers and employers contribute to the fund. All benefits are based on the contribution made by workers during their working life. In fact, benefits paid to the family/beneficiary will also be based on the deceased or injured worker's contribution record. Benefits are paid only to those who have made contributions. This plan is also known as the individual savings or capitalisation approach.

Social security schemes in Malaysia are financed either by publicly mandated defined-contribution or publicly managed defined-benefit methods. The first method of financing is fully funded by the National Provident Fund under a system of capital accumulation, whereas, under the second method of financing, schemes may be financed out of general revenue on a pay-as-you-go basis or at least a partially funded-basis under the annual assessment system. In Malaysia, the pay-as-you-go system is the primary method of providing retirement income. Under this funding mechanism, contributions collected from current workers are immediately used to finance the pension payment of retirees (Ibrahim, 1999). This pay-as-you-go method started off using the advance funded approach where a considerable amount of reserve was accumulated to be invested.

Limits and holes in the safety net

The Malaysian social security system has been an important achievement both for maintaining the living standards of individuals and as part of the wider project of becoming a modern, industrialised country. However, there are a number of limitations of the system, as it exists at the present time, as well as potential threats consequent upon more or less likely developments in Malaysia. For the purposes of this chapter they are brought together and classified as relating either to financial or exclusion issues.

Financial Issues

It could be argued that any national system of social security should provide a minimum socially acceptable standard of living before or after retirement and before or after disability or death occurs. These requirements are taken into consideration in the provision of the EPF Pension Scheme, but only loosely. According to the EPF financing method, ideally, members should not withdraw their savings until they retire. The main reason for that statement is because the level of the EPF savings is planned in terms of the income deemed necessary during retirement. EPF has defined income maintenance as equivalent to 50 per cent of the last drawn salary (Employees Provident Fund, 1991). This is based on benefits for manual, clerical and executive levels in the public sector and on certain assumptions such as continuous employment from the age of 16 for manual, 18 for clerical and 23 for executive level workers and a life expectancy of 75 years. This will indicate that at a 20 per cent contribution rate, the accumulated credit would produce an annuity equivalent to 230 per cent of the last drawn salary for manual, 158 per cent for clerical and 127 per cent for executive level workers. These levels will greatly surpass the 50 per cent cut-off level. So, those with continuous exposure (given that the assumptions of the simulation are satisfied) would have little difficulty in achieving what is deemed an adequate income.

At the present time, however, it is clear that there are a number of actual and possible developments which threaten the adequacy of these arrangements. The first and most general in the sense that it may impact on any capital fund concerns the success, in terms of capital growth, with which it is managed. The point here is that the EPF operates according to the national provident fund method. Under this method, the EPF can invest the accumulated balances in Malaysian Government Securities, shares or capital markets. As the accumulated balances are large and are expected to continue to grow, careful and cautious investment management and strategy are necessary. Mismanagement or an inappropriate investment strategy could adversely affect the viability of the present and future arrangements and benefits. To maintain inflation proofing, it is vital for the EPF to adopt a policy of maximising returns within generally safe investments while striving to achieve more balanced allocations towards inflation proof assets in the area of properties and equities. At the same time, the need to secure adequate funds for members upon retirement also dictates the Fund's risk adverse investment policy so as to ensure protection of capital. Retired individuals will remain vulnerable to severe inflation if investment management and strategy adopted are vulnerable in protecting members' benefits and rights. To prevent this vulnerability appropriate management and safer investment strategy need continually to be considered.

One principle of Malaysia health policy is equity. This means that all citizens should have an equal opportunity to have a healthy life and equal access to health services. To achieve this goal, the National Social Welfare Policy of 1990 promotes workplaces' moral or social obligation in helping the Government to deliver medical or health schemes covering not only workers but also their families. Similar to the system practised by a number of Asian countries such as Japan, it offers the possibility that every citizen will be covered by some kind of health insurance according to their occupations. However, it should be noted that the basic, underlying objective may be based less on notions of equality and more on a wish by the government to diversify the sources of health care spending.

In addition to these arrangements, the EPF Account III scheme consists of 10 per cent of a member's savings and can be utilised for medical care. There is an argument that this should be re-scaled. The basis for this is that, relatively, that amount is small compared to health care cost. Furthermore, as sickness particularly comes with old age, more money is needed to meet the health needs of older people.

With improving life expectancy (presently placed at 70 years) and a tightening labour market, the retirement age for Malaysian workers may be increased. This will, all other things being equal, increase the number of years a person can work to accumulate retirement fund, but it may also mean having to work harder in order to accumulate enough balances for a longer retirement period. It was noted earlier that the EPF has an important responsibility to provide adequate savings during retirement. Thus, the EPF must always ensure that the pre-retirement withdrawal and benefits schemes will not drastically reduce the member's saving. Maintaining a fine balance between the pre-retirement and retirement benefits can do this. Correspondingly, before a member decides to withdraw their savings prior to retirement, they must ensure that it will be used appropriately, that is for the use for which it is intended. As Mohammed (1993) has argued, however, such consciousness is only possible if the member understands the concept of savings with the EPF for retirement. Responding to this, the EPF perhaps has to consider playing a more significant and pro-active role in educating the public regarding its role as a retirement saving scheme.

As Malaysia successfully pursues the philosophy that development means growth with equality - a principle that has been embodied in all major social policies - more appropriate quality of life, increases in longevity and changes in demography will have impacts on the life of all Malaysians. Lower mortality rates and improved health means the next generation will live longer. As life expectancy is longer, society will need supplementary financial resources to finance those extra years of life and the increased health care costs. Contrary to this development, health care is covered in only a limited way by SOCSO. Moreover, SOCSO has to keep health care schemes available and affordable. Responding to this, EPF and SOCSO are trying harder to improve existing health care arrangements and to extend them to a more comprehensive scheme.

The conclusion for Malaysia may be similar to that in Britain, where the relationship between work and social security contributory benefits was very direct: other sources of support are vital. Drawing on community care concepts, which have brought together contributions other than public or private savings, various initiatives could, appropriately adapted, be introduced into Malaysian policy. Among the possible developments are: introducing occupational therapy care; introducing courses on occupational safety and health; upgrading medical facilities and services in all SOCSO Medical Boards; prolonging maternity leave; extending coverage to the self-employed and facilitating better benefits; and improving physical and medical rehabilitation programmes. It is possible that collectively such programmes could fulfil society's health and other social care needs. But, as always they would come at a price so that the challenge is not only deciding on the best forms of intervention to meet the needs of Malaysian society, but also establishing how the costs are to be met.

Exclusion Issues

The limitation here is that there are many sections of society that are excluded from the benefits of Malaysia's social security system. How could we include them inside the net? The Malaysian population was estimated to grow at an average annual rate of 2.3 per cent during the Seventh Plan period to reach 23.26 million by the end of the decade. (Malaysia, 1996). From this figure, about 63 per cent of the total population were expected to be in the working age group 15-64. The labour force was expected to grow at a rate of 2.8 per cent per annum to reach about 9.3 million by the year 2000. The labour force will also continue to have a young age profile, that is a high proportion of workers in the 15-34 age group. In 1990, the total number of employed population in Malaysia was 7 million (Table 3.2). However, there were only about 3.4 millions of these contributing to the EPF. Together, both the EPF and the Public Sector Pension Scheme covered only a total number of about 3.7 million Malaysian employees, so that about 3.3 million employed people - almost half the total workers - were still not covered by any retirement scheme (Mohammad, 1993). From this, it can be predicted that many of this 3.3 million group are exposed to poverty and hardship during their future, retired days.

Table 3.2 Malaysia: profile of labour force, 1990-2000

	1990	2000
Total labour force (000)	7,042.0	9,327.1
Labour force participation rate (%)		
Male	85	86
Female	47	49

Source: Malaysia (1996)

The statistics in Table 3.2 also indicate the trend, apparent now for some years, in female participation in the labour market. This reflects the achievement of the implementation of the National Policy for Women which was formulated in 1989 to stimulate greater female participation in the economy and labour market as well as improved access to education and health. Responding to this trend, there are attempts to create programmes appropriate to the needs of female workers. Efforts are focused on providing women with skills to cope with the twin responsibilities of family and career (about 75 per cent of women labour force are housewives). Under the Seventh Malaysia Plan (Malaysia 1996) among the strategies being implemented are:

- the provision of more flexible working arrangements and support facilities;
- providing more educational and training opportunities for women to improve their upward mobility in the labour market;
- improving further the health status of women, reviewing laws and regulations that inhibit the advancement of women in the economy;
- encouraging the private sector (as the private sector is the largest employer) to facilitate and set up more conducive working arrangements for women that take into account their multiple roles and responsibilities;
- the provision of flexible working hours, career breaks and other flexible work practice which will enable women to integrate work with household duties;
- providing assistance such as advisory and counselling services.

The lack of marketable skills has been recognised as a main factor constraining women's participation in higher skilled and better paying jobs. So, in addition to efforts to enhance human capital formation among women through technical, vocational and other relevant training programmes, the government may also amend the Employment Act, 1955. This is to permit women to be gainfully employed in part-time employment. Amendments to labour legislation may also aim at allowing employers to introduce flexible working hours. The existence of such possibilities implies that social security policy in Malaysia is being informed by an awareness of gender issues so that gender sensitive programmes undertaken by government and non-governmental organisations may become increasingly common.

The Future

The Government's approach to social security programmes as a rational approach to welfare can be seen through state subsidies to privatise and extend market principles to welfare provision and the reduction of certain taxes to provide incentives and activate welfare provision by the private and voluntary sector. It could be said that in the recent economic difficulties and recession, social security policy should take responsibility for creating more productive employment, enhancing skill levels of the workforce and sustaining higher productivity levels. Similar to the British experience, pursuing economic policies aimed at maintaining full employment is important because without full employment the contributory funding basis for social security provision could not be maintained. Indeed the method of financing adopted requires rising real wages and near full employment if sufficient funds are to be accumulated. In a situation where unemployment, recession and general market fatigue occur, then social security schemes should be prepared as a firm social security institution on which people can rely. Moreover, any investment strategy also depends on macroeconomic management and international monetary and trading systems. Greater inter-linking of national labour markets, as a result of the globalisation of economic activities, may worsen Malaysia's social security mechanism. Any such threats will affect the EPF benefits too so that such possibilities should be taken into consideration.

Finally, one of main issues about the future direction of Malaysia's social security system that needs to be highlighted here is self-employment schemes. In 1998 there were about 1,774,320 self-employed persons in Malaysia (Vijaya, 1999). Of those, 1,398,800 (78.8 per cent), were male and 375,520 female. The Seventh Malaysia Plan stated that in the 1995-2000 period about 37.4 per cent of all workers would be in agricultural, animal husbandry, forestry, fishing and hunting industries. However, a large segment of these occupational groups plus foreign workers and domestic maids are also still not covered by any retirement scheme. Even though they are brought within the scope and coverage of the enactment, it is only on a voluntary basis. There is a case then, for the existing Pension Schemes to be expanded in scope and coverage to all those groups. Indeed, it could be said that the fact that so many workers and their families are excluded from the schemes and many peoples are self-employed either in the urban or informal sectors constitutes the major challenge facing social security policy makers. Coverage could be extended to the self-employed groups, either in a form of the so-called 'onion approach' that is one based on the extension of coverage out from the existing schemes, or a separate scheme with special and secure benefit packages, or a set of several special schemes targeted on various groups in need.

Conclusion

Besides EPF and SOCSO, Malaysia also has private provident, life insurance and religious welfare funds. The *zakat fitrah* (Muslim tithe payable) contributions and many small welfare funds, which are being operated by village mosque committees, do provide continuous help to poor families and the needy in the community. This is done in Chinese and Indian communities too. The contributions are mostly in the form of a regular supplementary income. Though benefits from such funds are limited to small contributions and are payable in the event of marriage, injury, sickness, education purpose or death in a family, they do play an important function as a social security institution. Thus, as Malaysia has a very strong community and family organisation roots, this family and community support pillar could be used effectively in maximising social security. In the climate of self-reliance being promoted in Malaysia, more appropriate ways and means to co-ordinate the EPF and SOCSO with the family and community pillar with a caring, comprehensive and complementary social security institution should be considered. Indeed, this is not only a vital solution but also a future challenge.

References

Baharuddin, S.A. (1994), 'National Unity: Malaysia's Model for Self-Reliance', in INTAN, *Malaysian Development Experience: Changes and Challenges*, INTAN, Kuala Lumpur.
Employees Provident Fund (1991), *Annual Report*, EPF, Kuala Lumpur.
Ibrahim, R. (1999), *Pension Schemes: Available Options*, Paper presented at Seminar on Financial Security in Old Age, National Council of Senior Citizens Organisations Malaysia, Petaling Jaya.
ILO (1962), *The Trade Union Situation in the Federation of Malaysia*, Report of a Mission for the International Labour Office, Geneva.
Malaysia (1996), *Seventh Malaysia Plan 1995-2000*, Government Printer, Kuala Lumpur.
Mohamed, S. (1993), *Promoting Savings and Social Security Needs: Expanding the Role of the EDP in a Rapidly Growing Economic Environment*, Paper presented for the First Malaysian National Savings Conference, Kuala Lumpur.
Paguman Singh (1991), 'Social Security in Malaysia', in C. Nicholas and A. Wangel (eds), *Safety at Work in Malaysia: An Anthology of Current Research*, Institute of Advanced Studies, University of Malaya, Kuala Lumpur.

Row, F. (1988), *Law and Practice of Social Security (SOCSO) in Malaysia*, SOCSO, Kuala Lumpur.

Vijaya, K.R. (1999), *Old Age Financial Security for the Self-Employed*, Paper presented at Seminar on Financial Security in Old Age, National Council of Senior Citizens Organisation Malaya, Petaling Jaya.

Wad, P. (1997), *Enterprise Unions and Structural Change in Malaysia*, Paper presented to the ASEAN Inter-University Seminar, Universitas Rina, Pekan Baru, Indonesia.

4 For richer and poorer? Pension policy in the United Kingdom
TONY MALTBY

Introduction and overview

This chapter compliments those on community care (chapters 6 and 7) and considers the financial position of older people in the UK with a focus upon state provision. To provide some historical context, the chapter will outline the development of pension policy.[1] The central and linking themes of this book, the labour market, family values and support, and public expenditure will be at the heart of the analysis. This aside, there are three issues which have dominated the policy debate over the course of the twentieth century and shaped how policy on retirement and pensions in particular, has been implemented. These are, the ageing of the population, the increasing intervention of government in the lives of individual citizens and finally, the growth and development of retirement as a distinct phase of life.

In the UK, income after the state pension ages (presently 60 for women and 65 for men) is derived from a combination of three main sources, through occupational and personal pensions, benefit transfers from the state (e.g. Basic Pension, SERPS or Income Support and other state benefits) or from paid work. Additionally, a small percentage of the older population may have income from financial and other investments. The present retirement pensions structure is composed of three pillars:
i) The Basic Pension payable from the state to all those who have made sufficient National Insurance payments over the 'qualifying period' (for men 44 years, for women 39 years) and is funded on a pay-as-you-go basis.
ii) A State Earnings Related Pension (SERPS) or an occupational or private personal pension. Those who contract out of SERPS pay a reduced rate of National Insurance contribution as well as receiving generous tax breaks.

iii) Finally, and of increasing importance, means-tested safety net (social assistance) benefit presently called Income Support. Those who fail to qualify for the Basic Pension have to resort to Income Support. Currently 14 per cent of men and 51 per cent of women fail to qualify for this universal benefit because of an insufficient contribution record (Blackburn, 1999).

Employment income plays a relatively small part in the income of older people, although there is considerable variation from a European perspective. In recent discussions about future policy, the idea of extending the proportion of the older population that remain economically active either in full or part time employment has received some serious consideration.

Development of Pensions

Before the introduction of a state pension in 1908, most people worked until they were no longer physically able to. Workers could rely upon benefits from their small insurances from the Friendly Societies or the exigencies of the Poor Law when assistance from their families, the usual source of support, could no longer be counted upon. However, the Liberal government initiated the payment of a pension from the Exchequer with the passage of the 1908 Old Age Pensions Act. This was non-contributory, means-tested and paid to those who survived to 70 and who had not 'habitually failed to work'. It was therefore a payment to '...the very old, the very poor and the very respectable' (Thane 1978b). Coverage of the 1908 Act was extended to insured workers and their wives between 65 and 70 by the passage of the Widows, Orphans and Old Age Pensions Act (1925 Act) effective from 1928 and established the contributory principle, present in today's state pension scheme. Various other Acts of Parliament prior to the Second World War offered fine-tuning to the pensions legislation already on the statute book (see Macnicol, 1998; Maltby, 1994).

The National Insurance Act 1946 implemented the Beveridge Report (1942) in substance if not in detail (Hess, 1981) and established the basis of the post-1945 system of contributory benefits in the UK. Yet many pensioners relied upon Social Assistance benefits for a large percentage of their weekly income (Deacon, 1982). Titmuss (1955), prophetically commenting upon the rise of occupational pensions, anticipated 'two nations in old age', the majority whose supplementation came from Social Assistance and the relatively better off minority, who had an occupational pension. The number and coverage of these has increased since 1945 and presently approximately 50 per cent of the workforce are members of an occupational scheme. In 1961 the Conservative government introduced the Graduated Pension scheme through the National Insurance Act 1959 to allow for a small earnings related pension to supplement the 1946 flat-rate pension. However, the Graduated Pension was non-indexed and so has lost its relative value as a method of supplementation.

The Social Security (Pensions) Act 1975 created the state earnings related pensions scheme (SERPS), and the structure of the retirement pension system operating today. Annual indexation of the Basic Pension was based upon the retail prices index or earnings (whichever was the greater). The State Earnings Related Pension Scheme pension would be paid out on the basis of the best twenty years earnings, largely to accommodate for the broken career paths of many women (see Castle, 1975). The Act also introduced the Home Responsibilities Protection (HRP) from 1978 enabling those caring for relatives or children (mainly women) to protect their right to the basic state pension (Department of Social Security, 1991a).

However, from 1981 (under the government of Margaret Thatcher) indexation of the Basic Pension altered from earnings to prices, devaluing it by 20 per cent up to 1991 (Fry and Stark, 1991). Today it is worth 17 per cent of average earnings and by 2030 it is estimated it will be worth 8.6 per cent of average earnings. The assault on the state's primary role in pension provision was continued through a series of reviews (Hemming and Kay, 1982; Department of Health and Social Security, 1984; Department of Health and Social Security, 1985a)[2] which proposed that the states' role as a provider would decline and that of the private sector increase to

> ...encourage personal independence and return to the old notion of a benefit system which provides a floor on which individuals can build instead of a ceiling which locks them into indefinite dependency (Portillo, 1989, p.192).

The earnings related portion of the SERPS was modified, reducing entitlement by half (by £12 billion per annum by 2033) by altering the principle of earnings relation of 'best twenty years earnings' to that of 'lifetime earnings'. The revaluation of SERPS earnings was reduced from 25 per cent to 20 per cent and although subject to phasing over a ten-year period (from April 2000), will devalue the pension from 1978 by one-fifth. Additionally, widows who under the 1975 SERPS scheme could inherit the whole of their husband's pension (up to a ceiling) are now only entitled to half.

The contracting-out regulations of the 1978 SERPS were also altered through the Social Security Act 1986 (implemented from 1988) so that in addition to occupational pensions, 'defined contribution schemes', 'appropriate personal pensions' and money purchase schemes (more colloquially referred to as personal pensions) could be used to 'contract out' of SERPS. Take-up of these was encouraged through payment of a 2 per cent 'bribe' (or 'incentive') for the first five years up to 1993 against the advice of the Government Actuary. More recently, the pension age was equalised for men and women at 65 and will be phased over a ten-year period from 2010.

This privatisation of pensions (Labour Research, 1987; O'Higgins, 1984) gave full voice to the two nations in old age idea first outlined by Titmuss (1955). The reversion to lifetime earnings calculations and other changes has been detrimental to the majority of women. This is because women's employment careers tend to be disrupted and typically comprise of a period in full time employment up to marriage, a period out of employment whilst having children (euphemistically termed a 'career break') followed by a longer period in part-time employment whilst children are at school. This is followed by a return to full time work for a brief period up to retirement (Joshi, 1992; Joshi, 1989; Dex, et al 1996). Additionally, most occupational pension schemes reflect the actuarial and other practices present within the state schemes with respect to gender (McGoldrick, 1984), the model of pensions designed by men with men in mind. Section 53(2) of the Social Security (Pensions) Act 1975 made it a statutory requirement to provide equal access for women and men to such occupational schemes. However, the benefits that are provided are usually differentiated according to gender specific criteria, partly based upon the greater 'risk' of a women's longer life expectancy. The application of different pension ages, the structure and provision of dependants and survivors benefits (women members often do not receive such benefits) and in the scheme design, also favour a male working pattern rather than a female one, endorsing the model of the male breadwinner (McGoldrick, 1984). Part-time workers, predominantly women in the UK, are often excluded on the basis that they do not work sufficient hours or that the scheme only provides for full-time employees on an actuarial basis.

Present Position of Older People

The present position reflects the past and as Falkingham (1998) notes later life is now more often associated with financial insecurity than security. The previous section emphasised that concern for older people's income and 'welfare' has been predicated upon economic rather than social imperatives, linked to involvement in the labour market and more specifically in paid work. Central to pension policy and particularly since 1948, has been the notion of the 'male breadwinner'. This has had some very significant negative consequences for the income of women in later life (see Arber and Ginn, 1991) despite their numerical superiority within the population over 60.

Yet data derived from the Family Expenditure Survey has shown that pensioners' income in real terms has doubled since the early 1960s (Retirement Income Survey 1996). More recent data, derived from the Pensioner Income Series (Department of Social Security, 1997) shows that the incomes of the top 20 per cent of pensioners has increased by 70 per cent since 1979, whereas those of the lowest 20 per cent have risen by only 38 per cent. Although this is a general trend it does not appear to be related to any major shift of older people up the income distribution but instead to increasing inequalities among pensioners and largely attributable to the increasing numbers of (mainly male) pensioners retiring with good occupational pensions. Field and Prior (1996) show how women have lower access to occupational pensions than men, directly related to their position in the labour force (as part time, low paid workers) and their continuing role as care-givers within the 'family', both to children and older kin (see chapters on Community Care). They have also demonstrated how women are particularly affected by the falling value of the Basic Pension and SERPS and the general shift towards the gender biased private sector funded pension schemes.

Despite some upward trends, the incomes of all pensioner groups have declined in comparison with changes in average incomes overall. Consistently over recent years both single pensioners and pensioner couples have been over-represented in the bottom two-fifths of the income distribution. A quarter of single pensioners and pensioner couples have incomes below half average incomes of the whole population and the proportion in poverty (defined as half average income) was greater in 1992-3 than in 1979. Moreover, older people in the UK are less well off than their counterparts in other leading industrial societies (see Bosanquet, Laing and Propper, 1990). Among the poorest older people in the UK there are just under one million (10 per cent of the older population) living on incomes below the Income Support levels (the main means tested safety-net social security benefit). Ginn (1997) has shown how in the period 1993-95, 74 per cent of these Income Support recipients over 65 were women yet a significant number of eligible for this benefit do not claim it - nearly one in five of those eligible (Department of Social Security, 1995).

In an attempt to counteract these trends, the present government has introduced a Minimum Income Guarantee (MIG) for pensioners. Yet this has to be claimed and is means-tested. The Budget of March 1999 promised that the MIG would rise in line with earnings rather than prices so that by April 2000 for a single person it would be £78 and for a married couple £121. A one off payment of £100 was also announced which would be paid to all pensioner households to assist with higher fuel costs during winter. Although welcome, these policies mark a further shift started with the Thatcher administrations, towards a greater reliance upon means-testing. In response one organisation (Help the Aged) suggested that raising the Basic Pension to £75 would have cost about the same as the £3 billion cost of raising the MIG and the £100 winter payment, but would have helped more people (especially older women) for longer.

As for personal pensions the problem here is that only the Basic Pension is assured, the second tier component (i.e. the personal pension) depends on the outcome of investments. As one economist has put it 'a guarantee is replaced by a lottery' (Atkinson, 1991) and poses serious questions for the future fate of people whose investments fail to yield sufficient income. Added to this there was the widely reported scandal of the 'mis-selling' of personal pensions by a number of pension providers. Although the Major and Blair governments have taken action over this, largely through the massive and complex Pension Act 1995, it does raise important policy questions over the level of benefits such pensions will accrue when they mature and the salience and appropriateness of such a policy in the first place.

The Myth of the Demographic Time Bomb

The concern with population ageing and the notion of a 'demographic time-bomb' have for many years consistently dominated the policy debate. Indeed it has been an issue, which has helped shape the discussion on pensions policy. What has come to be called the 'ageing of the population' is clearly discernable within the UK and European society. In general terms, this is a result of a combination of declining birth rates and greater life expectancy: 'fewer babies, longer lives'. For example, in 1901 life expectancy at birth was 45 years for men and 49 for women whereas in 1996 the corresponding figures were 75 years and 80 years, almost a doubling of life expectancy at birth over the course of last century with higher numbers of people living twenty years or more in retirement. The mean age of the UK population will rise from 38 years to a projected 44 years by 2036, and the numbers of people over pensionable age from 10.7 million today to 11.8 million in 2010 (Shaw, 1998). Accompanying these demographic shifts a clear gendered imbalance has been created within the population over sixty: the feminisation of later life.

These changes raise significant policy dilemmas, particularly for pensions. Yet despite an acceptance of these facts, pensions policies in both private and public sectors have consistently adopted an androcentric framework, linked with policy on labour force participation: the 'work test' (Shragge, 1984). Indeed, the 1908, 1925 and 1946 Acts (Macnichol, 1998) are classic examples of this. Little acknowledgement is (and was) made of the different work and life histories of women that often result in their poverty in old age (Arber and Ginn, 1991; Maltby, 1994). The incidence of cohabitation, widowhood and divorce[3] mean that many women cannot rely on the financial support of a husband.[4] Nor can it be assumed that married women will be able to share their husbands' income equally (Ginn, 1998). Therefore, coupled with the feminisation of the older population there exists a feminisation of poverty in old age, a result of the main emphasis on providing for the 'worn out working man' and his dependent wife that has existed since (at least) the 1908 Act. Moreover, this trend towards population ageing is often viewed with apocalyptic alarm and cast by many as a demon in the shape of the 'demographic time-bomb'. Such a position has been one of the arguments propounded for (particularly) the state to withdraw from funding pensions (and thus assist in reducing public expenditure) (see Department of Health and Social Security, 1984; Department of Health and Social Security, 1985a; Department of Health and Social Security, 1985b). Many emerging economies, notably and famously Chile have accepted the rhetoric and have already taken this path (see World Bank, 1994).

On the contrary, this worldwide trend towards population ageing should be viewed as positive development, one of the dramatic results of the effects of social and economic policy enshrined within the 'welfare state' (see Thane, 1989). The UK is well placed to absorb the effects of these demographic shifts since its population aged earlier than the rest of

Europe and as Hills (1993, 1997) has shown, over the next fifty years the effect of these demographic shifts will result in a minuscule increase in public expenditure of 0.32 per cent of Gross Domestic Product (GDP) per year and a net rise equivalent to 0.8 per cent GDP over the next 50 years. Thus, this emphasis on the economic burden upon future generations has resulted in the creation of the modern and ageist myth of the demographic time-bomb. What is required is, in essence, a change of perspective, particularly by policymakers and pension advisors, to one that accepts the world-wide ageing of populations, an acceptance that a greater proportion of public expenditure should be targeted at this segment of the population. Participation in paid work is not the only way in which people make economically valuable contributions to society. More broadly, arguments based on this demographic burden thesis, have been employed largely for party political and ideological purposes. They are an attempt to underline the unproven benefits of shifting provision from the state towards the private sector and that present expenditures on SERPS pensions is unsustainable.

What is clear is that the recent changes in pension policy in the UK have pre-empted concerns of the kind apparent in some other EU countries about the combined effects of demography and the maturation of pension schemes on public expenditure. Moreover, the policy of holding the Basic Pension at its 1979 level while encouraging the growth of occupational and personal pensions will result in a sharper polarisation in income levels among future pensioners, with low paid, part-time employees (predominantly women) having the poorest prospects. Titmuss' thesis about 'two nations in old age' is sadly being fully realised.

A Re-definition of the Retirement Process

Accompanying the ageing of the population, the second of the triplex of issues that has shaped policy towards older people over the course of this century, has been the increasing intervention into the lives of older people of the state and government institutions. This is a trend not only noticed in the UK but more generally in the western industrialised world. The successive policies of governments have assisted the creation of the socially constructed notion of retirement and associated with this, in the context of this chapter, the payment of a pension at a defined age (Phillipson, 1982; Townsend, 1986). In the case of the UK, this accompanied a growing acceptance of older people as 'deserving poor'. Retirement in the western sense is thus largely a twentieth century phenomenon.

Over the twentieth century there was a significant transformation in the experience and meaning of old age. For a large proportion of the population, retirement and exit from the labour force now no longer coincide. Retirement (associated with receipt of a pension) is no longer the recognised entry point to old age and it is increasingly anachronistic as a definition of older people. Accompanying the development of a concept of retirement there has been a distinct shift towards the withdrawal of (in particular) older men over 65 from the labour market. Nearly 75 per cent were still in employment in the late nineteenth century, declining to one-third in the 1950s and 3 per cent today (Phillipson, 1998). The trend for those men below the pension age of 65 is equally as marked with presently just under 50 per cent of them not economically active. Similar although more complex shifts are noted for women over 60 (Walker and Maltby, 1997) and for most Western industrial nations (Kohli et al, 1991; Atkinson and Rein, 1993; Walker and Maltby, 1997).

Although increasing numbers of older people are leaving the labour force in different ways, through early retirement, partial retirement, redundancy, unemployment, disability and so on (Walker and Maltby, 1997), older people are living longer and healthier lives, driving back the threshold of frailty. Added to this is the paradox in which 'official' retirement (marked by receipt of the state pension) cannot occur before 65 (for men) or 60 (for women), yet a large proportion of mostly male workers have entered retirement earlier. The established pattern of long work and short retirement is changing to one of increasing length and complexity as a result of a combination of greater longevity and higher rates of long-term unemployment, particularly for men (Phillipson, 1998).

Recent research (Campbell, 1999) (replicating Walker, 1985) has determined that the employment rate of older workers is lowest among those close to state pension age. Since 1979 male employment has started to fall at an earlier age, 50 instead of 55, and the lower level of employment among all older workers means that the decline starts from a lower peak, as shown in Table 4.1 (Campbell, 1999). Overall female employment has increased dramatically over the last 8 years for each age group except for the over 55s, accounting for the expansion of low paid, flexible part-time work within the service industries.

This fall in employment is more a function of higher economic inactivity than the result of an increase in conventionally defined unemployment. Table 4.1 shows how employment and inactivity changes follow one another; with employment falling furthest among men aged 55-

64. Table 4.2 shows the contribution of each age group's employment to the total decline in male employment. Older men (and to a lesser extent men aged 18-25) have had a disproportionate share of the decline in male and female employment. Reduced employment among men aged 55-64 accounts for more than one-third of the decline in male employment. Men aged 50-64 account for nearly half of the decline in employment even though they are a relatively small proportion of the total population (Campbell, 1999).

Research studies have demonstrated that the main factors determining the longer-term decline in employment among older workers are demand related (Taylor and Walker, 1994). For example, older men are likely to work in declining industries which has increased their risk of redundancy. The available evidence suggests that, in the UK at least, it is not changes in the nature of work or new organisational forms of work but changes in the aggregate supply of employment (or demand for labour) that is still the main influence on the relationship between ageing and work. Moreover, policy on pensions has to a great extent attempted to reinforce the removal of 'worn out workers' from industry (Macnichol, 1998).

Table 4.1 Changes in employment, unemployment and economic inactivity rates, 1979-1997 (percentage points)

		Employment	Unemployment	Economic Inactivity
Men aged	18-24	-12.6	+6.6	+6.0
	25-49	-7.0	+1.6	+5.4
	50-64	-16.4	+1.0	+15.4
	55-64	-21.2	+0.9	+20.3
All men		-10.2	+1.9	+8.4
Women aged	18-49	+9.8	+0.2	-10.1
	50-59	+4.2	0.0	-4.2
	55-59	-0.5	0.0	0.5
All	not in last 10 years*	+0.3	+1.2	-1.4
	last 10 years*	-7.5	+0.4	+7.1
All of working age		-1.1	+1.0	+0.1

Note: *refers to the last 10 years of working age (i.e. age 50-59 for women, 55-65 for men).
Source: Campbell (1999)

Table 4.2 Contribution to changes in employment patterns, 1979-1997 (%)

		Each group's contribution to the change in:		Proportion of population (1997)
		Employment fall	Inactivity increase	
Men aged	18-24	12.9	7.4	10.5
	25-49	41.6	39.0	60.7
	50-54	10.7	11.3	11.7
	55-64	35.5	41.6	17.2
				100.0
		Employment increase	Inactivity fall	
Women aged	18-49	88.9	89.0	78.1
	50-54	11.2	11.0	12.3
	55-59	-0.6	-0.6	9.6
				100.0

Source: Campbell (1999)

Present proposals

It is clear that changes in the nature of retirement, both as a concept and as a process in the late twentieth century, together with the changing demographic processes mentioned earlier, require policymakers to rethink pension policy. Unfortunately, such change will be driven primarily by changes in the structure of the labour market processes (Macnichol, 1998) and, directly linked with them, the changing nature and understanding of familial relationships. That is the imperative of 'work testing' (Shragge, 1984) and the changing nature of patriarchal relations (Maltby, 1984). However, as we have noted, and especially since 1979, such change has also been driven by a desire to curtail public expenditure on pensions.

The present government's (Department of Social Security, 1998) pensions policy is a tidying up of the existing system alongside an enhancement of the 'partnership' between the state and private sector by suggesting that public expenditure should shift towards the private sector, from 60 per cent at present to 40 per cent by 2050. When fully implemented it will continue the shift towards the greater privatisation of pensions, and to the continuing rise of what Blackburn, (1999) has termed 'grey capitalism'. It reflects the views expressed by the World Bank (1994) which argued (from an economic libertarian view) for a 'multi-pillar approach', a rejection of pay-as-you-go (because of savings disincentives and costs to public expenditure) and the introduction of mandatory funded private pensions.

Improvements in the position of the poorest pensioners are a priority but achieved through provision of the MIG. It suggested that the Basic Pension would remain but shrink in real terms (by continuing its annual revaluation with prices). It poured scorn on the call, mainly from pensioner organisations, for an increase in the value of the Basic Pension. In order 'to boost the pension of the lowest paid' (those earning less than £9,000 per annum), the SERPS pension will be replaced from 2002 by a new State Second Pension (SSP). The benefits of SSP will be flat rate and are expected to be 40 per cent of average earnings (£2,300 per annum), double, it argues, what can be expected currently from a SERPS pension. As now pension credits will be given for all those caring for dependent relatives or children under five as well as to the long term disabled with broken employment records.

Those earning above £9,000 per year ('middle' incomes) and who are not members of an occupational pension scheme, will be encouraged to take out a funded 'stakeholder pension'. These should be operational from April 2001 and would be low cost, flexible and provided by the private sector. Clearly this is to allow them to undercut and ultimately reduce, the number of people paying towards a 'personal pension'. In order to encourage the shift towards stakeholder pensions, the 'contracted-out' rebate on National Insurance will be increased *rather* than insisting upon compulsory inclusion in such a scheme. Better education, better information and better regulation will be an essential element of the stakeholder pension structure. It proposed no change for those earning above £18,500 per annum, since most in this income bracket are well protected as members of either an occupational or other private schemes.

Although the language of this policy is very encouraging, providing what it terms 'decent' pensions, this can clearly have different meanings. Does 'decent' mean,

i) alleviation of pensioner poverty; ii) prevention of pensioner poverty; iii) giving the retired the resources to play a part in the community; iv) enabling the retired to retain their pre-retirement standard of living (Blackburn, 1999, p.32).

The answer to this question, present in all discussions on pensions since (at least) 1878, is only hinted at. Pension policy should at least aim towards the first of this list, although ideally it should start with the second and move towards the third and fourth; the full social inclusion of older people. The greater reliance within the present government strategy upon the *alleviation* of poverty through the MIG and eventually the State Second Pension, marks the continuation of successive government thinking since the 1908 Act: nothing has changed. Blackburn is correct in suggesting that the absence of any mention of the third and fourth aims (priorities?) on this list underlines the present Government's perception of their role, that pensions should be obtained through the private sector. This development of the 'partnership' between state and private sector, is merely the enhancement of 'grey capitalism' offering 'poor relief for the poor and tax relief to the rich' (Blackburn, 1999). Indeed Walker (1999) has recently commented that

> The government has set a policy course which will continue that charted by its predecessor to residualize the public sector as a provider of pensions and to undermine the universality of national insurance (p.526).

Conclusions

This push by most national governments towards the private sector for a solution to the pension conundrum flies in the face of the evidence. As Walker and Maltby (1997) reported, there is a strong indication of a very powerful intergenerational solidarity and full support across the European Union for the 'social contract'; that is the payment of contributions or taxes to fund pensions. Furthermore, when questioned about where the responsibility for pensions should lie, the state, employers or individuals, the majority of respondents in all European Union countries indicated that pensions should be funded from contributions or taxes. What is also evident is that although there is some resentment on the part of Europe's senior citizens about the low level of pensions in some countries, there is widespread agreement among them about the importance of their families.

In order to eradicate the harmful effects of poverty and social exclusion and thus encourage senior citizens within Europe as a whole to become full participants in their communities requires the removal of existing socio-economic barriers. Of vital importance is the provision of an adequate income for *all* older people, particularly older women, who often highlight in the poverty statistics of most countries. Combating age discrimination in employment, for which there is widespread support from electorates within Europe, is another priority since this would enhance employment opportunities for all older people and effectively place old age in a new light.

Notes

[1] Space prevents me from a fuller description and analysis. There are a number of texts providing a detailed analysis of this history. For the crucial period from 1878 to 1948 see John Macnichol's (1998) excellent text. For the period after 1948 there are texts dealing with specific periods including Schragge, 1984, Atkinson, 1991 and Maltby, 1994.
[2] For a full discussion see Creedy and Disney, (1988). For a detailed analysis of the introduction of pensions policy within the Social Security Act 1986 see Nesbitt, 1995 and 1991.
[3] The UK has the highest rates of divorce in the European Union, see Walker and Maltby (1997).
[4] Nor should they! My point is that much of the poverty in old age is a result of the contributory principle and the androcentric (and patriarchal) approach to social policy in this area of pensions. A pension should be provided as an individual right of citizenship. It is more often provided in the form of deferred earnings.

References

Arber, S. and Ginn, J. (1991), *Gender and Later Life*, Sage, London.
Atkinson, A.B. (1991), *The Development of State Pensions in the United Kingdom*, STICERD Welfare State Programme Paper No. 59, LSE, London.
Atkinson, A.B. and Rein, M. (1993), *Age, Work and Social Security*, Macmillan, London.
Blackburn, R. (1999), 'New Collectivism: Pension Reform, Grey Capitalism and Complex Socialism', *New Left Review*, 233 Jan/Feb, pp. 3-65.
Bosanquet, N., Laing W. and Propper, C. (1990), *Elderly Consumers in Britain: Europe's Poor Relations?*, Laing and Buisson, London.
Campbell, N. (1999), *The Decline of Employment Among Older People in Britain*, CASE, London.
Castle, B. (1975), *House of Commons Hansard*, 18 March, column 1492.
Confederation of British Industry, (CBI), (1991), *Pensions post-Barber: Equalising Occupational Pension Schemes*, Confederation of British Industry, London.
Creedy, J. and Disney, R. (1988), 'The New Pension Scheme in Britain', *Fiscal Studies*, vol. 9, pp.57-71.
Davidson, F. (1990), 'Occupational Pensions and Equal Treatment', *Journal of Social Welfare Law*, vol. 5, pp. 310-331.

Dawson, A. and Evans, G. (1987), Pensioner's Incomes and Expenditure in 1970-1985, *Employment Gazette*, vol. 95, pp. 243-252.

Deacon, A. (1982), 'An End to the Means Test? Social Security and the Attlee Government', *Journal of Social Policy*, vol. 11, pp.289-306.

Department of Health and Social Security (1984), *Population, Pension Costs and Pensioner Incomes*, HMSO, London.

Department of Health and Social Security (1985a), *Reform of Social Security Volumes 1, 2, and 3*, Cmnd. 9517, 9518 and 9519, HMSO, London.

Department of Health and Social Security (1985b), *Reform of Social Security: Programme for Action*, Cmnd. 9691, HMSO, London.

Department of Social Security (1991a), *A Guide to Retirement Pensions*, Leaflet No. NP46, HMSO, London.

Department of Social Security (1991b), *Options for Equality in the State Pension Age*, Cm.1723, HMSO, London.

Department of Social Security (1995), *The Pensioners Income Series 1993*, DSS Analytical Services Division, London.

Department of Social Security (1997), *Pensioners' Income Series 1995/6* Analytical Services Division, London.

Department of Social Security (1998), *A New Contract for Welfare: Partnership in Pensions*, Cm 4179, The Stationary Office, London (Also available at Http://www.dss.gov.uk/hq/pubs/pengp.index.htm).

Dex, S., Joshi, H., McCulloch, A., and Macran, S. (1996), *Women's Employment Transitions around Childbearing*, CEPR Discussion Paper no. 1408, CEPR, London.

Duffy, K. (1995), *Social Exclusion and Human Dignity in Europe*, Council of Europe, Brussels.

Falkingham, J. (1998), 'Financial (in)security in Later Life' in M. Bernard and J. Phillips (eds), *The Social Policy of Old Age*, CPA, London.

Field, F. (1998), Ministerial statement to the House of Commons, *House of Commons Hansard*, 26 March 1998, par 14.

Field, J. and Prior, G. (1996), *Women and Pensions*, Department of Social Security Research Report Number 49, HMSO, London.

Fry, V. and Stark, G. (1991), 'New Rich or Old Poor: Poverty, Take-up and the Indexation of the State Pension', *Fiscal Studies*, vol. 12, pp. 67-71.

Fry, V., Smith, S. and White, S. (1990), *Pensioners and the Public Purse*, Institute of Fiscal Studies, London.

Hemming, R. and Kay, J.A. (1982), 'The Costs of the State Earnings Related Pension Scheme', *The Economic Journal*, vol. 92, pp. 300-319.

Hess, J. (1981), 'The Social Policy of the Atlee Government', in W. J. Mommsen (ed), *The Emergence of the Welfare State in Britain and Germany*, Croom Helm, Kent.

Hills, J. (1993), *The Future of Welfare: A Guide to the Debate*, Joseph Rowntree Foundation, York.

Hills, J. (1997), 'How will the Scissors Close? Options for UK Social Spending', in A. Walker and C. Walker (eds), *Britain Divided*, CPAG, London pp. 231-248.
Joshi, H. (1989), 'The Changing Form of Women's Economic Dependency' in H. Joshi (ed), *The Changing Population of Britain*, Blackwell, Oxford.
Joshi, H. (1992), 'The Cost of Caring' in C. Glendinning and J. Millar (eds), *Women and Poverty in Britain: The 1990s*. Harvester Wheatsheaf, Hemel Hempstead.
Kohli, M., Rein, M., Guillemard, A-M., and Gunsteren, H. (1991) *Time for Retirement*, Cambridge University Press, Cambridge.
Labour Research (1987), *The Privatisation of Pensions*, LRD Publications, London.
Macnichol, J. (1998), *The Politics of Retirement in Britain 1878-1948*, Cambridge University Press, Cambridge.
Maltby, T. (1994), *Women and Pensions in Britain and Hungary*, Avebury, Aldershot.
Marshall, T.H. (1950), *Citizenship and Social Class*, Cambridge University Press, Cambridge.
McGoldrick, A. (1984), *Equal Treatment in Occupational Pension Schemes*, Equal Opportunities Commission, Manchester.
Nesbitt, S. (1995), *British Pensions Policy in 1980s*, Avebury, Aldershot.
Nesbitt, S.M. (1991), *Social and Economic Determinants of British Pensions Policy: A Contrast Between 1975 and 1988*, University of Sheffield, Unpublished PhD thesis.
O'Higgins, M. (1984), 'Privatisation and Social Security', *Political Quarterly*, vol. 55, pp. 129-139.
Phillipson, C. (1982), *Capitalism and the Construction of Old Age*, Macmillan, London.
Phillipson, C. (1998), 'Changing Work and Retirement. Older Workers' Discrimination and the Labour Market' in M. Bernard and J. Phillips (eds), *The Social Policy of Old Age*, CPA, London.
Portillo, M. (1989), 'The Reform of Social Security: A Government View', in A. Dilnot and I. Walker (eds), *The Economics of Social Security*, Oxford University Press, Oxford.
Shaw, C. (1998), '1996-based National Population Projections for the United Kingdom and Constituent Countries', *Population Trends*, vol. 91, pp.43-49.
Shragge, E. (1984), *Pensions Policy in Britain: A Socialist Analysis*, Routledge and Kegan Paul, London.
Taylor, P. and Walker, A. (1994), 'The Ageing Workforce: Employers' Attitudes Towards Older Workers', *Work, Employment and Society*, vol. 8, pp.569-591.
Thane, P. (1978a), 'The Muddled History of Retiring at 60 and 65', *New Society*, vol. 3, pp. 234-236.

Thane, P. (1978b), 'Non-Contributory versus Insurance Pensions 1878-1908' in Thane, P. (ed), *The Origins of British Social Policy*, Croom Helm, London.
Thane, P. (1989), 'Old Age: Burden or Benefit' in Joshi, H. (ed), *The Changing Population of Britain*, Blackwell, Oxford.
Titmuss, R.M. (1955), 'Pension Systems and Population Change', *Political Quarterly*, vol. XXVI, pp. 152-166.
Townsend, P. (1986), 'Ageism and Social Policy' in C. Phillipson and A. Walker, (eds), *Ageing and Social Policy*, Gower, Aldershot.
Walker, A. (1985), 'Early Retirement: Release or Refuge from the Labour Market?' *The Quarterly Journal of Social Affairs*, vol. 1, pp.211-229.
Walker, A. (1999), 'The Third Way for Pensions (by way of Thatcherism and avoiding pensioners)', *Critical Social Policy*, vol. 19, pp. 511-527
Walker, A. and Maltby, T. (1997), *Ageing Europe*, Open University Press, Buckingham.
Walker, A. and Walker, C. (1997), *Britain Divided*, CPAG, London
World Bank (1994), *Averting the Old Age Crisis*, Oxford University Press, Oxford.

5 Formal old age financial security schemes in Malaysia
MOHD. FAUZI YAACOB

Introduction

It has been said, not without justification, that health is a matter of prime importance to older people. Staying reasonably well helps them to remain independent and in constant engagement. But equally important in old age is financial security. In the West, financial security in old age is an element of what is broadly known as social security, which refers to the various measures undertaken by the government for protecting its population from economic distress caused by the stoppage of earnings due to sickness, employment injury, invalidity, unemployment, old age or even death. In Malaysia, public measures of such nature are of recent origin. It can be said that the forerunner to the present day social security measures was started only in the 1950s (Amin, 1982). Prior to that date, older people who could no longer work and had no savings had to rely on the resources of their families.

This chapter provides an overview of the formal schemes that have been developed to meet the needs for financial security of Malaysian workers in their old age. It traces the origin and development of schemes such as those administered by the Employees Provident Fund Board and the Social Security Organisation. It briefly discusses the Civil Service Pension Scheme. Issues pertaining to the coverage of these schemes and adequacy of their coverage will also be an important part of this chapter, as will discussion of the necessity of reviewing the current policy and practice of retiring from public service upon attaining the age of 55. It starts with a brief general description of sources of income for older people in Malaysia.

Sources of income for older people

In Malaysia, older people secure income from a number of sources: remittances from working children, savings, private insurance, pension, employment and the state. The importance of each of these varies with different groups of the older population. For example, private insurance as an old-age support scheme is generally restricted to only a section of the older population, usually the urban professionals and middle class. In 1994, only about 22 per cent of the population subscribed to insurance coverage. Tan et al (1999) suggest that considering that some may have taken multiple policies, the percentage of older persons with this benefit is expected to be small. Insurance payments are often in a lump sum upon maturity of the policy and serve as long term, old age financial security if it is prudently managed.

Employment as a source of income is important for a considerable percentage of older people. In 1990, only 52.4 per cent of the 55-59 age group were employed, 44.4 per cent of the 60-64 age group, and 30 per cent of the 65+ age group. The number of older men in the labour market is larger than the number of older women: 72.7 per cent as opposed to 33.1 per cent of those in the 55-59 age bracket. For those in the 65 and over age bracket, 30 per cent of males are still active as opposed to 10 per cent of females. Generally speaking, older workers are in the agricultural and informal sectors, both of which do not have a formal retirement age.

Monetary contributions from working children constitute an important source of income for many older parents. Children usually begin contributing part of their income to their parents when they start work. The size of the contributions varies with their earnings and generosity. The contribution is perceived by children as *balas jasa*, that is repaying parents for what they have done. The ideology of *balas jasa* is both religious and cultural. Throughout the ages, Muslim Malay parents have been transmitting to their children the notion and value of filial piety and that it is their duty to take care of their parents once they become old and frail. Such an ideology is also cherished and upheld by Chinese, Indians and other ethnic groups living in Malaysia. In the pre-industrial and largely rural Malaysia of long gone days, great emphasis was placed on this aspect of filial piety. The family, both nuclear and extended, provided the necessary assistance to each and every member of the group, more so for the older members of the group. In the largely traditional and agricultural setting, older people enjoyed a privileged position. They were accorded deference and often looked up to as wise and experienced, their views and advice were always sought. More often than not, in their sickness and ill health, they were well-looked after by the members of their immediate family. Generally, the care givers were the female members of the group, who form the backbone of the family. Until the advent of rapid industrialisation in the early 1960s, women's roles and functions were largely confined to the family and kinship domain. Their participation in the labour market had been minimal. Men, almost exclusively, provided the financial support.

The values and norms of the time demanded that these be strictly adhered to. Of late, however, the influence of these forces has been weakening. Rapid urbanisation, massive rural-urban migration and the increasing of women's participation in the labour market have led to changes in the family structure to result in the weakening of family support for older people. For example, the percentage of the older people living alone or not co-residing with adult children has risen, as shown by Tey (1995), who also noted that while those who do not work tend to receive support from children this is more important for rural females than other groups.

Apart from remittances from their children, personal savings form another important source of income for older people. Savings include cash in hand or in banking accounts, investment in land, houses, jewellery and, more recently, stocks, shares and unit trusts. For some, savings in these forms represent part of their income put aside for future use. In their productive years, they may have worked as employees or have been self-employed. To be thrifty or *jimat cermat* is an important value still considered to be important to be imbibed by young persons just embarking on a career. They are given advice by their elders that they should *sedia payung sebelum hujan*, literally meaning 'have the umbrella ready before it rains'.

For some other older people, these savings are linked to retirement benefits. Our attention is now focussed on these.

History, development and features of formal old age financial security schemes in Malaysia

Presently, there exist several formal social security and pension benefit schemes, such as those administered by the Employees Provident Fund Board (EPF), the Social Security Organisation (SOCSO), and The Armed Forces Board (LTAT). A section of Malaysian workers are covered by the

Civil Service Pension Scheme, which is the earliest old-age benefit scheme, created during the time of British Malaya. EPF was started in 1951 by virtue of the Employees Provident Fund Ordinance passed by the then Federal Legislative Council. SOCSO started operation in 1969 by virtue of the Employees Social Security Act 1969. In addition to legislation that gave birth to these organisations or institutions there are several other pieces of legislation that are related to workers' welfare. These include The Workmen's Compensation Ordinance 1952 and The Employment Ordinance 1955.

As mentioned earlier, the Civil Service Pension Scheme or the government pension scheme is the earliest of the formal old age benefit schemes. A non-contributory benefit scheme, it was created during the time of British Malaya but indigenised through a series of changes since its inception. There are no records to indicate when exactly the scheme was first introduced. A report by a committee of the then Federal Legislative Council surmised that the scheme was established only after 1875 for there was no record of its existence prior to that date (Wahid, 1970). The Civil Service Pension Scheme has been enshrined in the 1957 constitution under article 147. As defined by article 133, the civil service includes the military and police force, the judiciary and legal service, the federal and state administration service, and the railway and education service.

The basis of the scheme's present day implementation are the Pension Ordinance, 1951 and its amendments contained in the Pension Act, 1980. The scheme provides the basic elements of welfare and security for employees when they retire or for their dependants in the event of their death. It also includes protection in the event of accidents and sickness at the workplace. Employees in the Malaysian public sector retire compulsorily upon attaining 55 years of age. Compulsory retirement can also take place on other grounds, such as medical, organisational restructuring or renunciation of citizenship. An amendment included in the Pension Act 1980 makes it possible for an employee to opt for early retirement upon attaining 40 years of age, without affecting the previous practice of an early retirement option at the age of 50 for men and 45 for women. A public servant can also be asked to retire in the national interest if or when his or her service is needed elsewhere, in which case they are entitled to pensions and other benefits.

To qualify for a pension, an employee must have reached the retirement age, or the optional retirement age, or must have been medically boarded due to accident or disease. The scheme provides for a guaranteed minimum pension of RM180 per month on condition that an employee has served not less than 300 months or 25 years. The maximum amount payable to an employee upon retirement is equivalent to one-half of their last drawn salary. An employee who retires on medical grounds will be entitled to a minimum of one-fifth of their last drawn salary on condition they have served not less than 120 months or 10 years. The same benefit applies to employees who have been requested by the Government to serve in a non governmental organisation and who died in service. For employees who died in service, their dependants will be entitled to a pension payment of not less than one-fifth of the last drawn monthly salary. They will continue receiving the benefits until they lose that right, which occurs under the following circumstances: remarriage in the case of widows or upon reaching the age of 21 in the case of children.

Apart from the monthly pension payment, government retirees are also entitled to a gratuity and 'golden hand-shake'. A gratuity is a lump sum payment payable at the point of retirement, calculated on the basis of the last drawn salary and the number of months served. A 'golden handshake' is a facility accorded to public servants to accumulate up to a maximum of 90 days of their annual leave in exchange for cash payment at the end of their service, and is calculated on the basis of last drawn salary, inclusive of all allowances, and the accumulated leave, that being leave not taken on the ground of exigencies of service.

In contrast to the Civil Service Pension Scheme which is non-contributory, the EPF is fully-funded, the first of such schemes to be implemented in Malaysia. Set up in 1951, it has its history in the several provident funds that were in practice previously, set up by employers in the then thriving plantation and mining industries for their respective employees. Workers in these industries were largely from China and India and early legislation pertaining to labour was aimed at their protection. For example, the Indian Immigration Ordinance Fund, 1907, was aimed at controlling the recruitment of immigrants on a national basis and preventing abuse that arose from such recruitment of indentured labour. Labour Enactment (Mining) and Labour Enactment (Agriculture), introduced also in 1907, were aimed at protecting immigrant labour in the mining and agricultural sectors respectively (Amin, 1982). After the Second World War, the importation of immigrant labour was stopped. Most of the immigrant labour and their families had started to stay permanently and there was a substantial participation of indigenous population in the labour market. These developments had led to the realisation that there was a need to introduce a comprehensive set of labour legislation to protect the interest of the country's working population. The Employees Provident Fund Ordinance 1951 was a piece of legislation that arose out of such a need.

At the outset, the EPF's main objective was to provide low paying workers outside the government sector with financial protection when they retire, or in the event of disability or death if these occur earlier. Though formed officially in October 1951, the EPF received its first contribution only in July 1952. It required all workers aged 16 and above, earning less than RM400 per month and working in certain 'scheduled employment' to contribute to the fund. Scheduled employment then referred to, inter alia, estates of over 25 acres, organisations hiring at least ten workers, and employment with the government of the federation or any state or any municipality, town council, town board and local council. The monthly contribution payable by employees and employers were in accordance with a fixed statutory rate that amounted to 5 per cent for the employees and 5 per cent for the employers.

Over the last forty years, the EPF has been continually changed through a series of legislative measures. The changes are related to its scope of application, contribution rate, and benefits. For example, changes introduced in 1964, extended the scheme to cover workers earning up to RM500 per month working in organisations that employ three or more workers. In December 1967, its coverage was extended to Sabah and Sarawak. In 1977, the scheme allowed the self employed to voluntarily make contributions to the fund.

Changes were also made to the rate of contributions. The rate of 5 per cent payable by the employees and the employers respectively had been in operation since the EPF's inception. After August 1975, employees contributed to the fund 6 per cent of their salary, while employers contributed 7 per cent. Beginning from December 1980, employees contributed to the fund 9 per cent of their salary and the employers 11 per cent. Further changes in the rate of contribution were made in 1995 since when employees pay to the fund 11 per cent of their salary, with a contribution of 12 per cent by their employers.

Contributors to the EPF were allowed to withdraw the amount standing to their credit on attaining the age of 55, upon being physically and mentally incapacitated from engaging in further employment or when they leave the country with no intention of returning. In 1980, the law was amended to allow employees who attained the age of 50 to withdraw one-third of the amount standing to their credit, for such purposes as paying a deposit for the purchase of a house. A very significant and innovative change was introduced on 1 November 1994, providing for every members' account to be separated into 3: Account I, Account II and Account III, whereby 60 per cent of a member's contribution is kept under Account 1, 30 per cent in Account II and 10 per cent in Account III. No withdrawal is allowable from Account I until the member attains the age of 55 unless in cases of death, leaving the country or incapacitation from further employment. The rationale for this ruling is to ensure that every member has sufficient cash savings to provide during retirement. A member can withdraw savings from Account II for buying or building a house. Further withdrawals are allowed every five years from the previous withdrawal for the purpose of reducing or paying off the balance of a housing loan. They can also use part of the saving in this account when reaching 50 years of age, provided they still has some balance in the account. Account III is to be used for paying medical expenses of critical illnesses, and to take care of medical expenses not covered or partially covered by the members' employer. Thus medical treatment is not limited to the member, but also covers the members' spouse, children, parents and siblings. When a member attains 55 years of age, the three accounts are merged and there is a choice of any of the following modes of payment: lump sum, periodic payment, annual dividend or part lump sum payment of the balance in periodic payment. This innovation allows the saving in the EPF to be viewed and used as both retirement and pre-retirement benefit.

When the Government of Malaysia passed the Employees Social Security Act in 1969 and on 1 January 1970 set up the Social Security Organisation (SOCSO) in order to implement its provisions, the country moved a step further in the area of social security for its growing labour force. The schemes introduced by the Act and administered by SOCSO became the first in Malaysia to follow the internationally accepted social security norms. They are based on social insurance principles and the pooling of risks.

The Act provides for two social security schemes: the Injury Insurance Scheme and the Invalidity Pension Scheme, covering the three contingencies of industrial accident, occupational disease and invalidity. The Employment Injury Insurance Scheme, which is intended to cover the inadequacies of the Workmen's Compensation Ordinance, 1952, provides protection to insured persons against the contingencies of industrial accident and occupational disease arising out of and in the course of their employment. The Invalidity Pension Scheme, on the other hand, provides protection against the contingency of invalidity due to illness or infirmity from whatever cause.

The Employees Social Security Act 1969 applies only to those employees whose wages do not exceed RM500 a month and who will remain in the scheme even though their wages may come to exceed the amount so long as they remain with the same employer or other employer who is liable for coverage. Government servants are exempted from the purview of the Act, because they are already covered by the Pension Act; but employees of local authorities and quasi government bodies are covered. The Employment Injury Insurance Scheme and the Invalidity Pension Scheme are financed from contributions by the covered employers and insured employees. Contribution rates are income related and payable monthly. The contribution towards the Employment Injury Insurance Scheme, which works out to approximately 1.25 per cent of the employee's monthly wage, is solely borne by the employer. The contribution towards the Invalidity Pension Scheme, which works out roughly to 1.0 per cent of the employee's monthly wage, is shared equally between the employer and the employee.

The Employment Injury Insurance Scheme provides benefits such as: disablement benefit; medical benefit; dependant's benefit; constant attendance allowance; funeral benefits; supply of prosthetic appliances and aids; and rehabilitation. Disablement benefit is payable to an injured person who suffers from disablement as a result of an employment injury, and consists of three types: temporary disablement benefit; permanent partial disablement benefit; and permanent total disablement benefit. Temporary disablement benefit is paid in cash at a rate roughly equivalent to 70 per cent of the assumed daily wage for as long as the disablement lasts. Permanent disablement benefit is paid to an employee where an employment injury has resulted in permanent disablement as confirmed by a medical board. The loss of permanent capacity is assessed at 100 per cent for permanent total disablement and is paid at the full rate. For permanent partial disablement, the benefit payable is such percentage of the full rate as is proportionate to the loss of earning capacity assessed by the medical board, and is paid in the form of a monthly pension. However, if the injured employee's loss of earning capacity does not exceed 20 per cent, the injured employee is allowed to commute his monthly pension into one-lump payment.

Insured persons who suffer from disablement as a result of employment injury are accorded with medical benefit through a system of panel doctors appointed by SOCSO or from a government hospital. Injured persons who require hospitalisation are eligible for admission into second class wards at a government hospital. Dependant's benefit is payable to the dependant(s) of an insured person who dies from an employment injury. The benefit is payable to his widow, or widows, for life or until remarriage, and children (including those legally adopted) until they are 16, or 18 if they are in schooling.

The Invalidity Pension Scheme provides an insured person who suffers invalidity from employment injury a monthly pension throughout the period of invalidity or until their death. The quantum ranges from 25 per cent to 65 per cent of the insured person's average monthly wage. Constant attendance allowance is also payable to an insured person who is eligible for invalidity pension or permanent total disablement benefit if and so long as they remain so severely incapacitated as to constantly require the personal attendance and care of another person. The rate for such allowance is equivalent to 30 per cent of the daily rate of permanent total disablement benefit.

Issues about financial security schemes for older people

In the past, several issues have been raised with respect to financial support schemes for older people. In this chapter, discussion is limited to the issue of coverage of the scheme, adequacy of benefit and the policy and practice of retirement from public sector employment at the age of 55.

In 1995, Malaysia had a labour force of about 7 million, of which approximately 800,000 were in the public sector. The rest were employees in the private sector, and the self-employed in the urban informal and rural agricultural sectors. But available information indicates that a significant percentage of these workers are still not covered by any old-age financial security schemes. The Civil Service Pension Scheme covers only a section of the employees in the public sector, either in the federal or state service. Those in public service, not covered by the pension scheme, are covered by the EPF. Those in the private sector are covered by either the EPF or SOCSO. About 50 per cent of the country's labour force are covered by the EPF, and some by SOCSO (Vijaya, 1997). But, many are not covered by any scheme. These are largely the self-employed small-scale traders, farmers, fishermen and casual labour. Since they are not covered, they have to rely on savings, income transfers from their children or even social welfare assistance in their old age. In the past, some thoughts have been given to this group of workers. The EPF, for example, has made provision since 1977 for the self-employed workers to voluntarily contribute to the fund. But the response was not encouraging. As reported by Vijaya (1997), there were only 11,800 active self-employed members with the EPF as at December 1996. Arguably, a more concerted nation-wide campaign should be launched to encourage more self-employed to participate in schemes that will provide them with financial security in their old age.

Related to coverage, is the issue of compliance. Though it is required by law for employers to make contributions to EPF or SOCSO, cases of non-compliance are fairly common. In 1994, more than 23,000 cases of employers - approximately 10 per cent - failed to make contributions towards their employee's old-age fund. In 1995, there was a decline in number, but it is still significant at more than 14,000 cases, representing some 5.6 per cent of the total number of employers.

When the EPF was first set up in 1951, employees contributed 5 per cent of their salary and employers 5 per cent. The rate remained unchanged until the mid-1970's. Revised in a series of steps, it now stands at 11 per cent for workers and 12 per cent for employers. A question that continues to be pertinent is whether contributions of such proportions will provide adequate retirement benefit. The answer is not simple. Individuals vary in their perception of what is adequate for them. The rate currently in force seems to work quite well for higher income bracket, but it seems to provide a rather insufficient coverage for those who are in the lower income brackets. In this respect, it is worth noting that more than 60 per cent of the contributors to the EPF are earning RM1000 or less per month. As at December 1996, the average amount withdrawn at 55 was RM19,501 (Vijaya, 1997).

A similar scenario can be painted in relation to the 20,000 or so employees in the government sector, including the Police and Armed Forces, who retire annually. About 80 per cent are semi-skilled and unskilled workers. Only 5 per cent retire at the professional and managerial level and 3.4 per cent at semi-professional and technical level. The bulk of the retired workers from the semi-skilled and unskilled group, upon retirement, receive pensions of about RM300-350 a month, a sum well below the poverty line. This situation could be deemed to warrant a re-examination of the pension formula especially that affecting the lower income group. In this respect, it is worth noting that in Singapore the contribution rate to the state's Central Provident Fund amounts to about 20 per cent of the average worker's salary.

The third issue of concern is the retirement age. The current policy and practice in the public sector is that employees retire compulsorily upon attaining 55 years of age. Most formal private sector organisations also adopt a similar policy and practice. However, over the last two decades or so, trade unions and other non-governmental organisations have made calls for a review of policy and practice. In the light of significant demographic changes that have taken place in the country within the last two decades, such calls merit consideration. The most important of these changes is that, with the overall improvement in income and aspects of the quality of life, Malaysians live longer. There have been improvements in life expectancy over the years. In 1980, the average life expectancy at birth was 66.4 years for men and 69.5 years for women. By 1990, the average life expectancy for men had increased to 70.5 and for women 73.9 years. By the first decade of the next millennium life expectancy for men is expected to rise to 74 and for women 78. The greater longevity, coupled with general good health, implies that Malaysian workers have the capacity to contribute economically beyond the age of 55. Indeed, as has been discussed earlier, a significant percentage of Malaysians of that age are still in the labour market. Most are to be found in the rural agricultural and urban informal sectors, where no retirement age exists. But, they are so in other sectors as well, and their size will grow particularly as and when the service sector grows in importance in Malaysia's economy.

The issue about the appropriate retirement age (as well as the adequacy of the amount of the EPF pension) is not only one that follows from increased life expectancy. Thus, the decline of the extended family in Malaysia and, for some ethnic groups at least, a decline in birth rates (see chapter 7), may have increasing impact upon the amount and nature of family support that many older people will be able to rely. Moreover, the retirement age is also correlated with the phenomenon of fewer younger people entering the labour market. In Malaysia, it is not just a classic case of 'fewer babies, longer lives'. It is also related to the preference of the younger age groups, particularly those in the 15 to 20 age cohort, to delay entry into the job market. The majority of this age group opt to remain in school or college. To a certain extent, this phenomenon has contributed to the acute labour shortage that Malaysia experienced in the decade preceding the economic slow down of 1997. During that period Malaysia had to rely on foreign labour for its then growing manufacturing, construction and agricultural industries.

A review of the policy and practice relating to retirement age for Malaysian workers would bring this aspect of the labour situation into line with the policy and practice in other countries, at least with countries in the ASEAN region. Singapore, Indonesia, Philippines and Thailand have long pegged the retirement of their workers to an age beyond 55. In the developed countries like the United Kingdom, Germany, France and Holland, workers retire at 65. Further, in some other countries the authorities have even contemplated 'a decade of retirement' with pressure to abolish mandatory retirement before the age of 70, to be on a par with the legislation in the United States. The current position in Malaysia is that proposals have been made to the Cabinet that move in the common direction. These are quite conservative, however, with a recommendation of an increase to 58 years and only upon the recommendation of their respective heads of departments.

Conclusions

It has been shown that in Malaysia there exist several schemes that provide financial security for Malaysian workers in their old age. But it has also been shown that a significantly large percentage of the Malaysian workers are yet to be covered by any scheme. Even among those who are covered by any one of these schemes, there is the problem of the adequacy of the size of pensions. These problems are compounded by the policy and practice of the compulsory age of retirement which is, internationally, on the low side. A compelling argument for a review is the fact of longer life expectancy which gives rise to a situation of longer post-retirement years and perhaps a longer period of 'disengagement'. Equally important, the review would perhaps alter the current notion that many have that people transform into 'doddering geriatrics' once they turn 55.

References

Amin, N.M. (1982), *The Role of Social Security in National Development: A Socio-Economic Study in Malaysia*. A dissertation submitted in partial requirement for the degree of Doctor of Philosophy, Century University, California.

Ariffin, B.A. (1989), *Skim Pencen di Malaysia: Masalah Pembiayaan dan Langkah Untuk Mengatasinya*, A dissertation in partial requirement for Master in Public Administration, Faculty of Economy and Administration, University of Malaya, Kuala Lumpur.

Bond, J. and Coleman, P. (eds) (1990), *Ageing in Society*, Sage, London.

Chan, K.E. (1992), *Statistics and Trends of Population Ageing in Malaysia*, Proceedings of National Seminar on Challenges of Senior Citizens towards Vision 2020, Kuala Lumpur.

Chin, F.K. (1984), *An Evaluation of the Social Insurance Schemes in Malaysia*, A dissertation in partial requirement for Masters in Economics, University of Malaya, Kuala Lumpur.

Malaysia (1951), 'Pension Ordinance 1951', *Government Gazette*, Kuala Lumpur.

Malaysia (1957), *Pension Regulation 1957*, Percetakan Kerajaan, Kuala Lumpur.

Malaysia (1980), *Pension Act 1980*, Government Printer, Kuala Lumpur.

Tan, P.C. and Ng, S.T. (eds) (1997), Proceedings National Day For the Elderly, National Council of Senior Citizens Organisations Malaysia, Kuala Lumpur.

Tan, P.C., Ng, S.T., Tey, N.P. and Halimah Awang (1999), *Evaluating Programme Needs of Older Persons in Malaysia*, Monograph Series No. 1, Faculty of Economics and Administration, University of Malaya, Kuala Lumpur.

Tey, H.C. (1995), *Health Care and Socio-economic Support of the Elderly in Peninsular Malaysia*, Masters in Economics Thesis, Faculty of Economics and Administration, University of Malaya, Kuala Lumpur.

Tinker, A. (1996), *Older People in Modern Society*, Longman, London and New York.

Vijaya, K.R. (1997), *The Role of Employees Provident Fund (EPF) in Financing Old Age in Malaysia*, Proceedings National Day for The Elderly, National Council of Senior Citizens Organisations Malaysia, Kuala Lumpur.

Wahid, W.A. (1970), *Problems in Pensions Administration*, Project Paper in partial requirement for Diploma in Public Administration, University of Malaya, Kuala Lumpur.

Yaacob, M.F. (1998), *Retirement: What Is the Correct Age?*, Paper presented at National Seminar Towards Successful and Healthy Ageing, NASCOM and Department of Anthropology and Sociology, University of Malaya, Kuala Lumpur.

Yaacob, M.F. and Nordin, M.F. (1998), *Old-Age Financial Support Schemes in Malaysia*, Paper presented at Experts Meeting of Welfare Policies, East and West, Department of Anthropology and Sociology, University of Malaya, Kuala Lumpur.

6 Managing a mixed economy of social care: community care in Britain

ROSEMARY LITTLECHILD
LIZ ROSS

The Conservative government in Britain during the 1980s espoused an ideology which in relation to social care sought to control or reduce public spending through more effective management of resources, encouraged a mixed economy of welfare and introduced greater market competition between and within the different sectors. Concern with the cost of welfare and the creation of a 'dependency culture' alongside the demonstrable inefficiency of some state services led to the market and the private sector being seen as attractive options. Furthermore the private sector included the 'private' lives of families and friends as well as the voluntary and self help sectors. The promotion of the market was linked with the encouragement to 'look after your own'.

Chapter 1 outlined the concern of the governments in Britain since 1979 to reduce public expenditure and to eliminate waste and inefficiency from public sector welfare services. It identified three distinct but related changes in the delivery of services:

- a move to more efficient management;
- the introduction of market principles;
- an attempt to restore a sense of personal responsibility for meeting social need.

In this chapter we consider the impact of these changes in the field of social care for older people, people with physical or learning disabilities and people with mental health problems, focusing first on the major piece of recent legislation the National Health Service and Community Care Act 1990 (NHSCC 1990) and then considering more recent developments in this field following the election of the Labour Government in 1997.

Community care

Caring is 'not a cerebral concern, nor a character trait, but the concern of living active humans engaged in the processes of everyday living. Care is both a practice and a disposition' (Tronto, 1993, p.104). Where adults are unable to care for themselves on a day to day basis their care by others can include both caring *for* and caring *about* them in that physical caring tasks such as washing, feeding and being with people go alongside feelings of care about the person's well being and about them as a person (Clark, 1996). Historically care has been provided by four main agencies, the public sector, the voluntary sector, the family and through the private market (Symonds, 1998). Thus the provision of care has for centuries taken place within some sort of 'mixed economy' (Wistow et al, 1994), although the emphasis has shifted significantly at different points in time. The NHSCC 1990 incorporates aspects of at least three dimensions of the concept of 'community' (see, for example, Barnes, 1997) in that care is to be provided in the locality, where possible in people's own homes and by family or friends living close by.

The Act was a culmination of a century of policy and practice developments within social care and in reviewing the history and context of this legislation briefly a number of intertwined strands will be described.

The development of community care policy

Prior to industrialisation small scale community life in a predominantly rural setting incorporated the social care of adults within their social family structures. Industrialisation brought many people to crowded cities away from their families and close communities. During the nineteenth century public involvement in caring for people saw the development of large scale institutions for the poor, older people and those with disabilities who were unable to look after themselves. These institutions, some run by charitable organisations, were typically built in rural settings on the edges of towns and effectively separated these groups of people from the urban community.

In the first half of the twentieth century the large institutions of the nineteenth century remained, although some were now under the control of the local authorities. For those living in institutions such provision was associated with poverty, with a lack of family support and with the need to be controlled and separate from the rest of society. Following the Second

World War the National Health Service Act 1946 brought the mentally ill, people with learning disabilities and chronically sick older people into the mainstream health care system. The National Assistance Act 1948 required local authorities to provide residential care for older people unable to care for themselves and gave discretionary powers to local authorities to provide domiciliary services for those with physical disabilities. It was not until the 1960s that local authorities could provide meals at home and other local services to older people. Provision for those with physical disabilities remained minimal even after 1960 when the provision of domiciliary services became compulsory. The Chronically Sick and Disabled Persons Act 1970 placed a duty upon local authorities to register disabled people and provide services, but there were insufficient resources allocated to this to make a substantial impact. Many people remained dependent on voluntary sector services and the care of their families.

Meanwhile both preventative and after care for people with mental illness was discretionary. The Mental Health Act 1959 was the first piece of legislation to put forward the idea of the closure of the large hospitals and proposed that local authorities should provide local services, hostels, day centres and sheltered employment. However whilst during the following two decades there were fewer people living in institutional care and criticism of large institutions grew (see for example Goffman, 1968; Robb, 1967; Ryan and Thomas, 1980) there was no attempt until the 1980s to undertake major closures. With an increasing emphasis on 'normalisation' (Wolfensburger, 1972; King's Fund, 1980) and service user empowerment, (see for example Beresford and Croft, 1986) alongside challenges to the 'medical model' of care (Oliver, 1990), local authority and voluntary services within the community grew during the 1980s, albeit patchily.

During this period significant demographic and social changes were affecting family life. Increased proportions of older people within the population as well as changes in family structures, with increasing female employment, changing patterns of family life, including more divorce and children living with lone parents, and more geographic mobility are well documented. These changes in the second half of the twentieth century have had significant implications for home based care, given that such care has typically been undertaken by women within the family (Parker, 1990). Caring work, both formal and within the home, was, and still is, regarded as women's work and as such is associated with low status and low pay.

The history of British state involvement in social care has been described as 'the history of neglect' (Means and Smith, 1998 and see for example, Oliver, 1990; Fennell, Phillipson and Evers, 1988). The groups of people needing social care were perceived as unproductive, dependent and marginal to mainstream life. However by the 1980s there was pressure for reform and improved services both from the service users and from the wider political debate about the provision and financing of welfare services. Concern about rising costs of care, particularly for the projected increase in older people, the cost to the social security system of the provision of residential care and the high maintenance costs of large decaying institutions eventually prompted action by the government.

The National Health Service and Community Care Act 1990

Following a report by the Audit Commission (1986) the Conservative Government commissioned Sir Roy Griffiths to make recommendations on 'community care' policies as a whole. The key feature of the Griffiths report (1988) was that local authority social service departments (SSDs) should have responsibility for social care and that they should decide on social and not income grounds whether care was necessary. It would then be their responsibility to ensure that individuals obtained the necessary care from either the public or the private sector. If they were unable to pay, or payment was not covered by their social security benefits, then the local authority was to subsidise.

The NHSCC 1990 followed. The Act defines 'community care' in terms of both a way of organising the delivery of care and as an approach to the delivery of care. Such an approach puts value on the quality of life of the individual receiver of care and those caring for them with an emphasis on a needs led service which provides choice to the individual user. Following the Act the development of a market in social care involving the public, private and voluntary sector was significantly encouraged. For the first time the private world of the family and informal care was incorporated into the legislation thus shifting welfare responsibilities significantly from the public to the private areas of life.

The Act was effectively drafted to facilitate the partial privatisation of the local authority social care services and clearly aimed to ensure that the SSDs would decline as *providers* of services but would become the care managers who assessed the need for social care and purchased appropriate services from the voluntary and private sectors. For many social workers it meant a change in their role from practitioner to care manager. A new funding structure provided a single unified budget managed by the SSDs, incorporating the care element of social security allowances, thus shifting the funding of residential care from central to local government. A new specific grant was to promote social care for people with mental illness, with the health authorities acting as lead agencies in this case.

The 1990s have seen further legislation introduced by the Labour government. This by and large builds on the NHSCC 1990 and has continued to emphasise the three key elements identified at the beginning of this chapter. As we consider recent policy and practice developments in social care it is to these that we now turn.

A move to more efficient management

The 1980s and 1990s in Britain saw the introduction into the public sector of the concept of managerialism, described broadly by Cutler and Waine (1997) as 'the belief that the objectives of social services, such as health, education, personal social services or social security, can be promoted at a lower cost when the appropriate management techniques are applied' (p.xiv). The then Conservative government anticipated that in the field of personal social services, this would be achieved in a number of ways.

If, as some commentators suggest (Hudson, 1990; Lewis and Glennerster, 1996), the reforms of the NHSCC 1990 were driven by the government's desire to cut the central social security budget, then they have achieved their aim. The budget for the state funding of people in independent residential and nursing accommodation was successfully passed to local authorities in 1993 and they have had to devise their own eligibility criteria for its management. This has involved the means-testing of potential residents, the 'topping-up' of fees by families and the introduction of charging policies for more community care services by local authorities.

Not surprisingly, the criteria have been redefined in the light of resource pressures (Baldwin and Lunt, 1996) and services have been targeted at the most dependent people living in the community with the objective of keeping them out of residential care. Those people perceived as being at less risk are likely to find themselves receiving low priority (Means and Smith, 1998) or indeed denied any assessment of their needs (Davis et al, 1997). The Labour government has acknowledged this failing and is encouraging SSDs to focus on preventive strategies and effective risk assessment with the aim of targeting low level support for people most at risk of losing their independence (Department of Health, 1998a).

To this end it is proposing a prevention grant of £100 million over three years available for SSDs to work on agreed plans.

A key objective of the NHSCC 1990 was to clarify the responsibilities of agencies and so make it easier to account for their performance (Department of Health, 1989). However, disputes about boundary issues and ineffective multi-disciplinary working have been problematic for many people receiving care services (see, for example, Sheppard, 1995 and Croft-White, 1998). An area where the interface between health and social services has been particularly problematic is the admission and discharge of older people from hospital, with a 'vicious circle' of increased hospital admissions, earlier discharge, inadequate rehabilitation, increased need for residential care, and less to spend on preventative services, leading to more hospital admissions (Audit Commission, 1997; Henwood, 1997). Recent research funded by the Department of Health concluded that 'inter-agency and inter-professional collaboration is complex and difficult to achieve, but with the right combination of circumstances it is not beyond reach' (Hudson et al, 1997, p.193).

The Labour government has responded by issuing three key White Papers, 'The New NHS: Modern, Dependable' (Department of Health, 1997), 'Modernising Social Services' (Department of Health, 1998a) and 'Saving Lives: Our Healthier Nation' (Department of Health, 1999) and a supporting discussion paper 'Partnership in Action' (Department of Health, 1998b). These four documents contain the principal strategies for the reform of health and welfare services in the late 1990s, all of them emphasising a collaborative approach to providing services in order to promote public health, reduce health inequalities and help people maintain their independence.

The principle of partnership has been evident in a number of initiatives including:
- Primary Care Groups set up in April 1999 with representatives from social services on their governing body;
- Health Improvement Programmes outlining each health authority's plans for involving other agencies in their strategy to improve health and health care;
- Health Action Zones in local areas across the country providing a framework for a multi-agency approach to addressing ill-health and reducing health inequalities;

- The requirement on health and social services to produce Joint Investment Plans outlining how they will co-ordinate the delivery of services to vulnerable people.

Some of the barriers to effective joint working between health and social services have been due to the constraints imposed by the inflexibility of budgets for service provision. The government therefore intends to legislate in order to make it easier for the two agencies to pool budgets, transfer resources or offer more integrated services from within one agency (Department of Health, 1998b).

The commitment to partnership and cross-agency working at a strategic level is not in question; the difficulties of implementation have begun to be documented but the criteria for success must depend not purely upon the efficient use of public funds but also upon whether they are being used most effectively to the satisfaction of the public who use them. In an attempt to ensure that care is provided consistently and fairly throughout the country, the government has established clear objectives for service delivery, set out national priorities for improvements and is devising a social services assessment framework. In order to assess the effectiveness of the new approaches to the delivery of health and social services, new systems for monitoring performance will be established. A new statutory Health Development Agency will be charged with raising the standards and quality of public health provision. In social services, a key development will be the establishment of Regional Commissions for Care Standards, independent statutory bodies whose remit will include the registration and regulation of residential homes, nursing homes and organisations providing domiciliary social care services.

Whilst all the current government documents put great emphasis on public participation and involvement, what importance the government will assign to their perspectives on how well services are being delivered has yet to be seen.

The introduction of market principles

A key aim of the Conservative government in the early 1990s was to introduce market principles into both health and social care service provision. The NHSCC 1990 laid the foundations for the separation of purchaser and provider functions which was swiftly implemented in the NHS by the creation of Health Trusts and GP Fundholding initiatives. In 1997, the Labour government published its plans (Department of Health, 1997) to replace the internal market with a system of integrated care, based on partnership rather than competition. A number of these changes have been described in the previous section.

In social care the introduction of market principles took a different form. One of the key objectives of the community care reforms was 'to promote the development of a flourishing independent sector alongside good quality public services' (Department of Health, 1989) and to develop a market in social care provision. However, unlike many other local authority departments in the early 1990s, SSDs were not subject to 'compulsory competitive tendering' arrangements whereby they were *legally* obliged to tender outside their own in-house provision for service delivery. Nevertheless, local authorities were obliged to spend 85 per cent of the money transferred from the social security budget in 1993 on independent service provision. Initially this was largely spent on private or voluntary residential provision rather than on stimulating new kinds of home-based care. During this period there was an increase in the overall number of residential places, a dramatic increase in the number of publicly-funded places in private nursing and residential homes and a marked decrease in local authority residential provision and NHS continuing care beds.

Arrangements for contracting are varied and complex but there has been a trend for large private providers to dominate the market at the expense of small family-run businesses. As many fees paid by local authorities are not covering basic costs (Joseph Rowntree Foundation, 1998) corporate providers have the advantage of economies of scale and providing places at a lower unit cost. A similar picture is emerging in the provision of private domiciliary care which has been growing rapidly since 1993. The vast majority of this type of care is being provided by a few large suppliers offering block contracts to local authorities (Lewis and Glennerster, 1996). A survey of members of the United Kingdom Home Care Association (Young and Wistow, 1996) indicated that the 'spot contracting' (whereby local authorities purchase individual packages of care) as experienced by many small service providers, did not allow them the financial security to invest in the recruitment and retention of good quality staff, good working conditions and the maintenance of high standards of care.

Since the election of the Labour government there has been no return to the old-style provision of state services but rather some alterations to the way in which the market mechanisms work. Compulsory competitive tendering has been replaced with 'Best Value' as set out in the White Paper 'Modern Local Government: In Touch with the People' (Department of Environment, Transport and the Regions, 1998). Best

Value will apply to all local authority departments, requiring them to demonstrate that, regardless of the provider, services are delivered to clear standards which will cover not just cost but also quality and efficiency.

As noted earlier, a new system of regulation of care services will be established to replace the current arrangements where responsibilities are spread between local authorities, health authorities and the Department of Health. Eight new Regional Commissions for Care Standards will be created with Chairs appointed by the Secretary of State and representatives from local authorities, health authorities, user groups and providers on their management board. Key changes affecting care services to adults include the integration of registration for both residential and nursing homes, the same registration and inspection systems for public and independent homes and the registration of domicillary care agencies.

Whilst a market in care is clearly in place it is as yet too early to judge how effective this mixed economy is in ensuring a quality service and good value to the taxpayer. The Labour government has introduced regulatory measures which attempt to address these issues but it is, at the time of writing, unclear how far service users and their carers are experiencing individual choice and a needs-led service.

An attempt to restore a sense of personal responsibility for meeting social need

Personal responsibility for meeting the social care needs within the family extends both to the provision and the financing of care. The Conservative government emphasised the need for people to make their own provision for care as they grew older by saving and taking on personal pensions and insurance. One pressing issue on which the government has not yet taken action is the funding for long-term care of older people. Care which might have been provided free in NHS hospitals prior to 1993 is now more often being provided in private nursing homes with the user being liable to pay for the care, subject to means testing. Findings of a Royal Commission into the funding of long-term care for older people were published in March 1999 and recommended that all personal care (as opposed to accommodation or hotel costs) for older people, whether in their own homes or in institutional care should be free at the point of delivery and paid for through taxation. This would add another £1.2 billion to the annual bill. Two dissenters from the majority report recommended that free care should be restricted to those people requiring nursing services, estimated at a cost of £300 million. As yet the government has not announced any decision on this matter.

With regard to providing social care for older people, the Eurobarometer survey of the general public in Europe in 1992 found that in the UK about 58 per cent of the population thought that families are now less willing to care for their older relatives than they were in the past (Eurobarometer Survey, 1993). However the General Household Survey 1995 found that 1 in 8 of the adult population identified themselves as carers (Office of National Statistics, 1998). This figure accounts for 11 per cent of the male and 14 per cent of the female population. The GHS found that 45 to 64 years is the peak age for caring with 20 per cent of adults in this age group identified as carers. Most of these carers are not known to the social services. The 1995 GHS showed that 59 per cent of all people with an identified carer received no regular assistance from social or community health services and people who lived with their carer were much less likely to receive support from these agencies than those who lived elsewhere. Over a third of the respondents in the 1995 GHS defined themselves as sole carers. This is reinforced by the findings of a study by the Carers National Association (1996a) in which nearly half the respondents said they received no help with their caring responsibilities. Hardly the picture of a complex web of formal and informal services helping people to remain living at home in the community, rather one of isolated individuals, providing care usually for close family members.

Parker and Lawton (1994) have built up a typology of caring based on the tasks identified in the GHS. They distinguished between carers who offer intensive physical and/or personal care such as dressing or bathing, and those offering regular assistance, but of a more practical nature, such as shopping, cooking or household tasks. Preliminary comparison of the type of caring identified in the 1985, 1990 and 1995 GHS suggest that the proportion of relationships requiring personal and/or physical care has increased over the 10 years whilst the proportion requiring largely practical assistance has decreased. More carers are therefore involved in the most intensive caring activities. Such an analysis has been criticised as not being appropriate for those people caring for others with a long-term mental health difficulties who may well be totally independent in self-care skills but need other assistance or supervision requiring intensive support from their carers (Perring et al, 1990).

Given the changes in women's participation in the labour market, there are questions about the supply of carers, as women still provide the bulk of care to family members. An analysis which compares the 1985, 1990 and 1995 data (Parker, 1998) suggests that as more married women in the 18 to 34 age group now have paid work (70 per cent in 1995 compared to 50 per cent in 1975), there has been some slight reduction in the caring activities of those women under 44 years. However, these are women who are more likely to be involved in more practical helping activities rather than intensive personal or physical care. As an increasing number of women are going into full-time rather than part-time work and are withdrawing from the labour market more slowly, the pool of potential carers aged 45-64 available to provide the more intensive care is reducing. However, Parker (1998) questions whether this has had any significant effect on the proportion of women who *actually* provide care. The evidence suggests that many of those women are still combining work and extensive caring activities. The limited findings of studies on black carers (Atkin and Rollings, 1993) suggest that some of the physical, emotional and financial costs experienced by them are similar to those reported by white carers, but that their ethnicity compounds the experience, particularly in relation to loneliness, isolation and difficulties in communication.

The financial contribution of informal care compared to institutional or professional care varies (CNA, 1996b) but one of the most recent estimates (Nolan et al, 1996) is that it is worth between £33.9 and £39.1 billion, approximately 77 per cent to 80 per cent of all care provided. A crucial economic incentive of effective community care policy is therefore the continued support of informal carers.

Whilst care-giving by family and friends has always existed, it is only since the NHSCC 1990 that the term 'carer' has appeared in legislation (Twigg, 1994). Pressure from local and national groups for more formal recognition of the contribution that informal carers make to social care provision has resulted in some significant legislative and policy changes in the last decade. First, the Carers (Recognition and Services) Act 1995 gave carers the right to request an assessment of their ability to care and obliged SSDs to take that assessment into account when making decisions about providing services to the person being cared for. The legislation covers carers 'who provide or intend to provide a substantial amount of care on a regular basis' (Department of Health, 1995, p.2). Local Authorities were given no additional resources for the implementation of the Carers Act and the terms 'substantial' and 'regular' were not defined in the legislation. However the GHS data (Office of National Statistics, 1998) indicates that in 1995 nearly one-third of all carers spent more than 20 hours per week caring and 15 per cent more than 50 hours. In both cases the vast majority of carers lived with the person they were caring for. These are the carers whom one might expect to be eligible for an assessment under the Carers Act as providing 'regular and substantial' care.

The need to support carers has featured highly in the subsequent White Papers on welfare reform and in February 1999, the government launched a national Carers' Strategy (HM Government, 1999). It identified £140 million for local authorities to give carers regular breaks, promised legislation to allow carers to receive assessments independently of the person they care for and promised help for carers returning to work and further long term financial support.

Conclusion

By and large the Labour government has developed rather than changed the Conservative policies of the 1990s. There have been some changes in the organisational structure for service delivery, a freeing of restrictions for effective joint working between health and social services and systems established for increased monitoring of performance to specified standards. The mixed economy of care is now explicitly established within an increasingly regulated market. To date there is little evidence that the overall pressure on the British welfare system of 'more for less' (Cutler and Waine, 1997, p.146) is likely to change and 'the policy agenda will continue to be dominated by rationing rather than rights, and that guaranteed standards of service will only apply to those who are deemed most at risk and thus qualifying for a care package' (Means and Smith, 1998, p.240). Decisions still need to be made about future public expenditure for long-term care for older people and people with disabilities and greater clarity is required about the responsibilities of health authorities and social services departments.

Meanwhile, family members remain the primary carers for the majority of people requiring care in the community and their continued support is a crucial economic incentive for an effective and efficient community care policy. How both the changing demography and employment prospects of the cohort of people most likely to be identified as carers, and the changing patterns of family structure involving step-parents and grandparents will affect the patterns of care, has yet to be assessed.

References

Atkins, K. and Rolling, J. (1993), *Community Care in a Multi-racial Britain: A Critical Review of the Literature*, HMSO, London.

Audit Commission (1986), *Making a Reality of Community Care*, Audit Commission, London.
Audit Commission (1997), *The Coming of Age: Improving Care Services for Older People*, Audit Commission, London.
Baldwin, S. and Lunt, N. (1996), *Charging Ahead: The Development of Local Authority Charging Procedures for Community Care*, The Policy Press in association with the Joseph Rowntree Foundation and Community Care.
Barnes, M. (1997), *Care, Communities and Citizens*, Longman, Harlow.
Beresford, P. and Croft, S. (1986), *Whose Welfare? Private Care or Public Service*, Lewis Cohen Urban Studies Centre, Brighton Polytechnic, Brighton.
Clark, C. (1996), 'Caring, Costs and Values' in C. Clark and I. Lapsley (eds), *Planning and Costing Community Care*, Jessica Kingsley, London.
CNA (1996a), *Who Cares? Perceptions of Caring and Carers*, Carers' National Association, London.
CNA (1996b), *The True Costs of Caring*, Carers' National Association, London.
Croft-White, C. (1998), *Evaluation of the Homeless Mentally Ill Initiative 1990-1997*, Department of Health, London.
Cutler, T. and Waine, B. (1997), *Managing the Welfare State, Text and Sourcebook*, BERG, Oxford.
Davis, A., Ellis, K. and Rummery, K. (1997), *Access to Assessment*, Policy Press, Bristol.
Department of the Environment, Transport and the Regions (1998), *Modernising Local Government*, HMSO, London.
Department of Health, (1989), *Caring for People: Community Care in the Next Decade and Beyond*, HMSO, London.
Department of Health, (1995), *Carers (Recognition and Services) Act 1995: Policy Guidance*, HMSO, London.
Department of Health (1997), *The New NHS: Modern, Dependable*, HMSO, London.
Department of Health (1998a), *Modernising Social Services*, Stationery Office, London.
Department of Health (1998b), *Partnership in Action*, Stationery Office, London.
Department of Health (1999), *Saving Lives: Our Healthier Nation*, Stationery Office, London.
Eurobarometer Survey (1993), *Age and Attitudes: Main Results from a Eurobarometer Survey*, Commission of the European Communities, Directorate-General V, Employment, Industrial Relations and Social Affairs, Brussels.
Fennell, G., Phillipson, C. and Evers, H. (1988), *The Sociology of Old Age*, Open University Press, Milton Keynes.
Goffman, E. (1968), *Asylums: Essays on the Social Situation of Mental Patients and Other Inmates*, Penguin, Harmondsworth.
Griffiths, R. (1988), *Community Care: Agenda for Action*, HSMO, London.
Henwood, M. (1997), 'Discharge Account', *Community Care*, 6 November, pp. 28-29.

HM Government (1999), *Caring about Carers,* Stationery Office, London.
Hudson, B. (1990), 'Social Policy and the New Right - The Strange Case of the Community Care White Paper', *Local Government Studies,* vol. 16, pp.15-34
Hudson, B., Hardy, B., Henwood, M. and Wistow, G. (1997), *Inter-Agency Collaboration, Final report,* Nuffield Institute for Health, Leeds.
Joseph Rowntree Foundation, (1998), *A Fair Price for Care?,* Joseph Rowntree Foundation, York.
King's Fund (1980), *An Ordinary Life,* King's Fund Centre, London.
Lewis, J. and Glennerster, H. (1996), *Implementing the New Community Care,* Open University Press, Buckingham.
Means, R. and Smith, R, (1998), *Community Care: Policy and Practice,* Macmillan, London.
Nolan, M., Grant, G. and Keady, J. (1996), *Understanding Family Care,* Open University Press, Buckingham.
Oliver, M. (1990), *The Politics of Disablement,* Macmillan, Basingstoke.
Office for National Statistics (1998), *Informal Carers,* ONS Social Survey Division, Stationery Office, London.
Parker, G. (1990), *With Due Care and Attention: A Review of Research on Informal Care,* Family Policies Studies Centre, London.
Parker, G. and Lawton, D. (1994), *Different Types of Care, Different Types of Carer,* HMSO, London.
Parker, G. (1998), 'Trends in Caring 1985-1995' in Office for National Statistics Social Survey Division, *Informal Carers,* Stationery Office, London.
Perring, C., Twigg, J. and Atkin, K. (1990), *Families caring for people diagnosed as mentally ill : the literature re-examined,* HMSO, London.
Robb, B. (1967), *Sans Everything: A Case to Answer,* Nelson, London.
Royal Commission on Long-Term Care (1999), *With Respect to Old Age: Long-Term Care - Rights and Responsibilities,* Stationery Office, London.
Ryan, J. and Thomas, F. (1980), *The Politics of Mental Handicap,* Penguin, Harmondsworth.
Sheppard, D. (1995), *Learning the Lessons,* Zito Trust.
Symonds, A. (1998), 'The Social Construction of Public Care: From Community Care to Care by the State', in A. Symonds and A. Kelly (eds), *The Social Construction of Community Care,* Macmillan, Basingstoke.
Tronto, J.C. (1993), *Moral Boundaries: A Political Argument for an Ethic of Care,* Routledge, New York.
Twigg, J. (1994), 'Carers, families, relatives: socio-legal conceptions of care-giving relationships', *Journal of Social Welfare and Family Law,* vol. 3, pp.279-298.
Wistow, G., Knapp, M., Hardy, B. and Allen, C. (1994), *Social Care in a Mixed Economy,* Open University Press, Buckingham.
Wolfensburger, W. (1972), *The Principle of Normalisation in Human Services,* National Institute on Mental Retardation, Toronto.

Young, R. and Wistow, G. (1996), *Domiciliary Care: Growth and Stability?*, Report of 1996 Survey of United Kingdom Home Care Association Members, UKHCA, London.

7 Community care in Malaysia
FAIZAH YUNUS
SITI HAJAR ABU BAKAR

Introduction

In Malaysia, the public provision of personal social services has a long history, dating back to the early decades of the twentieth century (Mair, 1944). Since that time there has been an expansion in activities. Throughout most of the century, however, the scale of the care and support mechanisms, indeed the total public sector effort, has been small relative to the combined contribution of institutions such as the family and religious and voluntary organisations. In the sense of the social location of these institutions, it could be said that personal social services were truly community care.

With the accelerating pace of change, first following Independence, and later with the rapid economic growth of the post 1970 period - accompanied as they have been with deep social changes - the government has become more active. By the end of the millennium there has been a gradual build up of institutional arrangements, a legislative framework and programmes of care. Whereas collectively they constitute a considerably more sophisticated intervention than previously existed, the emphasis on the community remains the dominant one. There seems to be at least two reasons for this. Firstly, despite changes in the institutions of the family, organised religion and voluntary bodies, their positions in Malaysian society are collectively underpinned considerably more securely than their equivalents in most western countries. The community therefore is the primary locus of care and support. Secondly, policymakers in Malaysia have not sought to emulate the policies of some western countries - particularly the UK - of building large institutions such as mental hospitals, old people's homes and so on, that were prison-like in design, location and frequently regime. Rather, in Malaysia there has been a continued emphasis on supporting existing institutions.

This chapter is arranged into four sections. In the first we sketch out involvement with personal care and support, through its organisational arrangements, legislative frameworks, programmes and objectives. In the second there is an emphasis on the care of those who are physically disabled as a more detailed example of what the Malaysian approach has come to mean in practice. In the third section we provide information about recent and current changes affecting family life and which may have implications for the future of community care. The final section considers issues relating to the financing of community care.

The development of care and support services

The Organisational and Institutional Structures

The development of social welfare and community care in Malaysia began when the British colonial administration introduced a social welfare programme in 1912. A department was set up to help to improve the well being of migrant communities and the social development of indigenous local communities. However, due to financial pressures, the department was abolished during the depression of the 1930s. During the colonial period, in general, the scope of welfare services included education, labour, health and social services. There were also some community activities undertaken through various organisations such as community associations, village councils and co-operative societies.

In 1937, a separate social services department was created within the Colonial Office. (Mair, 1944). This served to centralise policies and activities that previously had been handled by each colony independently. Although the early development of a social services department focussed on labour conditions, the period was also both the beginning of systematic social services and one in which social work got recognition as a profession requiring special skills and knowledge.

The Department of Social Welfare Malaya was set up by the British Administration in 1946. During its early years, it only provided residual services, such as material assistance and shelter for displaced persons who were victims of the Second World War. In the course of the last fifty years, it has undergone several evolutions and has progressively expanded to fulfil its role in the development of the nation to encompass preventive and rehabilitative services and social development. As one of the main government agencies for social development, it has been placed under a succession of ministries. After Independence it was moved around between the Ministry of Labour and the Ministry of Health. It was given the status of a separate Ministry only in 1964, later changing its name from Ministry of Welfare Services to Ministry of Social Welfare Malaysia in 1982. Then from 27 October 1990, it became one of the departments under the Ministry of National Unity and Social Development.

Alongside the governmental organisations, religious and charitable organisations also provide social services. They have their own social network and social service system to help their local communities (Baginda, 1992). Thus, it is in the teaching of all the major religions followed in Malaysia - Islam, Buddhism, Hinduism and Christianity - to help the victims of misfortune. All have established arrangements for providing support and care. In addition, the spirit of charity and helping others has been a cultural tradition among the Malaysian populace. Consequently, a large part of the welfare services in Malaysia are carried out by voluntary organisations and they include the Malaysian Association for the Blind, Malaysian Association for Mental Health, the National Association for the Deaf, and The Good Shepherd Welfare. There is also the Malaysian Confederation of the Disabled which comprises many welfare societies. They receive financial support from the government and have played a major role in providing services for the care of children, youth, adults and older people. Even though they have limited financial resources, voluntary organisations have been expanding and widening their programme scope and coverage through donation and financial support received from individuals and the private sector. Many voluntary organisations are registered either under the Societies Act 1966 or under the Companies Act 1965.

The National Social Welfare Policy 1990

The nature and level of social welfare provision in Malaysia is framed by the National Social Welfare Policy which was formulated out of growing concerns over increased social problems that afflicted Malaysian society. The work to formulate this policy began in 1985 and was completed in early 1990, being approved by the Cabinet in May 1990. With it, social welfare has moved from its traditional rehabilitation approach into developmental and preventive areas. It focuses on the social well being of people and its goal was to secure and stabilise society in order to facilitate the nation's continued progress. It was perceived that in order to achieve this goal there would be a necessity, firstly, to inculcate the values of community living where everyone cares for others, secondly, to equalise opportunities for the less fortunate and the disadvantaged, and, thirdly, to nurture the spirit of mutual assistance and altruism at all levels of society.

In addition, the Policy specifically recognised that if these targets were to be achieved it would be necessary to develop a more professionalised care service in which agencies and social workers would need to be given training to develop theirs skills. Equally, it was recognised that attention would need to be given to community involvement and social education.

Social Welfare Programmes

Malaysia now has a wide range of social welfare measures including child welfare, adolescent welfare, welfare for older people, welfare for people with disabilities, welfare for women, family welfare, community welfare and volunteer welfare. They include:
a) The Social Assistance Programme which provides financial assistance through the following schemes:
* assistance to children
* assistance to older people
* allowance for handicapped workers
* launching grants for income generating activities
* public assistance
* school aid
* assistance to victims of natural disaster
* assistance for artificial aids/equipment

b) The Institutional Care Programme which provides residential facilities for children and older people who need substitute care because they have been abandoned, orphaned or have no place to live.

c) The Protection Programme is aimed at children, women and girls who are exposed to moral danger. The Child Protection Act 1991 provides for the care and protection of children from being neglected, abused or exploited by parents, guardians and others, and includes the provision of professional help and assistance to both children and parents or guardians. The Women and Girls Protected Act 1973 provides for the protection of women and girls exposed to moral danger.

d) The Prevention Programme on delinquency and family instability is provided through family development activities such as advice, guidance, counselling and supervision. The Juvenile Courts Act 1947 (Revised 1980), for example, provides for the well-being of juveniles. The Child Care Centre Act 1984 provides for the protection of children from possible neglect in their growth and development.

e) The Rehabilitation Programme provides community and institutional based reformation facilities for juvenile delinquents and wayward women and girls as well as training for people with disabilities, beggars and vagrants for re-integration into the mainstream of society. The programme focuses on physical, social, psychological, vocational, religious, recreational, sports and community involvement aspects.

f) The Production Programme provides community and centre based, income generating activities through the production of saleable goods. This programme caters for needy youths, people with disabilities, widowed and divorced women and recipients of social assistance schemes. It is aimed at the promotion of self-reliance, initiative, collective action and financial independence.

Care and support for those with disabilities

In Malaysia the term 'disability' is applied to all those with a physical, mental or sensory impairment. No country wide surveys have ever been carried out that provide knowledge of the exact number of persons with disabilities there are in the country. It can be said, however, that government statistics show that in 1996 there were 63,517 persons who had registered as having a disability with the Department of Social Welfare and that there had been an increase of 10.6 per cent compared with the registration at the end of 1995 (Ministry of National Unity and Social Welfare, 1996).

One of the limitations of the Malaysian approach is that there is no comprehensive law seeking to protect the interests of disabled persons, for example, that would ensure basic rights in such matters as education, skill training, employment, housing, public amenities and transport. There are, rather, a series of laws each dealing with a small aspect or single section of disabled people. The Employees Social Security Acts 1969, for example, establishes an Invalidity Pension Scheme that is managed by SOCSO. The scheme provides for payment of certain benefits where an employee becomes disabled due to injury or illness. Benefits are payable by all employers employing one or more people in any industry (though excluding employees of federal or state government, statutory bodies and local authorities) and once an employee is covered by the scheme, they remain protected. The Government has also introduced a new scheme, known as the Compensation/Ex-Gratia Payment for Civil Service Employees, to provide coverage for employees in the public sector who are permanently disabled while carrying out work-related duties or while on official assignments. The Workmen's Compensation Act 1952 provides for an employer's liability scheme under which employers are required to pay compensation to workers for employment related injuries.

Notwithstanding the disparate nature of the legislation, the Government has introduced a rehabilitation service for the disabled. This service is intended to help the disabled to be independent and subsequently to reach their maximum potential in all aspects of their lives. Both field services and institutional services are provided, the former including the issuing of identity cards, artificial aids and equipment, financial allowances for living costs, grants for small business start ups, and job placement schemes.

Community Based Rehabilitation

The Government has recently introduced a community based rehabilitation programme (CBR), an approach supported by WHO. This is a strategy within community development for the rehabilitation, equalisation of opportunities and social integration of all people with disabilities. It is implemented through the combined effort of disabled people themselves, their families and communities, and the appropriate health, education, vocational and social services.

CBR was pioneered by three WHO personnel. In 1983, the Malaysian Department of Social Welfare sent an officer and a medical doctor to evaluate and modify the approach during an Expert Group Meeting held in Manila. After the meeting, the Department of Social Welfare with the co-operation of Trengganu Department of Health set up a CBR project in the Batu Rakit District. With the help of local authorities and the co-operation of residents (including some with disabilities) the project was launched in 1984 and it was officiated by the Social Welfare Minister. It involved a *kampong* (village) with a population of 17,149 people of whom 277 had disabilities (this number representing 1.65 per cent of Batu Rakit District population).

An important principal in CBR is the involvement and participation by the community especially parents, relatives and neighbours. They play an important role in making CBR a success by motivating the local communities to inculcate a sense of responsibility and motivation to overcome common problems. Other CBR principles include: projects on which schemes are based should be cost-saving; they should systematically transfer 'care know-how' from the grassroots; they should avoid sending cases to rehabilitation institutions and hence decrease dependence on the government; and they should foster integration and total acceptance among the public that those with disabilities, as members of society, have rights.

Based on these principles, CBR is a project carried out at the community level and at home to:
- show the ability, competency and skill of those with disabilities towards excellence;
- emphasise community awareness and ensure acceptance and integration so the disabled do not feel they are less able and not useful;
- provide personal support to families with disabled member(s);
- foster support systems from local resources;
- help people to lead a normal life and show they have potential to excel and undertake activities to upgrade their living condition.

At the present time, there are 7 rehabilitation centres with a total of 992 participants. In addition to the training centres there are a total of 155 community based rehabilitation centres. In 1996 a total of 3440 people with disabilities received RM14,444,416 worth of financial aid. By comparison, in 1995 a total of 4835 disabled persons received RM3,351,274, so that there was a decrease in the number of recipients but an increase in financial value (see Table 7.1).

Table 7.1 Number of recipients of aid and expenditure by types of disability, 1995 -1996

Types of Disability	1995		1996	
	No. of recipients	Expenditure (RM)	No. of recipients	Expenditure (RM)
Sight	1157	816,252	836	3,444,306
Hearing	652	482,820	530	2,328,500
Physical	2333	1,764,737	1836	7,541,800
Mental	693	287.470	238	1,129,810
Total	4835	3,351,274	3440	14,444,416

Source: Ministry of National Unity and Social Welfare (1996)

The Department of Social Welfare plans to expand CBR throughout the community by opening a new CBR centre in every district. By 1995, a total of 135 CBR programmes were implemented, involving expenditure amounting to RM2,123,000 and providing services to about 1,770 people. The Department's own report on the CBR programme indicates the level of achievement (Ngah Mahmud, 1989). About 606 disabled children have benefited from the programme. 53 per cent of CBR studied functioned 8 hours a day and 31 per cent functioned with various activities between 3-5 days a week. Only 4 per cent carried out activities as little as twice a week. The study also showed that most CBR carried out everyday life activities, for example, how to eat and dress oneself, how to read, write and count. The study also showed that 42 per cent of parents involved themselves with the programme about which they had positive opinions. Within communities with a centre 93 per cent of residents said that they knew of its existence and activities.

Just as there are many ways to define and understand communities, they are many models of community care practice. Some models place much emphasis on mobilising people at the grassroots while others emphasise the technical nature of problem solving in the macro arena. A common thread running through many models is people working together to change the conditions that directly affect them in their daily lives. CBR can be referred to as bottom-up because it is a self-help, participatory model of community care practice. It is based on the premise that it is necessary to include the broadest possible participation. It places a great deal of emphasis on self-determination and democratic process. Professionals cannot change the community for the people, they must do that themselves. Professionals can provide encouragement, support, expert knowledge, and other resources. They can treat the members of the community with respect and dignity. They can work side-by-side with residents to create the conditions that make change and empowerment possible. They can help the residents develop knowledge, skills, and self-confidence needed to challenge the status quo. But the people themselves must define the problem and develop a plan for dealing with it.

In a sense it is an extension of the group work model. Considerable attention is given to group dynamics and in some cases the process through which the community defines its problems and develops strategies to resolve them is more important than the change itself. That is, the process of getting people together to discuss their common concerns and to plan for resolving specific problems is critical for effective community development.

Changes in the population and the family

In this section the focus of the chapter turns to one aspect of Malaysia - its people - that will continue to impact upon the nature, scale and definition of social problems to which the government may be expected to respond. But it is the people also, through their attitudes and abilities of different sorts, who will influence the nature of the feasible programmes. The aim here, then, is to provide a description and analysis of a number of trends in population and family formation and constitution that may come to have more or less effect upon community care.

Current estimates indicate that the Malaysian population increased at an annual rate of 2.7 per cent during the period 1991 - 1995, to reach 20.69 million in 1995 (Malaysia, 1996). The high growth rate is attributable to migrants from other countries (5.7 per cent per annum), as compared to the increase of only 2.1 per cent of Malaysian citizens (Table 7.2). The population structure consists of 34.1 per cent children below 15 years with 3.8 per cent in the age group of 65 and above. 62.1 per cent falls in the age group of 15 - 64 years. The changing numbers and proportions in each group are important for social care policies. The increase in population of the 14 years and under age group has created social issues such as the increasing need for childcare and for the development of infrastructure (schools, recreational centres etc.). The increase in population of age group 15 - 64 creates needs for more social development (higher learning institutions, sport and recreational centres, training centres) as well as for health services. Finally the increased numbers of older people have increased need for care, for gerontological services, and for infra-structure.

As elsewhere in the industrialising countries of Asia, there are important trends relating to marriage and families (Ariffin, 1999; Disney and McPherson, 1999). The average age at marriage has increased in recent decades, giving rise to a number of issues. The consequent fall in fertility has meant that household size becomes smaller. In addition, with the age at marriage increasing, the long period of bachelorhood has resulted in youngsters being exposed to freer lifestyles and anti social activities. At the same time there has also been an increase in women, both married and single, participating in the workplace. The social participation of women, in particular is changing not only the family's lifestyle but also the definition of the appropriate role division between male and female. This has some specific consequences for the future of community care since it reduces women's ability (and willingness) to care for family members. This creates a higher demand for child care (including nurseries, maids, etc.) and for services to support those family members who are old or have disabilities. This is tied to another change in households, namely the relative decline of the extended family so that the number of multi-generation households has decreased while there are increasing numbers of nuclear and single-member households (see Table 7.3).

Table 7.2 Population size: ethnic groups, age structure: Malaysia, 1995 -2000

	Population size (million people)			Average rate (%) of growth annually
	1995	1998	2000	
Total Population	20.69	22.18	23.26	2.3
Malaysian citizens	19.38	20.63	21.52	2.1
Bumiputera	11.95	12.91	13.61	2.6
Chinese	5.29	5.47	5.60	1.1
Indian	1.50	1.57	1.61	1.4
Others	0.64	0.68	0.70	1.8
Non citizen	1.31	1.55	1.74	5.7
Age Structure				
0 - 14 years	7.33	7.57	7.74	1.1
15 -64 years	12.60	13.77	14.62	3.0
65 and above	0.76	0.84	0.90	3.4
Distribution				
Urban	11.32	12.68	13.68	3.9
Rural	9.3	9.5	9.58	0.4

Source: Ministry of National Unity and Social Development (1996)

Table 7.3 Malaysia: average household size and rate of household types by stratum, 1980-1991

Household Type	1980	1991
Average Household Size		
Total households	5.2	4.8
Nuclear family households	4.9	4.8
Extended family households	7.1	6.5
Rate (%)		
Nuclear family household	55.2	59.9
Urban	50.4	58.7
Rural	57.7	61.1
Extended family households	27.8	26.4
Urban	29.3	27.2
Rural	27.0	25.7

Source: Department of Statistics (1998)

The 21st century is the 'century of the elderly' (Table 7.4). In many ways, the transformation of the family has influenced older people the most. People's sense of responsibility to provide support for parents has declined and the number of older people living alone or as a couple continues to increase. This age group has the highest consumption of health and social care provision, needing more intensive care because they are more prone to illness and because they form the majority of disabled people in Malaysia.

Table 7.4 Proportion of older people by age group Malaysia, 1990-2030

Year	55+ (%)	60+ (%)	65+ (%)	Total (%)
1990	8.9	6.2	4.0	19.1
2000	10.4	7.4	4.8	22.6
2010	11.9	9.0	5.9	26.8
2030	18.6	15.5	9.0	43.1

Source: National Population and Family Development Board (1990)

Financial issues

Insofar as these trends will generate new or additional needs to which the government may decide to respond, any new or additional services, whether primarily located in the community or not, will require additional resources. This is a fundamental issue for community care in Malaysia which can perhaps be most vividly highlighted by considering the financial contribution made by the government. Figures presented by Abdullah Malim Baginda reveal that in 1975 the budget for social welfare as a proportion of the total federal budget was 0.337 per cent, and that by 1990 this had declined to 0.230 per cent (Baginda, 1992). As a former Director-General of the Ministry of Social Welfare, it could be said that he had particularly useful insights into the adequacy of these budget allocations and it is worth quoting him at some length.

> It is evident that the quantum is grossly inadequate to support the individuals to meet their daily needs. Many attempts have been made in the past to increase the rate, but without success. If such a situation persists, we can be accused of happily maintaining people below the poverty level.
> We seem to persistently believe that the poor, the decrepit and the rejected could still seek the aid of their kin, neighbours and friends. We seem to ignore the fact that the attitude of our society is changing rapidly. They must have exhausted all possible avenues of help before braving themselves to submit to probing enquiries as to the state of their welfare and solicit meagre financial assistance.
> It is proposed here that the dignity of the human persons, poor as they are, should be upheld and if they deserve support, it should be adequate (Baginda, 1992, p. 384).

In his consideration of practical responses to what he appears to see as a problem of both under-resourcing and of attitude, he puts forward a number of suggestions. It is interesting to note that none of these involve larger amounts of federal funding, and that in the main they are proposals about using the existing allocations more efficiently. His first proposal follows from his observation that social welfare functions are carried out by a number of ministries and that the lack of integration may be tackled by locating them all under the Ministry of Social Welfare. Secondly, noting that the administrative costs of making payments directly to the public consume a major portion of an already small budget, he suggests payment through banks and post offices. Thirdly, the greater involvement of NGOs would reduce costs and leave the Ministry to take a more strategic and regulatory role. Finally, he considers the possibility of drawing on foreign funds from a variety of sources - private, non governmental, governmental and international.

Table 7.5 shows the size of the social services budget relative to total federal government expenditure in the years following the former Director-General's examination of the Malaysian system. The figures are not directly comparable with his, since in its reports the Ministry of Finance is including not only social welfare expenditure through the Ministry of National Unity and Social welfare (the definition used by Baginda) but also health care expenditure and some education (preschool) expenditure. Nevertheless, it remains clear that, by the standards of many more industrialised countries - even with the increases over the 1990s from 7.9 per cent to 9.1 per cent - there is rather a small emphasis on social spending in Malaysia.

Table 7.5 Social services operating expenditure

Year	Total Federal Expenditure (Million RM)	Expenditure on Social Services (%)
1990	33,405	7.9
1995	48,798	7.7
1996	55,982	6.9
1997	58,982	8.5
1998	64,124	9.2
1999	65,095	9.1

Source: Economic reports, Ministry of Finance (various years)

Conclusion

It could be said of community care in Malaysia that it forms the basis of personal social services, or personal care and support, now as it has done for at least the last century. It does not, in other words, as in Britain, constitute a new agenda that marks a break from older forms of institutional care. In relation to this, although it can be said that the government has taken important initiatives, such as with the CBR programme that has had successes in assisting people with disabilities, there are at least two important dimensions. First, its approach is very firmly based in communities, requiring the full involvement of users and their families if it is to be successful in its own terms. Second, the share of the national budget that the government has been willing to put into this, and other areas of the social services, has been small. Whether or not the government has achieved the optimal balance between economic and social objectives is an important issue and one which will become perhaps re-thought as population characteristics, family structures, values and gender roles change, making it less automatically obvious which community it will be that does the caring.

References

Arifin J. (1999), 'At the Crossroads of Rapid Development: Malaysian Society and Anomie', *Asia Pacific Families Journal*, vol. 1, pp. 23-43.

Baginda, A.M. (1992), 'Financing Social Services in Malaysia: Some Options', in C. K. Sin and M.I. Salleh (eds), *Caring Society: Emerging Issues and Future Directions*, Institute of Strategic and International Studies, Kuala Lumpur.

Department of Statistics (1998), *Senior Citizens and Population Ageing in Malaysia*, Population Census Monograph Series, No. 4, Kuala Lumpur.

Disney, H. and McPherson, A. (1999), 'Changing Family Structure and the Impact of Economic and Social Factors on Family Well-being', *Asia Pacific Families Journal*, vol. 1, pp. 44-54.

Lum, K.T. (1992), Welfare Need of the Elderly', in C.K. Sin and I. Salleh (eds), *Caring Society: Emerging Issues and Further Directions*, Institute of Strategic and International Studies, Kuala Lumpur.

Mair, P.L. (1944), *Welfare in the British Colonies*, The Broad Water Press, London.

Malaysia (1996), *Seventh Malaysia Plan 1996-2000*, Government Printer, Kuala Lumpur.

Ministry of National Unity and Social Development (1996), *Annual Report 1996*, Government Printer, Kuala Lumpur.

National Population and Family Development Board (1990), *Malaysia Country Report on Socio-Economic Consequences of the Ageing Population*, Government Printer, Kuala Lumpur.

Ngah Mahmud, M.H. (1989), *The Development of CBR in the Department of Social Welfare*, Unpublished paper, Ministry of Welfare, Kuala Lumpur.

Rothmans, J. (1995), 'Approaches to Community Intervention', in J. Rothmans, J.L. Erlich and J.E. Tropman (eds), *Strategies of Community Intervention*, Peacock Publisher, Itasca.

8 Britain's evolving health policies
MIKE McBETH

Introduction

The issue of health inequalities has become more important in British health policy. In May 1997 a Labour government replaced the Conservative government that had dominated politics throughout the twentieth century. The Conservatives had been ideologically closer to the views that differences in health and life expectancy were inevitable; and inequalities more generally tended to be regarded as mechanisms that might motivate individuals to improve their own economic circumstances. For Conservative governments since the beginning of the 1980s, poor health and lower than average life-expectancy were understood primarily as being a consequence of a combination of cultural and individual factors that resulted in individuals failing to pursue healthy lifestyles. For the new Labour government, health inequalities are regarded as also being caused by structural and economic inequity. State action, therefore, as well as individual behaviour change has become an important component in the drive to improve health.

To address health inequalities a more comprehensive set of policies is currently being devised. A tendency is emerging that encourages the breaking down of boundaries between organisations and departments and increased co-operation between the separate institutions that are involved in health and welfare. This so-called 'joined-up government' means that, increasingly, health policy is being regarded as something that should properly encompass the full range of socio-economic factors that affect the poor and marginalized. Therefore, anti-poverty strategies, tax and benefits policies, education, transport and housing are all being considered as important factors in the strategy of improving health. A shift from hospital-based health care systems towards primary care is also now underway along with reforms of the way that health care is delivered at the local level.

This chapter briefly examines the development of the British health service and the disparities in health that have been found. In particular, socio-economic inequities, gender diversity, regional inequalities and the contrasts between ethnic groups are considered. The role of the health service in dealing with health inequalities is assessed and the future of Britain's primary care services will be discussed in the context of their ability to work along with a range of other agencies to begin narrowing what has become known in Britain as 'the health divide'.

The development of health services

The relationship between socio-economic position and health is one that has been known for some time. During the great plague year of 1665 the relationship between mortality and social class was clear. Prosperous London residents used the weekly 'bills of mortality' to warn of rising death rates and these prompted many of them to temporarily leave the capital. By the middle of the nineteenth century, public health problems were becoming more acute as overcrowding and insanitary conditions particularly afflicted the poor. The population of Britain doubled between 1801 (the year of the first official census) and 1851, then doubled again in the next 60 years. Population growth was concentrated in the emerging industrial cities. At the end of the seventeenth century one in every four people lived in urban centres, but by the middle of the nineteenth century, that figure had reached one in two. Between 1851 and 1891 the urban population grew from 50 per cent to 72 per cent of the total (Laslet, 1983). Glasgow's population grew by 37 per cent between 1831 and 1841, Manchester and Salford's jointly by 47 per cent between 1821 and 1831 while the population of Bradford increased by 78 per cent in the same period (Flinn, 1965). Infectious conditions were the principal cause of death; with cholera, tuberculosis, typhus, scarlet fever and smallpox especially virulent.

One of the early pioneers of public health in Britain, Edwin Chadwick, published his 'Report into the Sanitary Conditions of the Labouring Population of Great Britain' in 1842, which demonstrated that the incidence of both deaths and disease were highest in the most overcrowded areas. Chadwick showed that the average age of death was related to social class, with labourers dying at 22 years of age on average, tradesmen at 30 and the gentry at 43 years. Two years later, a Royal Commission examined the proportion of children who died before the age of five years in Preston, they reported that 18 per cent of those who died were children of the gentry compared with 55 per cent who were the children of labourers, weavers and factory hands.

The death rate in Britain began to fall after about 1850 and Thomas McKeown (1979) has argued that more than sixty per cent of the decline could be attributed to a reduction in infectious conditions. Furthermore, the fall in infectious diseases predates any effective medical interventions. McKeown therefore attributes the falling death rates and increased life expectancy not to medicine, but to improvements in sanitation and rising living standards, which in their turn led to improvements in diets.

In spite of the success of preventive and public health, Britain's medical profession gradually established itself as the major influence in matters of health policy. In modern Britain, health care services are dominated by the collective state medical system, known as the National Health Service (NHS). The NHS was formally launched in July 1948. The medical professions were instrumental in ensuring that the NHS was dominated by the hospitals. This has resulted in a number of serious contradictions within the British health care sector.

The NHS was to be the 'jewel in the crown' of the British welfare state and was considered by many as a radical solution to improve health care services in Britain. William Beveridge in his 1942 report 'Social Insurance and Allied Services' (Beveridge, 1942, p.6), which has been widely taken as the basis for post second world war reconstruction, argued that Britain should set about 'slaying the five giants on the road to recovery', these were described as 'WANT, DISEASE, IGNORANCE, SQUALOR and IDLENESS'. In 1944 plans for a new health service were well underway and the Ministry of Health issued a white paper, which stated that the government,

> ... wanted to ensure that in future every man and woman and child can rely on getting all the advice and treatment and care they may need in matters of personal health; that what they get shall be the best medical and other facilities available; that their getting these shall not depend on whether they can pay for them or any other factor irrelevant to real need. (Ministry of Health, 1944, p. 5)

The four main principles of the NHS in Britain were that it should be comprehensive, uniform, universal and free at the point of use. Thus all medical conditions should be dealt with by the new NHS, the standard of service received should be the same across the country, everyone should have access to services and no direct charges should be levied on patients. It was hoped that with such a fair and equal service health inequalities would diminish. In addition it was expected that as the NHS worked to make those who were ill well, then the population would become healthier and thus the costs to the state of health care would diminish.

In the event, neither of these expectations were realised. After less than two years cash limits were necessary and in 1951 charges were introduced. As new technology and medical advances proceeded, what was possible quickly outstripped what was affordable. In addition, demographic changes, in particular the rise in the number of older people meant that extra demands were placed on the health service. In consequence more money needed to be spent year on year simply to maintain the existing level of provision. The NHS has consumed up to 6.2 per cent of Britain's gross national product (Appleby, 1992). By 1991 expenditure on the health service had risen to £26,000 million and spending had increased by more than 6000 per cent since its inception (Appleby, 1992). By 2004 spending on health is forecast to be approximately £68.7 billion, equivalent to 7.6 per cent of GDP (*The Guardian*, 22 March 2000).

In spite of the financial problems that were besetting the new NHS, a degree of complacency might be said to have developed in Britain in the wake of the establishment of the welfare state. In July 1957 Harold Macmillan, the Conservative prime minister said that most British people 'have never had it so good' (quoted in Tiratsoo, 1997, p.119). It was widely believed by the 1950s that the welfare state had succeeded in one of its main aims of abolishing poverty. Furthermore, the investment in the NHS would soon show that health inequalities were reducing. However, by the early 1960s academic research was beginning to question the extent to which the welfare state was meeting its goals. Poverty was found to be far more widespread than had been expected and analysis of the 1951 census suggested that health inequalities had not diminished. At first these rather disappointing developments were thought to be the result of a delay between the introduction of health and welfare services and their effects being felt. When analysis of the 1961 census suggested a widening of the gap between the most and least healthy, it was clear that the welfare state, including the NHS were failing and further action needed to be taken in order to enable the NHS to more properly meet its goals.

The fear of spiralling welfare costs became more acute in the mid-1970s with the economic crisis that was triggered by the sudden increase in energy costs as oil prices soared. The energy and subsequent fiscal crisis brought with it more serious challenges to the welfare consensus: could the nation continue to afford a comprehensive welfare state?

Inequalities in Health

While evidence in modern Britain suggests that during the twentieth century there have been considerable overall improvements in the nation's health, disparities between the most and least healthy have grown (see table 8.1). For example, life expectancy at birth for women is now almost 80 years, compared with only 48 in 1900; and for men life expectancy is now 75 years, compared with 44 in 1900. Over the same period infant mortality has fallen from over one in ten to six per 1,000 births (Office for National Statistics, 1995). Empirical evidence continues to indicate that people who are least well off tend to be ill more often and to die sooner. Furthermore, long-standing and disabling illnesses are more concentrated among the poor, unskilled and unemployed people of Britain.

Table 8.1 Age-standardised mortality rates per 100,000 people by social class, selected causes, men and women aged 35-64, England and Wales, 1976-1992

	Women (35-64)			Men (35-64)		
	1976-81	1981-85	1986-92	1976-81	1981-85	1986-92
All causes						
I/II	338	344	270	621	539	455
IIIN	371	387	305	860	658	484
IIIM	467	396	356	802	691	624
IV/V	508	445	418	951	824	764
Ratio IV/V:I/II	1.50	1.29	1.55	1.53	1.53	1.68
Coronary heart disease						
I/II	39	45	29	246	185	160
IIIN	56	57	39	382	267	162
IIIM	85	67	59	309	269	231
IV/V	105	76	78	363	293	266
Ratio IV/V:I/II	2.69	1.69	2.69	1.48	1.58	1.66
Breast cancer						
I/II	52	74	52			
IIIN	75	71	49			
IIIM	61	57	46			
IV/V	47	50	54			
Ratio IV/V:I/II	0.90	0.68	1.04			

Source: Harding et al (1997)

Note: Social Class I/II = professional, managerial, technical; IIIN = intermediate, non manual; IIIM = skilled, manual; IV/V = partly skilled and unskilled manual.

Class and Health

In order to gain an understanding of Britain's failure to match the improvements in health that had been evident in some other developed countries during the post-war period, a working group on inequalities in health was set up in 1977 by the then Labour government. The working group was chaired by Sir Douglas Black, the government's chief medical officer. The group was asked to review the evidence for health inequalities, to examine information about differences in health status between various groups in society, to consider the possible causes of such differences and their implications for policy, and to suggest further research.

The Black working party concentrated on class, gender and age differences in mortality and morbidity as the main variables for analysis. The Black Report (as it became known) was completed in 1980 and presented to the Conservative government. The report made compelling reading as it suggested that while mortality rates for men and women in social class I (professional) and social class II (managerial and technical) had fallen, rates for social class IV (partly-skilled) and V (unskilled) were the same or marginally worse. A man in social class V was 2 ½ times more likely to die before he reached retirement age than one in social class I. The Black Report made 37 recommendations for action to reduce inequalities in health.

The official responses to the findings were discouraging. In the foreword, Patrick Jenkin, then Secretary of State, argued that the cost of the policy recommendations was too high and there was insufficient evidence that they were necessary.

> It will be seen that the Group reached the view that the major causes of health inequalities are so deep-rooted that only a major and wide-ranging programme of public expenditure is capable of altering the pattern. I must make it clear that additional expenditure on the scale which could result from the report's recommendations ... is quite unrealistic in present or any foreseeable economic circumstances, quite apart from any judgement that may be formed as to the effectiveness of such expenditure in dealing with the problems identified. I cannot, therefore, endorse the Group's recommendations (Quoted in Townsend et al, 1988, p.4).

However, the Black Report generated tremendous interest and the findings were of such importance that the report became a landmark study in the development of an understanding of health inequalities in Britain. In the Black Report, material and structural factors were regarded as the most important explanation for inequalities in health. Such factors include,

...damp housing leading to increased amounts of respiratory infection; household overcrowding; inadequate diet associated with low incomes... poorly educated and informed parents; stresses leading to child abuse; a generally poor environment...the everyday strain of coping with a demanding young family in inadequate circumstances in areas suffering from multiple deprivation (Benzeval et al, 1995, p.19).

The Black Report was updated in 1987 with the publication of *The Health Divide*, which also set out to establish what progress had been made in dealing with the Black Report's recommendations. The updated report suggested that little progress had been made and that 'new challenges', particularly mass unemployment had led to increased health and social inequalities. The report concluded, 'there...has not been a recognisable national effort to tackle inequalities in health' (Whitehead, 1988, p.350).

Further evidence of class-based differences in health and life expectancy in Britain are to be found in a study of more than 17,000 civil servants (Marmot et al, 1991). The so-called 'Whitehall studies' classified individuals by their employment grade and showed that mortality rates were far higher than expected among the lower grade civil servants. The data from these studies suggest that mortality differences between social classes may be even greater than that observed when national census data is utilised (see Francome and Marks, 1996).

Gender and Health

Women are the main users of health services and comprise the majority of health service workers, however many critics have argued that generally speaking, women have not received appropriate care (see Nettleton, 1995 and Doyal, 1995). In the NHS, a tendency to prioritise the high technology, acute medical sector at the expense of services for the chronically sick, disabled, geriatric and mentally ill has a damaging effect on women because of their greater use of the chronic services.

The NHS is the largest employer in Europe and is also the largest employer of women in Europe. Internationally and historically, women usually provide general medical care and the NHS is in a strong position to lead the way in equal opportunities, yet is failing to do so (see Snell, 1996). Many feminist critics of the NHS have argued that it reflects patriarchal stereotypes of the nuclear family with men occupying the more senior decision-making roles, being assisted by women who generally occupy more passive caring positions (see Graham, 1987). Miles (1991) notes that in many Eastern European countries between 70-85 per cent of doctors are women, yet this is not the case in Britain. Over 70 per cent of the workforce is female, yet only 13 per cent of full time hospital consultants are women, while 90 per cent of nurses and midwives are women. Even where women are promoted to more senior positions, they tend to be in more 'feminised specialities' such as child psychiatry where 37 per cent of consultants are women compared to traumatic and orthopaedic surgery where only 0.5 per cent of consultants are women (Pascall, 1986).

One of the issues that attracts most concern in the treatment that women receive from the British health services is the over-medicalisation of women's reproduction that gives control over women's fertility to doctors (who are usually male). In order to obtain contraception, women must undergo medical examinations. Obstetricians generally exert technical control over the management of modern childbirth. Such control includes chemical or surgical induced labour, drugs to speed or delay labour, electronic foetal monitoring and increased caesarean deliveries. These interventions, often require hospitalisation and take childbirth decisions away from women, which has led Pascall (1986, p.166), to conclude that 'women do the work of reproduction; men control it'.

Ethnicity and Health

Data on ethnicity and health is still scant in Britain. In fact it was only in the 1991 Census that the government attempted to establish the number of people from various ethnic minority groups. The census revealed that 3 million people, or approximately 5 per cent of the total population were from a minority ethnic group, of these almost half were born in Britain (Government Statistical Service, 1993). The largest ethnic minority, comprising 1.7 per cent represents people who originated in the Indian sub-continent. The ethnic minority population is not evenly distributed throughout the country and tends to be concentrated in London and in Britain's inner city areas.

Research suggests that there is a prevalence in certain ethnic minority groups of strokes (Marmot et al, 1984), diabetes and coronary heart disease (Balarajan and Raleigh, 1993), and particularly in the Asian communities of tuberculosis, liver cancer and other infectious diseases (Whitehead, 1988). Also, babies of ethnic minority mothers are twice as likely to die in the first year of life as the average (Dunnell, 1993).

The causes of ethnic minority health inequalities are not fully understood. However, the non-white ethnic minority population in Britain is over-represented among the unemployed and disadvantaged. Studies have repeatedly made the link between poverty and ill-health so in this regard Britain's ethnic minorities face a more acute problem.

Regional Differences

The NHS was built upon a pre-existing health care structure. The old private and charitable hospital sector tended to be located in the more affluent areas where a wealthy local population could afford to maintain such institutions. Once the health service was established, the distribution of services was not consistent with a needs-led service. Indeed, Tudor-Hart (1971), famously coined the 'inverse care law' to describe the relationship between the need for health services and their apparent scarcity. The availability of good medical care tends to vary inversely with the needs of the population served, so the more prosperous areas have been provided with better medical services than poorer areas where need is greatest.

Generally speaking, the poorer northern and the inner-city areas have fared less well in terms of medical facilities than the wealthier south and rural or semi-rural areas. In 1976 a new national formula, designed to re-distribute health care resources on the basis of local needs, found that health care spending was almost 30 per cent higher in the most prosperous regions compared to the poorest. However, in a climate of economic retrenchment, any redistribution would result in cuts in service provision to the better-off areas and there were considerable protests. In 1991 the formula was amended and the prosperous areas, once again, began to benefit the most from the distribution of health care resources.

Health service reforms

As a result of its position as a state-managed service, the British health system has always been intensely politicised. It was originally organised into three distinct parts. The hospitals were the most important sector and teaching hospitals (attached to universities) were given special high status with their own boards of governors in direct contact with the Ministry of Health. Secondly, general practitioner (GP) services, dentists, opticians and pharmacists were allowed independent status and contracted their services out to the NHS. The third sector, administered by local authorities, included environmental protection, public health and personal health services including maternity and child welfare clinics, health visitors, midwives, health education, vaccinations, immunisations and ambulances.

As it became clearer that health spending was not likely to fall, administrative reforms that might make the existing system more efficient were sought. In addition, it was becoming apparent that certain patient groups were receiving less adequate care, particularly the elderly and mentally ill. The problem was thought to be located within the administrative system. There was a lack of integration of services and funding arrangements tended to replicate existing inequalities between regions and between services. Various government papers published in 1968 and 1970 made proposals for change, including one of administering the NHS through local government. The 1973 Health Services Act created a more streamlined NHS structure and around 90 area health authorities and local district committees were established as a means of improving local accountability.

Marketisation and Privatisation

As administrative changes failed to make sufficient impact on the cost of health services, more fundamental reforms were considered. The most important and far reaching recent modification has been the attempt to introduce the principles of the market. The Conservative governments of the 1980s began this process with the launch of compulsory competitive tendering, whereby contracts for ancillary services such as catering, cleaning and laundry were awarded to the lowest bidder – usually in the private sector. Such contracts were often won at the expense of workers' pay and conditions.

More fundamentally, after 1990, the Conservatives sought to pressure hospitals and other direct providers of health care and welfare services to compete with each other in order to lower costs. Hospitals were encouraged to effectively 'opt-out' of state control and to establish themselves as 'independent providers' of care services with their own management boards. General practitioners were also encouraged to become individual 'fund-holders', to manage their own budgets and to buy in services on behalf of their patients. In order to achieve the aims of competition, the funding of services was separated from the provision of services. Hence the division of the NHS into two distinct sections known as 'providers' and 'purchasers'. Local health authorities lost their management function and became responsible for assessing the health needs of their resident populations, making judgements about how the provision of services will be met and purchasing those services from health providers, such as the hospitals.

The role of management and administration in the health services has also received a boost. The white paper 'Working for Patients' (Secretary of State for Health, 1989) was the result of an investigation led by Sir Roy Griffiths into management in the health services (Department of Health and Social Security, 1983). Roy Griffiths was the managing director and deputy chairman of Sainsbury's supermarket chain. His report was trenchant in its criticisms of NHS management:

> One of our most immediate observations from a business background is the lack of a clearly-defined general management function throughout the NHS. By general management we mean the responsibility drawn together in one person, at different levels of the organisation, for planning, implementation and control of performance .... The centre is still too much involved in too many of the wrong things and too little involved in some that really matter (Department of Health and Social Security, 1983, pp.11-12).

Griffiths argued that the health authorities' system of consensus management resulted in a lack of energy and in a failure to think in innovative ways. The health service was likened to a mobile 'designed to move with any breath of air, but which in fact never changes its position...' (ibid.). The government accepted Griffith's proposals and introduced or strengthened management structures at each tier of the health service. Managers now have clear areas of responsibility and are often appointed on short-term contracts. Managers are usually concerned with handling budgets (sometimes this can be in a ward, a specialist unit, an entire hospital or health centre), negotiating contracts and administering information systems in order to monitor and refine budgetary and contractual arrangements. The management of budgets is increasingly being used to control activities in hospitals. Doctors must now work with business managers to agree activity rates in a unit. Budgets are linked to negotiated agreements concerning workloads, staffing levels, patient throughput and so on.

When Labour entered office in 1997, it was widely expected that major changes would be wrought on the organisation of the health service. This has not been the case and the present government have built upon the previous reforms. General practitioner fundholding has been extended in two ways: all GPs are involved and they must now work with local teams of health care providers such as district nurses, health promotion specialists and midwives, these are known as commissioning groups. The reasoning is that health local care providers are more likely than bureaucrats and managers at district level to be able to assess the health needs of each area.

Health inequalities revisited

In developed countries, inequality in income distribution, as opposed to the crude level of national wealth appears to be the most notable factor in explaining the size of health inequalities. Evidence appears to suggest that in terms of life expectancy, the distribution of income becomes one of the most important considerations when a country exceeds a gross national product per head of $5000 (Power, 1994, p.1154). During the last 25 years, as income inequality has widened in Britain, so has health inequality. As Wilkinson (1992, p.165) states,

> Cross-sectional evidence suggesting that there is a significant tendency for mortality to be lower in countries where a more egalitarian distribution of income does exist. That this relation has been identified in different groups of countries at different times and with different measures of income distribution suggests that it is robust.

The previous Labour government commissioned the Black Report and the new Labour government, elected in 1997, resurrected the issue of health inequalities and a number of policy documents have been produced that aim to tackle the issue. The 'Independent Inquiry into Inequalities in Health Report' (Department of Health, 1998), was undertaken by a team of investigators and chaired by Sir Donald Acheson, previously the government's chief medical officer. According to the Acheson Report, almost one in five working age households in Britain has no one in work, while one in five people are reported to have persistently low incomes. In 1996/97 four and a half million children were being brought up in families with below half average income, three times the number 20 years ago.

The Acheson Report represents the latest contribution to the health inequalities debate and emphasises the importance of the social environment and better social networks for tackling health inequalities. In addition, Acheson recommends a more co-ordinated approach to government activity across departments in order to better scrutinise the effects of policy on health inequalities. Particular emphasis is placed on raising incomes and improving people's knowledge so that they are more able to make meaningful decisions that will benefit their health.

Conclusion

The present government appears to have accepted the argument that lifting people out of poverty is the best way to reduce health inequalities. However, the commitment to raise standards for the poorest has been tempered by the government's cautious approach to public spending. Considerable inroads have been made in lifting people out of poverty, in particular the young and those in work. In addition, more people are in work now than ever before so tax revenues are rising. The government has also pledged to increase health service funding in real terms year on year. But with costs and demand also rising, (the NHS is treating more people now than it ever has before), there remain doubts as to whether sufficient resources are allocated to the health sector.

There remains much to be done to reduce health inequalities and to guarantee that the British health service meets the demands that the population place upon it. The government has argued that it will require at least a decade before the results of its strategies are apparent. For many, this is too long to wait and as criticisms of the service mount unprecedented numbers are choosing to be treated privately.

References

Appleby, J. (1992), *Financing Health Care in the 1990s*, Open University, Buckingham.

Balarajan, R. and Raleigh, S. (1993), *Ethnicity and health: a guide for the NHS*, Department of Health, London.

Beveridge, W. (1942), *Social insurance and allied services*, (Cmd. 6404), HMSO, London.

Benzeval, M., Judge, K. and Whitehead, M. (eds) (1995), *Tackling Inequalities in Health*, King's Fund, London.

Department of Health (1998), *Independent Inquiry into Inequalities in Health Report*, The Stationery Office, London.

Department of Health and Social Security (1983), *NHS Management Inquiry: Report*, Chairman: Roy Griffiths, Department of Health and Social Security, London.

Doyal, L. (1995), *What Makes Women Sick? Gender and the Political Economy of Health*, Macmillan, Basingstoke.

Dunnell, K (1993), *The Health of the Nation Conference Proceedings*, NE and NW Thames RHA, London.
Flinn, M. (ed) (1965), *Report on the Sanitary Conditions of the Labouring Population of Great Britain, by Edwin Chadwick*, Edinburgh University Press, Edinburgh.
Francome, C and Marks, D. (1996), *Improving the Health of the Nation*, Middlesex University Press, London.
Government Statistical Service (1993), *1991 Census: ethnic group and country of birth: Great Britain*, vol. 2, HMSO, London.
Graham, H. (1987), 'Women, Health and Illness', *Social Studies Review*, September, pp.15-20.
Harding, S., Bethune, A., Maxwell, R. and Brown, J. (1997), 'Mortality Trends Using the Longitudinal Study' in: F. Drever, and M. Whitehead (eds), *Health Inequalities: Decennial Supplement: DS Series no.15*, The Stationery Office, London.
Laslett, P (1983), *The World We Have Lost*, Methuen, London.
Marmot, M.G., Adelstein, A.M. and Bulusu, L. (1984), 'Immigrant Mortality in England and Wales 1970–1978', *Studies on Medical and Population Subjects*, no. 47, HMSO, London.
Marmot, M.G., Smith, G.D., Stansfield, S., Patel, C., North, F., Head, G., White, I., Brunner, E. and Feeney, A. (1991), 'Health Inequalities among British Civil Servants: the Whitehall II Study', *The Lancet*, vol. 337, pp. 1387–1393.
Miles, A. (1991), *Women, Health and Medicine*, Open University Press, Milton Keynes.
Ministry of Health (1944), *A National Health Service*, Cmnd 6502, HMSO, London.
Nettleton, S. (1995), *The Sociology of Health and Illness*, Polity, Cambridge.
Office for National Statistics, (1995), *Social Trends*, HMSO, London.
Pascall, G. (1986), *Social Policy: A Feminist Analysis*, Tavistock, London.
Power, C. (1994), 'Medicine in Europe: Health and Social Inequality in Europe', *British Medical Journal*, vol. 308, pp.1153–1156.
Secretary of State for Health and others (1989), *Working for Patients*, HMSO, London.
Snell, J. (1996), 'Room at the Top?', *Nursing Times*, vol. 92, pp.26–27.
Tiratsoo, N. (ed.) (1997), *From Blitz to Blair: A New History of Britain Since 1939*, Weidenfeld and Nicolson, London.
Townsend, P., Davidson, N. and Whitehead, M. (1988), *Inequalities in Health and the Health Divide*, Penguin, Harmondsworth.
Tudor Hart, J. (1971), 'The Inverse Care Law', *The Lancet*, vol. 1, pp.405–412.
Whitehead, M. (1988), 'The Health Divide' in P. Townsend, N. Davidson, and M. Whitehead (eds), *Inequalities in Health and the Health Divide*, Penguin, Harmondsworth.
Wilkinson, R.G. (1996), *Unhealthy Societies: The Afflictions of Inequality*, Routledge, London.

9 Getting well in Malaysia
ROZIAH OMAR

Introduction

Following Independence in 1957, transformation of the economic, social and political scene in Malaysia has provided avenues for an accelerated quality of life for all. Thus the high rates of economic growth over several decades, combined with poverty eradication programmes, contributed to reducing the incidence of poverty in Peninsular Malaysia, from 49.3 per cent in 1970 to 29 per cent in 1980 and 9.5 per cent in 1995. Structural modifications not only reduced poverty, as well as created a more equal distribution of wealth among the ethnic groups, but at the same time improved the health status for all.

Prior to Independence, the people in Malaya suffered many health problems, especially poverty related ones. Diseases such as malaria, malnutrition, TB, anaemia and many communicable diseases were evident. Women, especially in the rural areas, had few opportunities to get education and poor access to family planning. Many died from complications during pregnancy and labour, suffered anaemia, and were often at the mercy of untrained birth attendants in the villages. Policy makers, especially during the post NEP period, have reacted to these problems by gradually implementing strategic interventions. Realising the importance of a healthy population for nation building, the government emphasised the importance, for its balanced development agenda, of developing its health sector. The Rural Health Service (RHS) and Maternal Child Health (MCH) became central in these attempts to improve health and increased budget allocations were made to promote health care. Despite the fact that even with the increases, the budget allocation for health remained relatively small, these efforts have succeeded in improving the status of maternal and child health, as well as eliminating most of the communicable diseases.

Notwithstanding these considerable achievements, it has been argued that Malaysia's health care is not equitable and accessible to all (see Chee, 1990). As this chapter will show, there are particular concerns relating to the health of low income groups in both rural and urban areas. Furthermore, inequalities may worsen if the government proceeds with proposals to privatise support services for public hospitals. For many years, severe criticisms from various groups voicing their doubts about privatisation were directed at the government for its wish to reduce the public provision of health care. Learning from the experience of others, and due to the strong voice of the lobbyists against privatisation, the government has recently decided to pull back its plan. Given that decision, a question to be asking is: what is the direction forward for Malaysian health care? As Malaysia moves closer to becoming a developed country, is she adequately equipped to face the health issues and problems related to its developed status including the increasing costs of health care and the challenges of the burden of lifestyle diseases and modernisation?

Trends in health status

Progressive economic development, accessibility to education, better access to medical care have all influenced positively the well being of the population. Table 9.1 shows selected indicators over time. Thus, in 1980, the crude death rate in Malaysia was one of the lowest in the region. The crude death rate in Peninsular Malaysia in 1997 was much lower than the average 8 per thousand in Asia or 9 per thousand in the world as a whole (Tan, 1992). Malaysia's infant mortality rate is already less than 20 per thousand (Chee, 1990) and ranks second among the ASEAN countries in terms of its infant mortality rates (Tan, 1992). Likewise, at 0.2 per 1,000 live births, the maternal mortality rate has decreased to levels below those pertaining in most other countries in the region.

Table 9.1 Selected indicators for health status in Malaysia

Indicators	1980	1990	1995	1997
Life Expectancy at Birth - Men	66.7	68.9	69.4	69.6
Life Expectancy at Birth - Women	71.6	73.5	74.2	74.5
Crude Birth Rate	30.9	28.4	25.9	25.8
Crude Death Rate	5.3	4.7	4.6	4.5
Doctors per 10,000	2.8	3.9	4.6	6.6
Dentists per 10,000	0.5	0.8	0.85	0.86
Infant Mortality Rate (per 1,000)	24.0	13.0	10.4	8.8
Toddler Mortality Rate (per 1,000)	2.0	0.9	0.8	0.6
Maternal Mortality Rate (per 1,000)	0.6	0.2	0.2	0.2

Source: Ministry of Health Reports

However, as positive as these indicators are, looking more closely there are a number of concerns, some apparent now, some constituting challenges for the future. Thus, for all the health indicators in Table 9.1 there are considerable variations of health status between different states in the country. The west coasts states such as Penang, Johor and Selangor have much better health indicators than states in the east, such as Kelantan and Trengganu. Also, whereas the overall improvements could be said to be dramatic, important questions for the future include: how to improve further, and what can be done to eliminate the gaps? A specific indicator that needs to be highlighted is the increasing life expectancy in Malaysia. In 1998, the life expectancy for men in Malaysia was 69.5 and 74.1 for women. It is estimated that by the year 2020, the life expectancy for women will be 80.4 and for men 75. The manifestations of an ageing population will provide a different set of challenges for the policy maker and society as whole (Omar, 1993; Omar, 1994; Omar, 1999).

The development of the provision of health care

The Role of the Ministry of Health

Having established the need to provide health care, the Malayan government set up a department of health in 1957 to address the burden of ill health and disease. Today, it has grown to a ministry with a strong vision, supported by a budget and a sophisticated health delivery system to suit specific needs of the population.

The vision of the Ministry of Health (MOH) is to achieve a nation of healthy individuals, families and communities, through a health system that is equitable, affordable, efficient, technologically appropriate, environmentally adaptable and consumer friendly with emphasis on quality, innovation, health promotion and respect for human dignity, and which promotes individual responsibility and community participation towards an enhanced quality of life. The hallmark of the vision is the focusing of efforts to generate rapid growth in the health care sector so that all Malaysians will be able to enjoy a better quality of life. Improvements in health services, eradication of poverty, greater access to health education and social amenities will in return benefit the health status of the nation.

As Malaysia has progressed, the challenges faced by the Ministry of Health have become tougher and more complex. With economic progress, different lifestyles became established and these resulted in epidemiological change. Lifestyle diseases are seen as replacing many of the communicable diseases as more and more Malaysians are dying and suffering from heart diseases, cancer and HIV/AIDS. However, many argue that these lifestyles diseases, often referred to as diseases of modernisation, are superimposing on diseases of poverty (Chee, 1990; Tan, 1992; Omar, 1997). There are sectors of the population that are still prone to malaria, the recent Japanese encephalitis and dengue. The main burden of some of these communicable diseases are still prevalent especially among the marginalised and impoverished groups in Malaysia such as the Orang Asli (Baer, 1999). The establishment and strengthening of programmes to cater for these health burdens poses a major challenge, the pursuit of which will require the MOH to work more closely with other agencies.

Health Expenditure

In conjunction with the setting up of the Ministry to form and lead policy and implementation of health care policies, the government also provided financial support. In common with the position in other countries this public support, along with private expenditures, constitutes a major share of the national resource. Thus, in 1990, world health expenditure amounted to US$1,700 billion or 8 per cent of global revenue. Of this amount, 10 per cent was spent on health by the developing countries of Africa, Asia and Latin America. In 1990, the United States spent 12.7 per cent of its GDP on health. By 1994, it increased to 14 per cent and was expected to rise to 18 per cent by the year 2000. Malaysia's health expenditure has increased. As a proportion of the national budget there has been an increase from 1.91 per cent in 1971 to 3.94 per cent in 1996. Despite this increase, Malaysia is one of those countries in the region that still spends relatively small budgets on health (see Table 9.2). As noted by Peabody (1999, p.139):

> As expected, total expenditures (both public and private) per capita rise with income. However, the percentage of GDP does not seem to be strongly correlated with income. Several poor countries, such as India and Nepal spend large percentages of their GDP on health, while some wealthier countries, such as Malaysia and Singapore, spend relatively small percentages.

Table 9.2 Health expenditure in selected Asian countries

Country	Population 1995 Millions	GNP Per Capita 1995	Per Capita Expenditures on Health (1990 - 1991 $US)			Health Expenditures as Percentage of GDP, 1990-1995		
			Total	Public	Private	Total	Public	Private
Hong Kong	6.2	22990	748	144	604	4.3	1.9	2.4
Indonesia	193.3	980	12	4	8	1.5	0.7	0.8
Korea	44.0	8260	390	160	230	5.4	1.8	3.6
Malaysia	20.1	3890	77	33	44	3.0	1.3	1.7
Singapore	3.0	26730	547	316	231	3.5	1.1	2.4
Taiwan	21.2	12790	515	268	246	4.9	2.6	2.3
Thailand	58.2	2740	73	17	59	5.3	1.4	3.9

Source: Peabody (1999)

In the development of budget allocations for Malaysia over the period 1986-1995, it is clear that the bulk of the government health expenditure was allocated for curative health care such as the construction of hospital and patient care services. In addition, a significant portion was allocated to training with only a small amount for public health services. With the Seventh Malaysia Plan (1996-2000), the government has shifted the priority (see Table 9.3). The bulk of the expenditure was now to be allocated to promotional and preventive programmes and facilities. While there are good reasons - rising cases of lifestyle related diseases, for example – to focus on health promotion, the Malaysian government continues to allocate public subsidies to improving district hospitals and decentralising the health services in small towns.

Table 9.3 Development allocation for health, 1996-2000

Programme	Sixth Malaysia Plan	Seventh Malaysia Plan
Patient Care Services	2,070.3	1,831.6
Hospitals	1,537.0	1,159.7
Upgrading and Renovation	533.3	671.9
Public Health Services	293.6	655.7
Urban Health	66.5	183.3
Rural Health	131.8	400.0
Environmental Health	95.8	72.4
Other Health Services	134.5	162.7
Total	2,498.4	2,650.0

Source: Malaysia (1996)

Rural Health Service

Throughout all the five year plans, health care budgets have reflected the pattern of the needs of both rural and urban areas. Thus there has been a recognition that the poor especially in the rural areas may not be able to afford health care. Indeed this has become so central to the health agenda of the MOH that in the key strategies of the Seventh Malaysia Plan, the commitments to reduce inequity is inseparable from the overall agenda. Accordingly, one of the key roles of the MOH is to remedy the unequal access of health care among the rural population in Malaysia especially those who live in isolated areas of the Peninsula and East Malaysia.

Over the past forty years, the Malaysian government has made concerted attempts to improve the well being of the rural population. It has developed a special branch of the health care system, known as the Rural Health Service (RHS) to develop health facilities and direct provision of free services to the rural population. The RHS network forms the base for curative and preventive health programmes, including family health, vector borne disease control, environmental sanitation and health education. It is organised in a two-tier system, in which a health centre is designed to serve between 16,000 to 20,000 population, while a single community clinic (*Klinik Desa*) should serve between 2,000 to 4,000 population. Improvements in the organisation of the RHS has led to greater access. Estimates from the Malaysian Medical Association support this, stating that less than 7 per cent of the population live with no access to a static clinic within a radius of 5 km (Malaysian Medical Association, 1980). Government data also show that more than 95 per cent of the population in the Peninsula, and 70 per cent of those in East Malaysia have access to static health facilities (Kandiah, 1993). The RHS, then, constitutes a significant intervention facility for the majority of those in the rural areas. Consequently, the RHS especially through its Maternal Child Health Clinic (recently changed in name to Family Health) plays a crucial role in improving the health of women, especially poor, rural women.

Addressing Gender Inequalities in Health

In Malaysia the particular health needs of women have long been recognised. Thus, the Maternal Child Health (MCH) service in Malaysia was a product of the British legacy, introduced in 1923 with the setting up of midwifery services in the Straits Settlements. In the period prior to the Second World War, services were implemented to address the health problems of women, and practices such as family planning, nutrition and immunisation were introduced. However, due to manpower shortages and lack of funds, many of these programmes were limited to only a handful of urban women. When the war came to an end in 1945, malnutrition and communicable diseases were rampant.

From 1948 to 1957, the MCH was upgraded in terms of its services and numbers. In 1956, the MCH services came to the forefront of the administration to form an important adjunct to the National and Health Development Programme. More clinics were opened and personnel were trained in Singapore and England. However, most of the services were located in the bigger towns. The rural areas especially in the east coast states were neglected. Over the decades, this strategy has been partly responsible for the differential health status of the states and ethnic groups in the country. But, after Independence in 1957, there was a new political will to improve the well being of the Malays leading to the development of the MCH services in various villages. New interventions were set up, central to these being curative and preventive services, particularly services to improve maternal and child health.

Family planning was aggressively promoted to stop excess fertility. The National Family Planning Board was established in 1966 and endorsed the idea of the need for women to control their fertility. However, the Family Planning programmes are problematic for many Malay women and men because of the apparent conflict with Islamic values on contraception. This was nevermore so than in the 1980s when Malaysia went through a period of Islamic revivalism, and in 1985 when the Prime Minister announced the objective for Malaysia of achieving a larger population of 70 million (see Petchesky and Judd, 1998). However, studies have shown an increasing use of contraception among Malaysian couples. More women currently use contraception earlier and continue to use it at older ages. Data for 1984 and 1994 showed that half of the currently married women were using a method of contraception compared to about one third in 1974 (see Zulkifli et al, 1996).

Ante natal care, which forms a major part of the MCH services, has improved in its coverage dramatically after the 1980s. A recent estimate shows that ante natal coverage at government facilities covered a total of 516,876 (about 72 per cent) pregnant women in 1996. Immunisation coverage has improved each year, as have post natal visits and delivering at hospitals or by trained birth attendants. However, in line with the government objective to improve wellness, the Seventh Malaysia Plan has expanded the MCH unit to become the Family Health Development division with three main sections, Primary Care, Family Health and Nutrition.

Privatisation

Proposals to introduce privatisation to the Malaysian health care service were first put forward in 1983, with the government viewing this restructuring process as an alternative to reducing government activities in certain sectors, and subsequently reducing public spending. In 1991, the Privatisation Master Plan was introduced, based on several key objectives including:

- To reduce the financial burden and administrative tasks of the government;
- To increase efficiency and improve national productivity;
- To expedite economic growth;
- To reduce the size and involvement of the public sector in the economy;
- To aid the achievement of the objectives of Malaysia's development policies.

Previously when justifying the need to privatise, one of the main reasons given was to increase the efficiency of services. Private sector participation in the field, as well as in medical education, was encouraged for cost-sharing of the growing health expenditure. Privatisation has also increased for services within government agencies such as laundry, transport and catering (Zulkifli et al, 1996). The government also planned to privatise certain health institutions, to provide expertise and service for patients from neighbouring countries. The privatisation of health care and its related services was viewed as a new paradigm in health care organisation in Malaysia. The government argued that this new concept would change the total management of health to a more efficient organisation.

The National Heart Institute was the first medical institution to be privatised in Malaysia. There has also been encouragement of the expansion of the private sector in the provision of health care facilities. Thus in 1985 there were 135 private hospitals containing 3,666 beds while in 1997 there were 219 and 8,936 respectively. Most are located in urban areas, with approximately 60 per cent of the beds in private hospitals being in Penang, Selangor and Kuala Lumpur.

The critique of the private sector in health produced by the Malaysian Medical Association (1980) focused on the conflicting values of commercial business and those of medical professionals. Private sector medicine functions on a profit basis, and hence its tendency is to focus on urban middle income and privileged areas of society. This trend has been exacerbated because of the attractive remuneration given to physicians and specialists. The setting up of private hospitals has increased the cost of health care and, as a result, the private sector has to charge their patients high fees. Furthermore, most of the services are geared towards curative services especially services for women and the modern diseases. Many of the private hospitals are maternity homes, and specialist centres for cardiovascular disease, diabetes and cancer.

It is interesting to note that all the lobbying by the Citizens Health Initiative (CHI) and the Malaysian Medical Association (MMA) has succeeded. For many years the MMA has taken the position that privatisation of health care should not be implemented until there is in place a national health care financing scheme, a country wide primary health care system and integration of the private and public health care sectors. The CHI under its Citizen Health Manifesto argues that the government has a responsibility to ensure that the quality and delivery of health care services will not be compromised and that low income groups, the elderly and the chronically ill will not be denied access to health care as a result of privatisation. The control of health care costs is often a struggle among conflicting interests over the priorities of a society. However, in response to such concerns, the government has said that it will take measures during the Plan to make sure that quality of care will not be compromised for the sake of profit and the prime objective of the medical profession will not be sacrificed. The Private Healthcare Facilities and Services Act 1998 has replaced the former act, the Private Hospitals Act 1971. The latter was originally implemented in order to ensure that exploitation of the consumer would not occur and that any profit making objective did not override the value to provide equality in health care (Malaysia, 1996). The new Act gives more and wider powers and jurisdiction to the MOH.

Further issues in Malaysian health care

Whereas privatisation constitutes what is probably the major policy issue in health care in Malaysia, there are a number of other current policy debates and concerns particularly relating to urban areas.

Urban Environment

Malaysia is working aggressively towards becoming an industrialised country by 2020. With this vision, massive industrialisation projects are undertaken. Industrialisation is also related to urbanisation. Malaysia's major cities, especially Kuala Lumpur, continue to expand rapidly as a direct result of migration from rural areas and from other countries (see chapter 11). Both industrialisation and urbanisation have greatly impacted on the environment. For example, problems of air pollution are beginning to appear. Malaysia's Klang Valley, in which Kuala Lumpur is located, is polluted not only because of its huge numbers of cars transmitting exhaust fumes into the air, but also the polluted air from factory wastes. Fumes such as hydrocarbon, carbon monoxide, mercury and others are extremely hazardous to health, evidenced, for example, in the correlation between levels of hydrocarbon and of diseases of the lung. One consequence has been a shift in the pattern of diseases experienced by those living in urban areas, relative to those living in rural areas.

Urban Lifestyles

Lifestyle diseases have come to the forefront of health policies not only in developed countries, but more so in the developing countries where primary preventive measures are still likely to be effective (World Health Organization, 1995). Among the present lifestyles, associated with city living, that are influencing health are factors such as changing of diet, smoking, physical inactivity, and the stress of urban living. The general pattern of diseases in Malaysia is that lifestyle related diseases are now superimposed onto health problems related to poverty (Chee, 1990). There is an increase in those diseases, such as cardiovascular, diabetes, obesity, accidents and cancer, related to 'modern living'.

Urban Poverty and Health

Poverty causes ill health by depriving individuals or families of basic necessities of life such as adequate nutrition, shelter, healthy environment and quality health and medical care. Many studies have shown that health and poverty are interactive, and the poor are often less healthy than the rest of the population. Low-income families have less opportunity to enjoy good health, they experience under-nutrition, malnutrition and face difficulties in getting proper medical care (Tee, 1986; Luft, 1978).

It was noted at the start of the present chapter that, in general, levels of poverty in Malaysia have reduced in recent years. Thus, the number of urban poor households declined by 34 per cent from 84,600 in 1995 to 55,400 in 1997. Nevertheless, it has long been acknowledged that there are certain diseases that afflict the poor more than the well to do. Because of their overcrowded housing, poor sanitation, restricted access to good medical care and so on, the urban poor are exposed to diseases such as parasitic infection, and vector borne diseases. Serious overcrowding and lack of basic amenities add to the hazards of the old diseases with new problems such as pollution, traffic accidents, juvenile delinquency, drug addition, absence of psychological support from an extended family group, alcoholism and mental illness (Khairuddin, 1984).

To add further to the problems, the large numbers of illegal immigrants into the cities have brought with them the old communicable diseases such as typhoid and tuberculosis. Their presence causes more strain on the already inadequate resources such as housing, social services, medical care and other services. The problem is one facing not only the Ministry of Health but also those responsible for areas such as immigration, education and housing. Moreover, it is a problem that may be exacerbated as the Malaysian economy fully recovers from the late 1990s recession and again expands its demand for low income labour, thus drawing in more migrants from other countries in the region.

Conclusion

Malaysia aims to be a nation of healthy individuals, families and communities, through a health system that is equitable, affordable, efficient, technologically appropriate, environmentally adaptable and consumer friendly. Applying this vision, the government has developed a sophisticated health care network throughout the country which promotes curative and preventive health as well as emphasising individual responsibility and community participation. The health statistics have shown great improvement for Malaysians, be they men, women or children.

However, it is difficult to deny that, although the Malaysian government has indeed developed many health programmes and is very proactive in terms of its health strategies, there remain inherent weaknesses in some of these programmes, especially at the implementation level. The delivery of health care to the very poor, the elderly and to those who live in isolated parts of the country poses particular problems. For instance, the Rural Health Service currently does not provide the rural poor especially older people with the same opportunities to gain access to the same quality and efficient healthcare as their urban and younger counterparts. In addition, the budget for health and health expenditures must be fair and just so as to ensure that all groups of the population will be enjoying health sector reforms at each level of the health care system. It might be deemed unfair, for example, if the government decided to spend large resources on high tech medicine and direct less funds to the most basic services to the rural areas, the very poor and the old.

In this chapter, emphasis has been on the implications of features of many health care reforms which include the increasing role for private hospitals and other forms of privatisation. These are issues of interest to many. Privatisation of health care has expanded in terms of numbers and functions. Change is always needed to enable adaptation to different situations and environments. Though the government has announced its intention to cancel its plan to privatise health care, it is important to realise that, in the future moving to the 2020 society, new health care reforms may be needed.

References

Baer, A. (1999), *Health, Disease and Survival: A Biomedical and Genetic Analysis of the Orang Asli of Malaysia*, COAC, Petaling Jaya.
Chee, H.L. (1990), *Health and Health Care in Malaysia*, IPT, University of Malaya, Kuala Lumpur.
Kandiah, N. (1993), *Maternal Health Services. Status of Maternal Health Services in Malaysia*. In Technical Meeting on Maternal Health, SEAMEO-TROPMED. May 25-27, Kuala Lumpur.
Khairuddin, Y. (1984), 'Urban Primary Health Care', in Y.H. Yip and K.S. Low (eds), *Urbanization and Economic Development*, Institute of Advanced Studies, University of Malaya, Kuala Lumpur.
Luft, H.S. (1978), *Poverty and Health: Economic Causes and Consequences of Health Problems*, Cambridge University Press, Cambridge.
Malaysia (1996), *Seventh Malaysia Plan 1996 - 2000*, Government Printers, Kuala Lumpur.
Malaysian Medical Association (1980), *The Future of Health Services in Malaysia*, MMA, Kuala Lumpur.
Omar, R. (1993), *Elderly in Malaysia: Problems and Role of the Government and NGO's in Handling the Welfare of the Aged*, Proceedings International Conference on the Elderly, Singapore Action Group of Elders and International Federation of Ageing, Singapore.
Omar, R. (1994), *The Malay Woman in the Body: Between Biology and Culture*, Fajar Bakti, Kuala Lumpur.
Omar, R. (1997), 'Health, Disease and Development: The Malaysian Experience', in *Meeting the Health Challenges of the 21st Century*, Partnerships in Social

Science and Health Science, Philippine Social Science Council and APNET, Philippines
Omar, R. (1999), *Challenges for the 21st Century: Ageing and Care in Malaysia*, Proceedings Asia Pacific Regional Conference for International Year of Older Persons, The Hong Kong Council of Social Services and Department of Hong Kong Social Administration, Hong Kong.
Peabody, J.W. (1999), *Policy and Health: Implementation for Development in Asia*, Cambridge University Press, Cambridge.
Petchesky, R. and Judd, K. (1998), *Negotiating Reproductive Rights: A Study of Women's Views and Practises in Seven Countries*, International Book on the IRRRAG Research Findings, Zed Press, New York
Tan, P.C. (1992), 'Consequences of Population Change', in, T.P. Chang, T.N. Peng, A. Kassim and Z.A. Rashid (eds), *Malaysia: National Level Analysis*, Faculty of Economics and Administration, University of Malaya, Kuala Lumpur.
Tee, E.S. (1986), *Poverty, Malnutrition and Health*, paper given at ISIS National Conference on Poverty, Kuala Lumpur.
World Health Organisation (1995), *Lifestyle Changes and Their Impact on Health of Women in Western Pacific Region*, Women's Health Series, vol. 5, Manila.
Zulkifli, S.N., Rashidah, M.A. and Rashidah, S. (1996), *Reproductive Health in Malaysia*, paper given to Conference on Reproductive Health, APNET, Cebu City, Philippines.

10 Housing policy in Britain
JOHN DOLING

During the present century there have been a number of processes and events, common to western European countries, which have helped to shape their housing policies. Firstly, the linked processes of urbanisation, industrialisation and modernisation were already well advanced by the onset of the century so that policies have not been primarily about accommodating rural migrants in search of jobs, but rather satisfying those already living in cities. Secondly, the Second World War left a common legacy: as a result of the slowing down or complete cessation of new construction activity during the war years and, in some countries, of enemy action, there were huge shortages of housing. In all countries there were political pressures to mobilise national resources in order to satisfy housing need. Thirdly, whereas the three decades following the ending of the war were characterised by steady economic growth that facilitated the expansion of state supported welfare, including housing, from the mid-1970s economic pressures have created downward pressures on public budgets.

In Britain these economic pressures have been associated with a marked change of direction in housing policy. Following the ending of the Second World War, the government pursued a model of housing provision, supported by an expanding economy and full employment, in which there were strong elements of central planning and public provision, based on principles of need and equity. The main objectives were related initially to eradicating the shortages and later to upgrading the quality of housing for everyone. Gradually - turning to rapidly after the late 1970s - this has been superseded by a second model, supported by a more uncertain economy and high unemployment, and based on markets, devolved decision making, ability to pay and inequality.

The aims of this chapter are, firstly, to outline the main developments over time in the state-market mix in Britain and, secondly, to discuss some of the tensions found in current policy.

The development of housing

State Provision 1945-70

In 1945, the population of Britain was - indeed had been for some decades - heavily concentrated in urban areas, not just in the capital but also in the great Victorian, industrial towns of the Midlands and the North. This urbanisation had been based largely on rental housing provided by private companies and individuals, and even though the importance of this sector had declined, numerically, over the preceding 30 years, it still housed around half of all households. The sector housed, though not exclusively, many of the poorer households, whereas those with higher incomes - again not exclusively - had become home owners. Home ownership had in fact increased its proportion of the housing stock in the inter war years; so too had local authority housing which accommodated households from all parts of the income distribution, though particularly skilled manual workers.

The subsequent continuity of these developments reflected the fact that by the start of the war, Britain had established 'a framework of housing policy in a recognisably modern form' (Malpass and Murie, 1994, p.64). This was to prove significant in the context of the two major housing issues that were apparent at the end of the war. The first was, given attempts to establish systems that would aid attacks on squalor and enhance the welfare of citizens, how to ensure housing of an acceptable standard being affordable by people in all income groups. Considerable thought was given to how this was to be achieved, with Beveridge, in particular, discussing how, given that there were large regional differences in their levels, housing costs could be incorporated within the new social security system. Although no immediate solution was seen to the geographical variation problem, so that housing was to be treated outside the system, the significance of the anomaly was reduced because the existing mechanisms for rent setting - rent control in much of the private rented sector and exchequer subsidies in the local authority sector - meant that in general rents were far below market levels.

The second, though in some senses the prior, issue, was how to build large numbers of houses very quickly. Estimates at the time indicated that if all households were to be provided with their own homes the shortfall was as much as 4 million dwellings (Holmans, 1987). A consequence was the widespread sharing of homes, homelessness and the development of a squatting movement. The latter involved the illegal occupation, in rural areas, of disused army camps and, in the towns, of existing buildings such as offices and apartment blocks (Berry, 1974). In some cases the squatters were evicted but the more fundamental solution of course was to build as quickly as possible. And this is precisely what the newly elected Labour government did, using the model that had proved so successful in the war: central planning of the factors of production with implementation by local authorities. This determination reflected another consequence of the war, namely the change in 'public opinion and attitudes in an egalitarian direction, with much increased support for reliance on government in preference to markets' (Holmans, 1987, p.95).

In the first few of the post war years new housing production was dominated by the public sector, resulting in a rapid increase in the size of the local authority stock. In the 20 years of the inter war period, local authorities had built 1.3 million homes, a figure that had almost doubled by the end of 1953 (Holmans, 1987), and by 1965 had more than trebled to 3.9 million (Malpass and Murie, 1994).

In addition to the growing size of the public sector, a number of other aspects of post war housing policy are important. After the election of a Conservative government in 1951 the private sector was increasingly involved in production to the extent that throughout the period from 1950 to 1980 as a whole, the two sectors contributed about equal proportions. Almost all the private sector building was housing for home owners so that with this tenure along with council housing increasing in numbers, there was a related decline of the private rented sector (see table 10.1).

Table 10.1 Housing Tenure, Great Britain (%)

	Owner occupied	Housing association	Local authority	Private rented
1900	10	-	-	90
1950	29	-	18	53
1961	42	-	26	32
1971	51	-	31	19
1981	57	2	30	11
1991	66	3	21	10
1998	69	4	18	9

Source: Department of Environment Statistics

In common with many other western countries, then, Britain had addressed the problem of housing shortage with a large scale programme of new construction based on strong state interventions, organising the factors of production and balancing out the needs of different areas of the economy. This was the era of, what Harloe (1995) termed, 'mass' social housing; an era characterised by the notion that western states should ensure provision on the basis of need rather than supply and demand. Notwithstanding the broad similarities there were some specific differences. In the liberal regime states - Canada, Australia and US - where, removed from the main theatres of war, housing shortages had been far less and state involvement in housing was much more subdued; there was very little development of social housing sectors. In the mainland European countries, on the other hand, social housing sectors developed to a considerable size, but they were largely based on non-state intermediaries: non-profit making associations and companies, even private landlords, but in each case state regulation and subsidy achieved similar ends. What was different about the British approach, therefore, was the dominance of the local state as the provider of social housing, an outcome, as Donnison and Ungerson (1982) noted, that bore more similarity to the communist, east European countries.

Changing Direction: 1970-1980

The achievement of the British approach was that by 1970 it had produced a large sector - providing housing for about 1 in 3 households - with a significant proportion (though certainly not all) being of high quality in terms of space and fittings. Rent pooling across the large stocks of housing held by each local authority meant that the rents on individual properties could be lower than the market rent. In combination with a benefit system that provided financial assistance to those tenants with the very lowest incomes, allocation could be based on principles of need and not constrained by the ability of tenants to pay out of their own resources. With many larger households, in particular, being able to get housing of a value far beyond their own means, the local authority sector constituted a major redistributive mechanism.

This large social sector sat alongside - in some senses uneasily so - an even larger private, home owning sector. They represented quite different principles: one based on egalitarianism and de-commodification; the other based on inequality and markets. Actually the two sectors, along with the subsidy systems that supported them, contributed to a major division in British society. Lower income groups were supported in obtaining adequate or even better housing only in the public sector, whereas higher income groups could obtain more subsidy by entering home ownership and indeed the higher the income, the more subsidy obtained. The housing system therefore sustained a structural inequality penalising the poor if they moved into home ownership and the rich if they moved into public housing. This contributed to what has been termed a consumption cleavage whereby stratification developed on the basis of the different material interests of those who consume through the public and those who consume through the private sectors, with those material interests coming to have ideological and political expression (Saunders, 1990).

In fact, such issues were characteristic of the housing debates in the 1970s. With a shortage of housing no longer being statistically or politically a particular concern, and as governments struggled with the rapidly-worsening, economic instability and stagnation, however, the housing problem became re-structured so that distributional or consumption issues came to dominate. Unlike earlier decades when, as more than one commentator has pointed out, the differences in political rhetoric of the two main political parties became muted when translated into action (see Heidenheimer et al, 1975), in the 1970s their respective actions became more distinctive. Thus the Conservative government in office as the decade opened, set about transforming public housing, reducing levels of new production, and, most significantly, beginning a process of shifting the subsidy structure from the production side - which kept rent levels below market levels - to the consumption side - where the impact of higher rent could be reduced by means tested payments to individuals. This was also a shift from universal benefit (at least in the universe of public sector tenants) to individual benefits, which had the effect of deepening the structural inequality of housing tenure. The Labour government, elected in 1974, both repealed this legislation, so reverting to production side subsidies, and, as part of its strategy of attempting to solve the country's economic difficulties by increasing public expenditure, greatly increased new local authority housing production.

But, by the end of the 1970s there was seemingly a new consensus in which both parties perceived a reduced role for public housing. The new alignment began with the realisation by the Labour government that it could not sustain the then current level of public expenditure. It turned to the International Monetary Fund for assistance, their request being granted but only with the proviso that the government cut back on its expenditure. This it did, with the cuts in the housing programme being particularly severe. The erosion of Labour support was further signalled when the results of a major government review of housing, published in 1977, came down in favour of a future more oriented toward home ownership (Doling, 1983).

Reverting to the Market: 1980 Onwards

The manifesto on which the Conservative party had fought and won the general election in 1979, promised a continuation, indeed an acceleration, of the shift toward home ownership. In reality, the shift was even more dramatic, it quickly becoming clear that in the housing sphere the rhetoric about 'drawing back the frontiers of the state' to re-assert the role of markets meant a huge reduction in the size and role of public housing. Although the precise, statistically-defined objective was not clearly laid out, the view quickly developed that home ownership should and could be expanded to some 80, if not 90, per cent of households, with the public sector playing a minor, safety net role (Doling, 1994a).

This radical restructuring of the housing system was to be achieved through a number of government actions. Firstly, in its first year in office the government determined over a four-year period to reduce total public spending by £2,800 million, with the housing programme alone to be subject to a £2,582 million cut. The long run impact has been the reduction in new social housing construction - from around 150,000 in the mid 1970s to around 20,000 in the mid 1990s (Doling, 1994a). Secondly, the government revived the plans of a decade earlier to shift subsidy away from reducing rent levels across all public housing, encouraging them to rise rapidly - eventually to market levels - with subsidy being available on a means tested basis to those households with the lowest incomes. The impact of this change was to withdraw subsidy from any but the lowest income tenants, having the effect of making it financially more attractive for most income groups to enter home ownership. Finally, the government introduced legislation - the Housing Act 1980 - that gave most public sector and some housing association tenants the right to purchase their dwelling. Provided that certain conditions were met, the local authority (and housing association) could not turn down an application to buy. Moreover, there were large financial inducements with, depending on the length of the tenancy, the sale price being up to 50 per cent lower than the market value. In response to this package many tenants bought their homes - a million by 1986, and 1.7 million by 1996 - with a consequent reduction in the size of the public sector (Table 10.1).

A widely supported analysis (see, for example, Tosics, 1987) portrays all western European governments responding to their economic problems in ways similar to those of Britain, that is by pursuing strategies of privatising their housing sectors by switching more responsibility to market mechanisms and private resources. Even if this has been a general trend, it is clear that the strategies have varied considerably in detail. Indeed, there is evidence, throughout the 1990s at least, that far from privatisation, in some respects some European countries maintained, sometimes increased, their relative commitment to public support. Specifically, in those countries that, in response to economic difficulties, have pursued Esping-Andersen's Scandinavian route (see Chapter 1), there have actually been increases in the contribution that social housing made to total housing production. For these countries social housing production was seen as part of their strategies of attempting to maximise employment through public investment (Doling, 1994b). In these countries, therefore, there have continued to be a large annual addition to the stock of dwellings, available to people on the basis of non-market criteria.

By the second half of the 1980s it had become increasingly apparent in Britain that the expansion of home ownership to its then current level had become problematic (Doling, 1994a). Firstly, the rate of council house sales had slowed down considerably. The first tranche of sales had comprised mainly those tenants with incomes sufficiently high to make the transfer to home ownership financially desirable and feasible But now increasing numbers of those left in the sector had low incomes. The policy response took the form of new legislation in 1988 that attempted to achieve greater market involvement in housing in ways other than simply increasing the size of the home ownership sector. The Act enabled private landlords to let dwellings at market rents, the argument being that getting rid of rent control would attract private investment into the sector (Coleman, 1989). Further, it provided the means whereby public housing could be transferred, en masse, to other owners, perhaps a housing association or a private company. Such large scale voluntary transfers, as they were labelled, were intended to hasten the erosion of the public sector and to achieve a plurality of landlords. Finally, the Act introduced a different subsidy arrangement that encouraged housing associations to seek larger shares of their development capital from private financial institutions.

Following an eighteen year period of Conservative government, New Labour, elected into office in 1997, has made only minor changes of direction in housing policy: some relaxation of spending by local authorities and small amendments to the legislation dealing with homeless people, for example. In fact, it has continued with the belief held by the Conservatives that the housing market could be a major source of macro-economic instability and that reforms were necessary in order to reduce the volatility of house prices. The solution to this has been seen as being located with the system of mortgage interest rate subsidies (MIRAS) that hitherto had been seen as one of the incentives for people to increase their demand for housing. In a series of steps, and in line with neo liberal views of the undesirability of state intervention, the value of MIRAS has been reduced.

Current issues in housing

One observer has described the current housing policy system as having a major fault line dividing it into two separate parts (Kleinman, 1998). On the one hand, for the majority of the population who are relatively contented with their housing circumstances, policy is based on the home ownership solution. In some ways – as we will examine later – the driving force here is to be found in imperatives associated with the maintenance of economic growth. On the other hand, there is a minority, many of which live in social housing, whose housing and other circumstances may be far from satisfactory. For these groups, much of the policy responses might be said to be less to do with housing per se and more with social security and other considerations. In fact, it could be argued that the current housing system is problematic in a number of ways for those on both sides of the fault line.

The Sustainability of Home Ownership

From the perspective of neo liberal ideology the desirability of the increasing attachment to home ownership is clear. The state-directed decline of the size of the local authority sector and the growth of home ownership have ensured the increasing dominance of markets and consumer choice in housing production and allocation. Moreover as MIRAS has been withdrawn so home ownership itself has experienced less state intervention, while the withdrawal has also lead to a downward pressure on taxation. Much the same point could be made about the reductions in welfare safety nets for home owners: the reduction of social security payments for those with mortgages who become unemployed and the encouragement of private insurance (Burchardt and Hills, 1997; Ford et al, 1997). On this view, then, the housing market is being restructured in ways consistent both with people's preferences and with the sort of low taxation, low public expenditure economy deemed necessary in order to compete in the global market place.

Yet, in other respects, the congruence between what are seen to be economic imperatives and consumer satisfaction is not so clear. The market itself, despite expanding in numbers, has been characterised by volatility in the 1980s and low demand in the 1990s. The period of volatility took its most extreme from during the boom and bust between 1986 and 1989, with the bust being precipitated by a rapid hike in interest rates (Maclennan, 1997). Because most mortgages in Britain were variable rate the increase was immediately passed on to the house buyer. Together with increased unemployment this had the consequence that repayment difficulties expressed in terms of arrears and repossessions escalated rapidly to levels never previously experienced in Britain. (Doling, 1994a). The overall reduction in demand also resulted in a decrease, in both nominal and real terms, of house prices. The significance of this was tied to the post war history of house prices, which had never, at least on any great scale, decreased to the extent that home ownership had been looked upon as an absolutely safe form of investment. But at the end of the 1980s, not only did most home owners perceive that the value of what for many was their principal asset decline, but for those who had only recently purchased, taking a loan of a high percentage of the price, they entered a new situation of owing more than they owned. By 1993, it was estimated that more than two million households were experiencing 'negative equity' (Doling, 1994a) and the market remained depressed throughout most of the 1990s.

High levels of mortgage arrears and possessions and prices, that are as often falling or static as they are increasing, could be taken as evidence that the sort of buoyancy formerly associated with the market - indeed its very essence as a safe, high-return investment offering ideal housing solutions - is no longer apparent. Significantly, this lack of buoyancy is not confined to Britain. Information recently published by the Council of Mortgage Lenders (1997) gives indications of national price trajectories, suggesting that, throughout the 1990s, in most western European countries real prices were broadly static if not actually falling. In other European countries there appears to be no equivalent to the data produced by the Building Societies Association in Britain on mortgage arrears and possessions, but there have been some ad hoc surveys - for example,

Kosonen (1995) presents evidence of high levels of both arrears and negative equity in the Scandinavian countries in the 1990s - and/or anecdotal evidence (Forrest et al, 1999). On these bases, it is possible to conclude that housing markets in many western, European countries have, during the 1990s, been depressed in terms of price trajectories with new production being at a reduced level and with evidence of repayment difficulties.

A paper published in 1995 (Doling and Ford, 1995) posed three alternative models for understanding these developments in home ownership in Britain. These have relevance also for understanding the European wide nature of the phenomena. The first model interprets them as merely being the consequence of a temporary downturn in a market that has previously been characterised by cyclical behaviour. On this model there is nothing unusual about the last decade, except perhaps the duration of the downturn, and eventually the market will return to 'normal'. The second model similarly argues that market actors and institutions have now realised that they made many poor decisions in the past but as they learn from those mistakes and put other policies and practices into place, the market will eventually recover. The third model posited that there have been structural changes affecting demand, consequent upon developments in labour markets. The processes of global capitalism have been creating new labour markets characterised by high levels of unemployment, job insecurity and widening income differentials. The negative impact of these processes on many actual, and potential, home owners have been exacerbated, in some countries, by government policies that, as well as reducing housing subsidies, have liberalised financial and labour markets and reduced the insurance afforded by welfare arrangements. Overall, taking out a loan to buy a house has often become riskier because continuity of income is less certain and because welfare safety nets are less effective, which, in turn, has reduced the previous certainty about the investment potential of home ownership.

Actually in a context of the present high levels of job insecurity it might be argued that renting is a more appropriate form of housing provision (Doling and Ford, 1995). This has the advantage for the household that there is no necessity to be committed to a long term loan, against the promise of uncertain income, and any investment risk is borne by a landlord. Sluggish home ownership markets in Britain have been characterised by low levels of mobility (Maclennan, 1997) so that, insofar as renting is characterised by easy, that is quick and low cost, access and egress, it may more enable households to adjust housing consumption to their incomes and to be sufficiently geographically mobile to enable relocation in pursuit of new employment. In other words, if flexible labour markets are a necessary response to globalisation, home ownership, as presently experienced in Britain, may be a force for inflexibility.

Residualisation of Social Housing

While the situation faced by many home owners is problematic, the continued diminution of the social sectors has created other sets of problems. Increasingly, those left in the sector receive an income from the state, many because they are retired and many because they are unemployed. In addition, the homes that have been sold to private individuals and organisations have been mainly drawn from the better parts of the stock: suburban houses have been transferred, less desirable high rise dwellings, located in inner city areas remain. Many are in a poor state of repair. Large parts of the social sector, therefore, now consist of physically run-down estates, characterised by numerous social and economic problems such as high levels of crime, vandalism, drug taking, ill health and poor educational attainment. In these senses, public housing has become a welfare sector, often geographically segregated and providing accommodation for those who are unable to pay for private housing of a reasonable standard (Forrest and Murie, 1988). Far from being a prize to be aspired to, for most people in most parts of the country, social housing may be considered, at worst, an undesirable option, and, at best, a short-term solution, little more than a stepping stone. Insofar as public intervention is concerned it is directed not so much at housing per se but at re-engaging people with mainstream society - the so-called fight against social exclusion - by tackling crime, raising educational attainment levels including job training, improving health standards and employment creation.

Housing Shortages

Numerically, Britain has a surplus of housing over households. But, regionally and sometimes locally this is not everywhere the case. The problem has arisen because of the changing geography of employment. Over the last two decades, many of the manufacturing plants as well as primary industries such as iron and steel and coal mining located in the northern parts of the country have closed down. During the same period there has been an increase in service jobs particularly in London and other parts of the south. The resulting migration of labour in search of employment has had important consequences. On the one hand, in those regions exporting labour there is frequently a surplus of housing with some local authorities having little alternative but to demolish unlet apartment blocks. On the other hand, in London in particular, the shortages of housing are resulting in rapidly rising prices, overcrowding, squatting, and homelessness (Balchin, 1995). Even by 1990, there were estimated to be 30,000 squatters in London (Burrows and Walentowicz, 1992). In short, there is a changing or re-urbanisation of Britain that has many of the characteristics of earlier urbanisation phases and there is a case for re-orienting policy to address the problem of housing lower income groups, often newcomers to the city.

Again, this is not confined to Britain. There is considerable evidence that the phenomenon of homelessness is growing in most European countries (see Friedrichs, 1988) leading to the conclusion that 'all experts are agreed that homelessness has become an increasing problem during the 1980s' (Hedman, 1994:43). This view has become clear also to the tourist in major European cities for whom there is continued reminder of the problem in the numbers of people living on the streets. The western city, as one observer, has commented 'engender[s] widening gaps between haves and have-nots, an increasing likelihood of social conflicts, displacement, poverty for those left behind by labor market changes, and, for some, homelessness' (Daly, 1996. p.6).

Concluding remarks

Housing policy in Britain in the post war period has taken different forms, with the emphasis at the beginning of the period being on state involvement, particularly through local authority housing, and more recently on market processes. Over the half century, with increases in both the size and the quality of the stock, there have been considerable improvements in people's housing experiences. Whereas the improvements in the average have always disguised variations, the housing system manifests a number of limitations. On the one hand there are increasing numbers of people who are being excluded from housing all together and, on the other, home ownership is no longer ensuring high quality experiences for many. The limits of the home ownership solution are also apparent in the context of the development of a competitive national economy since buying a house may be inconsistent with the development of a flexible labour market and it may also act as a source of inflexibility. From a policy perspective the dilemmas are stark: reducing the size of the local authority sector and increasing home ownership fit well with the development of a low taxation, low spending economy, but the outcomes are both increasing personal risk and rigidities in labour supply. The problems faced by those at the lower end of the income distribution are also severe. The changing geography of employment and the regional shortages of housing are exacerbating problems of homelessness and squatting. In this respect there is some measure of similarity in the challenges facing housing policy makers in both Malaysia and Britain

References

Balchin, P. (1995), *Housing Policy: An Introduction*, Routledge, London.
Berry, F. (1974), Housing: *The Great British Failure*, Charles Knight, London.
Burchardt, T. and Hills, J. (1997), *Pushing at the Boundaries*, Joseph Rowntree Foundation, York.
Burrows, L. and Walentowicz, P. (1992), *Homes Cost Less than Homelessness*, Shelter, London.
Coleman, D. (1989), 'The New Housing Policy: A Critique', *Housing Studies*, vol. 4, pp.44-57.
Council for Mortgage Lenders (1997), *European Mortgage Review No 11*, CML, London.
Daly, G. (1996), *Homeless Policies: Strategies and Lives on the Streets*, Routledge, London.
Doling, J. (1983), 'British Housing Policy 1974-1983: A Review', *Regional Studies*, vol. 17, pp.475-478.
Doling, J. (1994a), 'British Housing Policy 1984-1993: A Review', *Regional Studies*, vol. 27, pp.583-588.
Doling, J. (1994b), 'The Privatisation of Social Housing in European Welfare States', *Environment and Planning C*, vol. 12, pp.243-55.
Doling, J. (1997), *Comparative Housing Policy: Government and Housing in Advanced Industrialized Countries*, Macmillan, London
Doling, J. and Ford, J. (1991), 'The Changing Face of Home Ownership: Building Societies and Household Investment Strategies', *Policy and Politics*, vol. 19, pp. 109-118.
Doling, J. and Ford, J. (1995), 'The New Homeownership: The Impact of Labour Market Developments on Attitudes Toward Owning Your Own Home', *Environment and Planning A*, 28, pp.157-172.
Donnison, D. and Ungerson, C. (1982), *Housing Policy*, Penguin, London.
Ford, J., Kempson, E. and Wilson, M. (1997), *Bridging the Gap? Safety-Nets for Mortgage Holders*, Centre for Housing Policy, York.

Forrest, R. and Murie, A. (1988), *Selling the Welfare State: The Privatisation of Public Housing,* Routledge and Kegan Paul, London.

Forrest, R., Kennett, P. and Leather, P. (1999), *Home Ownership in Crisis: The British Experience of Negative Equity*, Ashgate, Aldershot.

Friedrichs, J. (1988), *Affordable Housing and the Homeless*, Walter de Gruyter, Berlin.

Harloe, M. (1996), *The People's Home: Social Rented Housing in Europe and America,* Blackwell, Oxford.

Hedman (1994), *Housing in Sweden in an International Perspective*, Boverket, Karlskrona.

Heidenheimer, A., Heclo, H. and Adams, C. (1990), *Comparative Public Policy*, St Martin's Press, New York.

Holmans, A. (1987), *Housing Policy in Britain: A History*, Croom Helm, London

Kleinman, M. (1998), 'Western European Housing Policies: Convergence or Collapse', in M. Kleinman, W. Matznetter and M. Stephens (eds), *European Integration and Housing Policies*, Routledge, London.

Kosonen, K. (1995), *Pohjoismaiden Asuntomarkkinat Vuosina 1980-1993: Vertaileva* (Nordic Housing Markets in 1980-1993: A Comparative Analysis) Palkansaajien Tutkinuslaito, Helsinki.

Maclennan, D. (1997), 'The UK Housing Market: Up, Down and Where Next?' in P. Williams (ed), *Directions in Housing Policy: Towards Sustainable Housing Policies for the UK*, Chapman, London.

Malpass, P. and Murie, A. (1994), *Housing Policy and Practice,* Macmillan, London.

Saunders, P. (1990), *A Nation of Home Owners*, Unwin Hyman, London

Tosics, I. (1987), 'Privatization in Housing Policy: The Case of Western Countries and Hungary', *International Journal for Urban and Regional Research*, vol. 11, pp.61-77.

11 Public housing policy in Malaysia
MOHD. RAZALI AGUS

Introduction

In Malaysia, as elsewhere, the rapid industrialisation and economic growth - a feature of the post Independence period, and particularly the last quarter of a century - has been accompanied by rapid urbanisation. In part this has been the result of migrants from other countries in the region (especially Bangladesh, Indonesia and Thailand) coming to take up the numerous job opportunities. Migration from elsewhere in Malaysia has also been significant partly due to the implementation of the urban strategy under the New Economic Policy (NEP), the Malaysian government's development policy for the period of 1971-1990 (Malaysia, 1971; Malaysia, 1976; Malaysia, 1981). The NEP, introduced in 1971, sought to solve the problems of economic, ethnic and regional imbalances in the country. It envisaged the restructuring of Malaysian society in housing, commerce and industry. Urbanisation, industrialisation, and Bumiputra participation form a central strategy of the NEP, with the non-Bumiputras being encouraged to be partners in the economic activities (Agus, 1989c; Agus, 1989d; Salih, 1979).

The role of urbanisation in the NEP was first stated in terms of the development of housing estates and industrial centres in new areas and the migration of rural Bumiputras to urban areas (Malaysia, 1971; Agus, 1989d). This was deemed to be essential to achieve economic balance between urban and rural areas. In the Third Malaysia Plan (1976-1980), Fourth Malaysia Plan (1981-1985) and Fifth Malaysia Plan (1986-1990), the strategy was further elaborated to include a number of elements (Malaysia, 1976; Malaysia, 1981; Malaysia, 1986). First, the spreading of urban development rather than perpetuating its concentration in particular regions. The development of new housing estates and industrial centres in the less developed rural areas was to help to achieve a more balanced distribution of economic activities, particularly, in underdeveloped rural areas. Second, the integration of the development of these centres and their hinterlands in order to bring greater urbanisation and industrialisation to the rural areas. Third the strengthening of linkages among the various new housing estates, industrial centres and new townships through the development of a denser system of urban centres and specialisation. This was to ensure the spread of industries, housing estates and more importantly, urban employment opportunities and services to a wider range of the urban and rural communities (Salih, 1979).

These policy objectives were pursued in a context where in the main urban centres - particularly Kuala Lumpur and other centres in the Klang valley - the increased numbers of people and the increased general wealth brought about by economic growth, resulted in tremendous pressure on the housing stock. Thus, even at the end of the 1970s it was apparent that the supply of housing was failing to meet the needs not only of the poor but also many of the middle income groups (Tan, 1983). Housing policy then and subsequently has responded in a number of ways. For middle and higher income groups, the government has, inter alia, facilitated, directly or indirectly, the establishment of budget allocations and financial institutions that have, in turn, facilitated the growth of good quality, home ownership (Thillainathan, 1989). It is the aim of the present chapter, however, to concentrate exclusively on policy relating to the housing needs of low income groups. These include some who have migrated to the cities from rural areas or from countries elsewhere in the region or are longstanding, but poor, city dwellers, as well as poor groups remaining in rural areas - but all characterised by their low incomes and limited capital. As a consequence, many live in low quality housing, with some in squatter settlements.

In addition to examining general housing policy developments directed at these groups, the chapter also examines the particular case of the upgrading of squatter settlements in Kuala Lumpur. It does so against the need, recognised by government, to improve physical structures whilst not destroying social ones, that is of maintaining and supporting socio-cultural values and networks.

Low-income housing policy

One of the major social objectives in the Malaysian development plan is the provision of cheap housing as a basic social need based on the concept of a home-owning democracy. Under this concept, the public low-income housing programme was implemented and targeted specifically towards rural poor communities whose incomes were below RM300 a month (Agus, 1989b). This was the first time that the local population, particularly the Bumiputras, was included in a major social programme in a national development plan. Prior to Independence in 1957, the concept of public housing was known as 'the institutional quarters'. Under this concept, the British administration provided housing facilities for the upper-class British employees who worked in public institutions such as schools, police stations, hospitals, and district offices (Sendut and Tan, 1979; Agus, 1987). The only programme aimed at providing housing for the Malaysian people was concentrated on the resettlement of Chinese residents in the New Villages all over the country during the Emergency (1948-1960) (Agus, 1986; Agus, 1992). This programme was part of the strategy of the British administration to weaken the support for communist insurgents.

Public low-income housing has been given a high priority in Malaysian development plans since 1971 (Malaysia, 1971; Lim, 1982), with a major portion of the public housing budget being allocated for low-income housing projects. There was an increase of low-income housing expenditure from 43 per cent in the 1971 period to 68 per cent in the Sixth Malaysia Plan (1991-1995) (see Table 11.1). In terms of absolute costs, the increases have been even greater.

In the Sixth and Seventh Malaysia Plans, housing policy has been directed at attaining the objectives of the New Development Policy (NDP) and the Second Outline Perspective Plan (OPP2) (1991-2000) (Agus, 1995a; Agus, 1995b). Under the NDP and OPP2, housing policy is a continuation of the NEP programmes but a new element of privatisation of public low-cost housing was introduced to solve the housing problem for the poor and lower income communities (Mokhtar, 1993; Othman et al, 1982). Under the privatisation programme, the federal government envisaged the housing sector playing the leading role in providing stimulus to economic growth and in spearheading further industrialisation and urban development (Drakakis-Smith, 1977; Agus, 1986a; Agus, 1989a).

Table 11.1 Public low-income housing expenditure, 1971-2000

Development Programme	Allocation (RM Million)	Percentage
Second Malaysia Plan, 1971-1975	102	42.5
Third Malaysia Plan, 1976-1980	633	32.2
Fourth Malaysia Plan, 1981-1985	1,700	41.8
Fifth Malaysia Plan, 1986-1990	2,000	50.0
Sixth Malaysia Plan, 1991-1995	2,013	52.3
Seventh Malaysia Plan, 1996-2000	3,340	54.5

Source: Malaysia Plans (various years)

The emphasis of housing policy under the NDP and OPP2 is still on facilitating the development of low-cost houses for low-income communities based on the human settlement concept. Under this concept, first introduced in the Fifth Malaysia Plan (1986-1990), the provision of social facilities, such as schools, clinics, and community halls, was to be emphasised, in addition to the provision of basic infrastructure facilities and the promotion of economic opportunities (Malaysia, 1991). This is a continuation of the national development strategy to upgrade the quality of life of the rural and urban communities and to promote national unity. Thus, the low-income housing policy under the NDP and OPP2 emphasised the enhanced role of the private housing developers in the national economy and the greater support to be provided by the government agencies.

In 1996, the Deputy Prime Minister announced a new strategy to resolve low-cost housing needs of the country. The announcement emphasised the role of the Employees Provident Fund (EPF) in low and medium-cost housing projects throughout the country. According to the EPF authorities, 60 per cent of the new housing units will be low-income to be sold at RM25,000, 20 per cent will be in the medium-low range to be sold at not more than RM60,000 and the remaining 20 per cent will be medium-cost to be sold at not more than RM80,000 (Malaysia, 1996). This is in line with the Ministry of Housing and Local Government's plan to build 800,000 houses under the Seventh Malaysia Plan (1996-2000). The federal government had proposed to build 68 per cent low and low-medium cost units, 22 per cent medium-cost housing and 10 per cent high-cost housing (Malaysia, 1991; Malaysia, 1996).

Incorporating squatter communities in housing development

Although there appears to be adequate housing for all the people within the country, there is considerable disparity in the quality of housing. The largest areas of concern are among the lower income groups, especially the communities that occupy squatter settlements. Formally, the status of the settlements is illegal but the Kuala Lumpur City Hall, at least, has taken a more tolerant position. Nevertheless, it is accepted both centrally and locally that as a matter of priority squatter settlements must be upgraded.

The Malaysian government, however, early realised the limits of the public sector's production of low-income housing projects (Lim, 1982; Sen, 1986). There was also a growing body of sentiment among housing developers and professional bodies that the public sector is choked with too many responsibilities. Hence, it cannot be expected to change itself rapidly to meet new targets of constructing units of low-income houses, especially in redeveloping the squatter settlements in major urban areas. Since the public sector could not do the job alone, a new policy was formulated to incorporate new sectors such as private developers and squatter communities in the housing development programmes. In fact, the private sector has been called upon to provide the leading role and dynamism in the Malaysian economy. As early as 1969, the Malaysian government proposed that the public sector facilitates the private sector investment in large-scale development (Malaysia, 1971). However, this participation was limited to public works and agricultural development.

In 1981, the federal government provided further encouragement to the private sector, to play the leading role in providing stimulus to economic growth to spearhead further development in public housing programmes. Both the public and private sectors co-operated and participated actively in the construction of houses for the lower income groups. This strategy was aimed at reactivating and stimulating the construction sector as well as creating and providing more employment activities. The private sector's role in the partnership is now seen as one of the ways to improve its public image. The private sector is often stigmatised for perpetuating the interests of the middle and upper classes as well as its own profit maximisation motives (Johnstone, 1982; Drakakis-Smith, 1977; Agus, 1995a). The private sector is willing to invest in the low-cost housing projects because government land is used for housing. They have to pay a very low premium on land identified for low-income housing projects. Also, the public sector reduces the administrative delays in converting land for housing (Lim, 1982; Tan, 1983).

Another aspect of the public-private co-operation is the incorporation of the squatter community by policy makers in the low-income housing policy (Mokhtar, 1993; Agus, 1993b). In this policy, squatter settlements are identified, planned and redeveloped by the private housing developers. Both the commercial and residential units are constructed by the private housing developers and the relocated squatters are guaranteed low-income housing units sold at RM25,000 or less. In implementing this policy, the Malaysian government has provided general guidelines on the concept of partnership between the private and public sectors and the participation of the lower income communities in public housing programmes (Malaysia, 1991; Malaysia, 1996).

Squatter settlement in Kuala Lumpur

As a result of rapid urbanisation and industrialisation in Malaysia in the last two decades, there is a greater increase in urban population density, with the attendant problems. Increased density means greater demands on the existing land for housing, employment opportunities and services. The continuing migration of the rural poor has literally transformed rural poverty into urban poverty (Drakakis-Smith, 1977; Othman et al, 1982).

Squatter problems are more acute in Kuala Lumpur than other cities in Malaysia. There are several reasons that have contributed to these problems. First, Kuala Lumpur, as the centre of administrative and commercial activities in Malaysia, has attracted a large number of rural-urban migrants. Second, the government wanted Kuala Lumpur to have a balanced ethnic composition of the population. Third, this is also part of the government's strategy to create a new Bumiputra community that actively participates in commerce and industry.

According to statistics from the Kuala Lumpur City Hall in 1984 there were 4.9 per cent or 11,800 households living below the poverty level that is with a monthly income less than RM350. In 1987, the figure had increased to 5.2 per cent or 12,200 households. According to the recent Kuala Lumpur City Hall data for 1992, out of the total 190,899 squatters, 12.1 per cent had household monthly income less than RM300 (City Hall, 1992). The Co-ordination and Implementation Unit (ICU) of the Prime Minister's Department estimated that there were about 13,100 hardcore poor households whose income was less than RM202 a month in urban areas in Peninsular Malaysia (Malaysia, 1986; Malaysia, 1991). The surveys on household incomes carried out amongst the squatters in Kuala Lumpur between 1983 and 1992 provide some indication of their standard of living. More than two-thirds earned less than RM500 a month (Agus, 1994; Agus, 1992d). However, some of these squatter settlements are not too badly off in terms of access to social and health amenities.

Although the status of settlements is illegal, the government has since the mid-1980s, taken a more tolerant attitude towards squatters and squatter settlements. The accommodative gesture by the government is a pragmatic approach in dealing with the problem and with long term political strategies (Agus, 1995a). The government wanted a balanced population distribution ethnically and encouraged the Malays to migrate to urban areas. This is part of the government strategy to change the character of the urban population which was dominated by the Chinese before 1971.

According to Kuala Lumpur City Hall data there were about 25,000 squatter families and a total squatter population of 103,370 living in the city in 1970 (see Table 11.2). Malays comprised about 20 per cent of this figure, Chinese, 67 per cent, and Indians 13 per cent. The following decade saw a rapid increase in the squatter population, to 46,000 squatter families and a total population of 236,101 by 1980. It was the Malay squatter population that grew most rapidly in the seventies, followed by the Indians and the Chinese. It will be noted, however, that the Chinese squatters declined over the period as a percentage of the total number, from 67 per cent in 1970 to 53.6 per cent in 1980.

Table 11.2 Squatters by major ethnic groups in Kuala Lumpur, 1970-1992

Ethnic Group	1970	%	1980	%	1992	%
Malay	20,674	20.0	70,830	30.0	65,364	34.2
Chinese	69,258	67.0	126,464	53.6	85,023	44.5
Indians	13,438	13.0	38,807	16.4	40,512	21.1
TOTAL	103,370	100.0	236,101	100.0	190,899	100.0

Source: City Hall (1993); Agus (1995)

During the period of 1980-1992, the Malay and Indian squatter population comprised slightly higher proportions of the total, while the Chinese squatters declined from 53.5 per cent in 1980 to 44.5 per cent in 1992 (City Hall, 1992). The slight decline in total population in squatter settlements and the redevelopment of selected squatter settlements between 1980 and 1992 reflect the direct policies of City Hall. The movements of squatters were monitored regularly, and controls were imposed both on the expansion of existing squatter settlements and on the formation of new ones. About 200 squatter settlements still remain in Kuala Lumpur, located in various areas between the central business district and the periphery of the city (Agus, 1994).

Migrants however continue to replace the relocated squatters. Overall the number of squatters has decreased from 45,048 squatter households, for a total squatter population of 234,693 living in 32,066 dwellings in 1990 to 36,168 squatter households with a total population of 190,899 squatters living in 34,353 dwellings in 1992. According to data from Kuala Lumpur City Hall, the financial allocation for public low-cost housing is inadequate (Mokhtar, 1993; Abdullah, 1982). In the Sixth Malaysia Plan (1991-1995), City Hall planned to build 30,396 units of low-cost housing costing approximately RM703 million, however, only RM79.35 million was approved by the federal government. Thus, only 4,424 units were built by Kuala Lumpur City Hall in the 1991-1995 period.

Upgrading squatter settlements

The process of squatter redevelopment is difficult due to the lack of available and suitable land in urban areas. Nevertheless such an exercise does take place wherever possible. A redevelopment programme was set up by Kuala Lumpur City Hall to ease the overcrowding of the squatter settlements. Under the public and private partnership this has been implemented by Kuala Lumpur City Hall since the second-half of the Fourth Malaysia Plan (1981-1985). According to City Hall, 11 out of 13 squatter settlements have been redeveloped by private housing developers (see Table 11.3). The number of projects is expected to increase to 21 involving a total area of about 1,500 hectares. The number of squatter dwellings affected in this programme is about 10,000 units, with the entire programme expected to accommodate 35,000 low-income households (Mokhtar, 1993; Agus, 1993b; Agus, 1994).

Between 1978 and 1988, the city relocated about 45,606 squatters first to transit areas and later to public low-income housing schemes (City

Hall, 1992). Squatters were thus moved about from single-unit dwellings with few, if any, of the basic amenities, to temporary wooden row houses with about ten dwellings in each unit. From there, they were eventually transferred to five story 'walk-ups' or, commonly, to high rise units. A large number of squatter families thus had to undergo a period of rapid adaptation, beset with discontinuities, to live in more settled conditions with the advantage of all the basic amenities. Wegelin's detailed study of three federal government low-income housing projects in Kuala Lumpur city revealed that re-housing of squatter communities in low-income housing brings substantial improvements to the housing environment or the rehoused households in physical terms. The improvements include sanitation, piped water, electricity, security and privacy in their own houses (Wegelin 1978).

Table 11.3 Sustainable low-income housing in Kuala Lumpur, 1996

Location	Developer	Units Planned	Year Completed
Desa Pandan	Pandan Maju	1672	1990
Kg. Pasir Wdb	Danau Kota	1900	1996
Sri Sentosa	Bedford	1846	1989
Kg Puah/Chubadak	Sentul Murni	1260	1996
Kg Bakti selayang	Pandan maju	142	1992
Tmn Intan Baiduri	McKen	720	1991
Bukit Kepong	Titikaya	620	1993
Taman Kuchai	Farizar Devt	500	1991
Taman Miharja	Miharja Devt	700	1992
Sg Besi	Sobena Maju	1020	1996
Desa Pantai	Perumahan Negara	1140	1996

Source: City Hall (1999)

Urban sub-cultures and community development

A community may be defined as the smallest territorial unit in which individuals and families can carry out most of the activities thought important and necessary for daily life. This means that the community is the basic unit with a relatively complete culture. It incorporates social, economic, technological, political, religious and aesthetic customs in sufficient balance to enable members of each community to live well-rounded lives within its scope. Examples are a city, a town, a settlement or a village. But the idea of community as a goal which people may achieve has become prominent. In the west, the growth of towns and cities and their redevelopment to provide public housing has led to an awareness of the lack of cohesion and identity of large sections of the population. In answer to this need community centres have sometimes been established to provide recreational and cultural activities for the people, and to give an opportunity for democratic organisation of the residents of a new area. In fact, a community centre is an association, and only in so far as it is deliberately an association with limited and specified ends can it serve the specific needs of a differentiated urban population.

The concept of urban life in Western society has been suggested by Louis Wirth's essay, 'Urbanism as a Way of Life' (Wirth, 1938). In it, Wirth developed a 'minimum sociological definition of the city' as 'a relatively large, dense and permanent settlement of socially heterogeneous individuals' (Wirth, 1939, p.50). From these prerequisites, he stressed the major outlines of the urban way of life. He highlighted that number, density and heterogeneity created a social structure in which primary group relationships were inevitably replaced by secondary interactions that were impersonal, segmental, superficial, transitory, and often predatory in nature. As a result, city residents became anonymous, isolated, secular, relativistic, rational and sophisticated. In the Malaysian context, the evidence from sociological and anthropological studies suggests that Wirth's statement must be revised. Multi ethnic groups maintain and promote their cultural identities through various religious activities and institutions in squatter settlements and new housing schemes.

This discussion aids an understanding of the development of Malaysian policy and practice with respect to the upgrading of squatter settlements. The implementation of the concept of human settlement in lower income communities was further improved by focusing on the participation of the target groups in the planning process. The new element in the community development among these communities is also in line with the Malaysian government's Vision 2020 programme to create social justice, economic development and quality of life in the housing sector. The planning of sustainable low-income housing is not merely confined to the housing needs of the urban poor but also to the improvement of job opportunities, socio-cultural facilities and physical infrastructure in order to enable the targeted communities to maintain their respective cultural institutions and values. At the same time, they also promote community development by participating in their socio-cultural, religious and economic activities.

This development will set the pace to enable Malaysia to become a fully developed nation by the year 2020 not only economically, but also in terms of quality of life, ecological considerations, and continuation of socio-cultural values in urban areas. More importantly, greater public participation in socio-cultural activities provides opportunities for the residents to be involved in community development programmes such as *rukuntetangga* or *hari keluarga*. Low-cost sustainable housing will ensure other aspects of community development and socio-economic considerations will be given better attention in the future.

Against this background, and with a new emphasis on the low and medium-income housing, private housing developers were given a greater role in constructing low-income housing in the country, including Kuala Lumpur. It is the policy of Kuala Lumpur City Hall to resettle the squatters into planned housing estates with adequate infrastructure facilities and socio-cultural amenities (Wegelin, 1978; Johnstone, 1981; City Hall, 1992). Under the sustainable low-cost housing programme, the provision of socio-cultural facilities such as schools, clinics, religious facilities and community halls is emphasized. In addition to the provision of basic infrastructure facilities, the promotion of *rukun tetangga, hari keluarga, harikebangsaan*, and *rakan jiran* programmes are encouraged. Inter-ethnic relations usually occur on a formal or informal level, either within or outside the framework of organisational structures. Even the bare minimum of participation in the community involves accommodative and co-operative action, either in the market place, the work situation, the religious centre, the school, or the community hall. Often individuals representing different ethnic and cultural groups co-operate in the main concerns of life without ever becoming intimate in their personal contacts, and without entering each other's personal lives.

The psychological, cultural, and ecological barriers separating them may be high, but co-operate they do, nevertheless. In countless instances, the city is the scene of interpersonal contacts which cut across ethnic and cultural boundaries but which are warm, intimate, and informal. In the course of time, whether the inter-group relationships are formal or informal, there are reciprocal influences, sometimes manifested in the transmission, through borrowing or imitation, of cultural forms of objects that have some symbolic or utilitarian value. But if the inter-ethnic contacts are both intimate and prolonged, if individuals representing different cultural backgrounds enter intimately into each other's lives and experiences, this assimilative process results in a fusion of cultures and sub-cultures and a blending of the heritages of the people involved.

For the Malay squatters, the practice of *rumah terbuka* during religious celebrations such as *Hari Raya Puasa* is not only confined to fellow muslims. Other ethnic groups such as Indian and Chinese squatters continue to enjoy the hospitalities of their muslim hosts. In the Melaka study (Agus, 1985), it was found that a very high percentage of respondents (95 per cent) visit their Malay neighbours. In a recent study (Agus et al, 1993) in Kuala Lumpur and Subang Jaya of low-cost housing, a large percentage of respondents visit their neighbours and this is a positive social environment. Festive seasons of the three major ethnic groups in Malaysia give a good reason for establishing contacts with neighbours and for developing neighbourly relations. *Hari Raya Puasa*, Chinese New Year and *Deepavali* constitute good occasions for visiting in the low-cost settlements. This phenomena is probably relevant to Malaysia mainly due to her unique multi-ethnic society and social-cultural history.

Conclusions

While the importance of the redevelopment of squatter settlements has been largely ignored in planning and urban development in developing countries, Malaysia has recently given new emphasis to the provision of sustainable low-cost housing in major urban areas. More importantly, the concept of human settlements maintains family and community developments which promote urban neighbourliness and social integration among various ethnic groups. The recent development of the private sector's role in the partnership with the local authorities should be able to balance the need for profits with a positive response to the socio-economic needs of the lower income groups. Sustainable low-income housing increases the possibilities of the environmental improvement as well as for the socio-cultural development of the squatters and other lower income groups. This could be one of the major challenges of planning housing development and cultural integration for the twenty-first century in Malaysia.

References

Abdullah, T. (1982), 'Housing Finance-Policies and Objectives', *Development Forum*, vol. XIII, pp. 53-61.

Agus, M.R. (1983), 'Politik Perumahan Awam Kos Rendah di Malaysia: Satu Nota,Manusia dan Masyarakat (Jurnal Jabatan Antropologi dan Sosiologi UniversitiMalaya)', *Siri Baru*, vol. 4, pp. 57-70.

Agus, M.R. (1985), 'Hubungan Kejiranan di Rancangan Perunahan kos Rendahdi Melaka' (Neghbourhood Relations in a Low Cost Housing Programme), *Jurnal Persatnan Sejarah Melaka*, no. 9, pp. 84-92.

Agus, M.R. (1986a), *The New Role of the Public and Private Sectors in Implementing the Special Low-Cost Housing Program: The Malaysian Experience*. Paper presented at the International Symposium on Housing, Ministry of Construction, Japan and City of Yokohama.

Agus, M.R. (1986b), *Politik Dalam Perumahan (Politics of Housing)*, Gateway Publishing House, Kuala Lumpur.

Agus, M.R. (1987), 'Peranan Kerajaan Dalam Pengagihan perumahan Awam Kos Rendah di Malaysia: Satu Kajian Perbandingan' (The Role of the State in Distributing Low-Cost Housing in Malaysia: A Comparative Study), in K.S. Jomo, H.M. Khalid and S.H. Ali (eds), *Pembangunan di Malaysia: Perencanaan, Pelaksanaan dan Prestasi*, Persatuan Sains Sosial Malaysia, Kuala Lumpur.

Agus, M.R. (1989a), *New Housing Policy in Malaysia: Public and Private Cooperation for the Development of Low-Cost Housing*, Paper presented at the Sixth Inter-schools Conference on Development: Emerging Issues in the Third World Housing Policies, 1990's and Beyond, Centre of Development Planning Studies, University of Sheffield, U.K.

Agus, M.R. (1989b), 'Public Sector Low Cost Housing in Malaysia', *Habitat International*, vol. 13, pp. 105-115.

Agus, M.R. (1989c), 'Urbanization and Low-Income Housing in Malaysia', *Journal of Population and Social Studies*, vol. 2, pp. 205-221.

Agus, M. R. (1989d), 'Impact of Urbanization on the Urban Malays of Malaysia: Problems of Homeownership of the Lower Income Groups', Sarjana: *Jurnal Fakulti Sastera dan Sains Sosial*, Universiti Malaya, vol. 5, pp.113-132.

Agus, M.R. (1992a), *Pembangunan Perumahan: Isu dan Prospek (HousingDevelopment: Issues and Prospects)*, Dewan Bahasa dan Pustaka, Kuala Lumpur.

Agus, M.R. (1992b), 'Housing Development and the Urban Kampungs', Manusiadan *Masyarakat, Siri Baru*, vol. 7, pp. 30-44.

Agus, M.R. (1992c), 'Spatial Patterns in a Growing Metropolitan Area -Kuala Lumpur', *Malaysian Journal of Social Research*, vol. 1, pp. 33-48.

Agus, M.R. (1993a), *Keselesaan Penghuni dan Pilihan Bakal Pembeli Perumahan Kos Rendah di Terengganu Darul Iman (Dwellers' Satisfaction and Choices of Low-Cost House Buyers in Terengganu Darul Iman)*. InstitutPengajian Tinggi, Universiti Malaya, Kuala Lumpur.

Agus, M.R. (1993b), 'Penempatan Setinggan Perlu Dibangunkan Semula' (Squatter Settlements Should be Redeveloped), *Dewan Masyarakat*, vol. 31, pp.28-30.

Agus, M.R. (1994), 'Urban Growth, Poverty and the Squatter Phenomenon in Kuala Lumpur', in J. Ariffin. (ed), *Poverty Amidst Plenty,* Pelanduk Publications, Petaling Jaya.

Agus, M.R. (1995a), 'The State and Low-Cost Housing in Peninsular Malaysia', in C.B. Tan and R. Talib (eds), *Dimensions of Traditionand Development in Malaysia,* Pelanduk Publications, Petaling Jaya.

Agus, M.R. (1995b), 'Pembangunan Perumahan Wargakota' (Housing Development for City's Residents), in H. Abdullah (ed), *Titian Warna Sejarah Pembangunan dan Perubahan Citra Kuala Lumpur,* Penerbitan Sejarah, Kuala Lumpur.

Agus, M.R. and Rokiah, T. (1992d), 'Social Problems and Health', *Southeast Asian Journal of Tropical Medicine and Public Health*, vol. 181 (Supplement 3), pp. 84-93.

Agus, M.R., Othman, M.N. and Ong, F.S. (1993), *Residential and Commercial Electricity Consumers in Subang Jaya and Bandar Baru Bangi,* Institut Pengajian Tinggi, University of Malaya, Kuala Lumpur.

City Hall (1982a), *Laporan Tahunan 1982,* Dewan Bandaraya Kuala Lumpur.

City Hall (1982b), *Draft Structure Plan. Kuala Lumpur,* Dewan Bandaraya, Kuala Lumpur.

City Hall (1984), *Kuala Lumpur Structure Plan,* Dewan Bandaraya, Kuala Lumpur.

City Hall (1992), *Deraf Laporan Akhir Banci Semula Setinggan WilayahPersekutuan 1992,* Dewan Bandaraya, Kuala Lumpur.

City Hall (1993), *Bancian Semula Setinggan Wilayah Persekutuan Kuala Lumpur 1992,* Dewan Bandaraya, Kuala Lumpur.

Drakakis-Smith, D. (1977), 'Housing the Urban Poor in West Malaysia: The Role of the Private Sector', *Habitat International*, vol. 2, pp. 5-6.

Johnstone, M. (1981), 'The Evaluation of Squatter Settlements in Malaysia', *Journal of Southeast Asian Studies*, vol. 19, p.1.

Johnstone, M. (1982), 'Residential Construction and Financial Institutions in the Periphery: A Case Study from Peninsular Malaysia', in I. Ahmad and M.J. Jamaluddin (eds), *Geography and the Third World,* Penerbit Universiti Kebangsaan Malaysia, Bangi.

Laws of Malaysia (1976), *Town and Country Planning Act, 1976* (Act 172), The Government Printer, Kuala Lumpur.

Lim, C.T. (1982), 'Implementation of Low-Cost Housing Under the Fourth Malaysia Plan', *Development Forum*, vol. XIII, pp. 1-9.

Malaysia (1971), *Second Malaysia Plan, 1971-1975,* Government Printer, Kuala Lumpur.

Malaysia (1976), *Third Malaysia Plan, 1976-1980,* Government Printer, Kuala Lumpur.

Malaysia (1981), *Fourth Malaysia Plan, 1981-1985,* Government Printer, Kuala Lumpur.

Malaysia (1986), *Fifth Malaysia Plan, 1986-1990*, Government Printer, Kuala Lumpur.
Malaysia (1991), *Sixth Malaysia Plan, 1991-1995*, Government Printer, Kuala Lumpur.
Malaysia (1993), *Mid-Term Review of the Sixth Malaysia Plan, 1991-1995*, Government Printer, Kuala Lumpur.
Malaysia (1996), *Seventh Malaysia Plan, 1996-2000*, Government Printer, Kuala Lumpur.
Mokhtar, L.I. (1993), 'Urban Housing With Special Emphasis on the Squatter population of Kuala Lumpur', in K. Othman (ed), *Meeting Housing Needs: Issues and Policy Directions*, ISIS and Friedrich Ebert Stiftung, Kuala Lumpur.
Monershinghe, N. (1985), 'Research Needs and Priorities in Housing and Construction in Malaysia', *Habitat International*, vol. 9, pp. 37-57.
Othman, A.H., Talib, R. and Osman, S (1982), 'Malaysia and the Housing Problems: Searching for Solutions', in I. Ahmad and M.J. Jamaluddin (eds), *Geography and the Third World*, Penerbit Universiti Kebangsaan Malaysia, Bangi.
Salih, K. (1979), *Urban Development in Malaysia*, Working paper No. 74-3, United Nations Centre for Regional Development, Nagoya, Japan:
Sen, M.K. (1986), 'Problems and Obstacles from the View of the Construction Industry', in *Institute of Strategic and International Studies, Target 80,000: Malaysia's Special Low-Cost Housing Scheme*, ISIS, Kuala Lumpur.
Sendut, H. and Tan, S.H. (eds) (1979), *Public and Private Housing in Malaysia*, Heinemann, Kuala Lumpur.
Tan S.H. (1983), 'Low-Cost Housing in Malaysia: a Review of Public Sector Involvement', in Y.M. Yeung (ed), *A Place to Live: A More Effective Low-Cost Housing in Asia*, IDRC Publications, Ottawa.
Thillainathan, R. (1997), Homeownership in Malaysia: An Analysis of Trends and Issues', *Housing Finance International*, vol. 12, pp. 15-23.
Wegelin, E. (1978), *Urban Low-Income Housing and Development*, Martinus Nijhoff, Leiden.
Wirth, L. (1938), 'Urbanism as a Way of Life', *American Journal of Sociology*, vol. XLIV, pp. 3-24.

12 Crime and penal policy in Britain

MIKE NELLIS
DAVID STEPHENSON

Introduction

Rhetorically at least, official policy towards offenders throughout the twentieth century in Britain has been concerned with reformation and rehabilitation, although in practice, in the sentencing philosophies of the courts and the administration of the penal institutions (at least for adults), retribution and deterrence have never been wholly supplanted. The meaning of reformation and rehabilitation has in any case changed over time. They were originally conceived of in moral terms, exhorting offenders to live by the precepts of the Christian faith, and sometimes offering them basic practical assistance to do so. This emphasis began to be supplanted by psychology and sociology in the 1930s, and the period between the 1950s and the 1970s became the high-water mark of official commitment to 'scientific rehabilitation'. During this period criminology expanded as a university subject at postgraduate level, initially taking forward a government-based research agenda into the causes of, and solutions to, crime. Influenced by radical theoretical developments in sociology, however, criminology became an independent academic discipline, prepared to criticise official policy, and has remained so despite the decline of the rehabilitative ideal in the 1980s and 1990s.

The breadth and complexity of the ways in which crime and criminal justice are now studied in Britain, the abundance of data and the diversity of perspectives, is perhaps the first major difference with Malaysia. This imbalance makes the comparative criminological task (Nelken, 1997) unusually difficult, so this chapter is perhaps best seen as a precursor of proper comparative work, rather than an instance of it. It concentrates on key features of criminal justice policy in Britain in the past ten years, but will occasionally refer back beyond this period to illuminate (from the British side) why measures such as corporal and capital punishment which continue to be used in Malaysia were discontinued in Britain. It will seek to acquaint Malaysian readers with some of the issues which preoccupy British criminal justice policy-makers, and professionals, and their critics at the beginning of the 21st century.

In this context 'Britain' encompasses three different criminal jurisdictions (England and Wales, Scotland and Northern Ireland). There are sufficient similarities between them to make it meaningful to speak of 'British criminal justice', but also distinctive legal, administrative and cultural differences. The pace of change has differed in each of the three jurisdictions. Scotland has managed to retain a welfare-orientation in its response to young offenders for much longer than either England and Wales and Northern Ireland. Developments in Northern Ireland have been affected by a history of violent civic strife between the Protestant and Catholic communities, and the terrorist organisations who purport to represent them. The terrorist threat has had significant implications for policing and security in England and Wales, while the miscarriages of justice associated with the sentencing of alleged terrorists was a major cause of the crisis of confidence in British criminal justice in the early 1990s, triggering the creation of a special body, the Criminal Cases Review Commission, to investigate alleged miscarriages (Blom-Cooper, 1997).

Most of this chapter will relate to England and Wales (the largest of the three jurisdictions, the most written about in the criminological literature, and the one with which the authors are most familiar), but occasional reference will be made to the others. Coverage will necessarily be limited, and only the briefest sketch can be given of the administrative structures of criminal justice. Responsibility for crime policy rests largely with two government departments, the Home Office and the Lord Chancellor's Department, although the Department of Health retains some key responsibilities for young offenders, and also for mentally disordered offenders, including three 'special hospitals' where the most serious such offenders are detained. The 'criminal justice *system*' usually refers to five agencies - Police, Crown Prosecution Service, Courts, Probation Service and Prison Service, although the extent to which they act as an integrated system is problematic, and under review at the time of writing. There are 42 police areas in England and Wales, accountable, like Probation Services, in part to local committees, in part to the Home Office. The (lower) magistrates courts are staffed by 30,000 magistrates (lay people who see the work as an expression of public service) and deal with less serious crime. The (higher) Crown Courts, of which the highest is the Old Bailey, in London, are staffed by 2000 judges and Recorders (experienced legal professionals appointed by the Lord Chancellor) to deal with more serious cases. A wide-range of voluntary organisations, national and local, have historically campaigned for legal and penal reform, and provided services to offenders; more recently, it is through voluntary organisations that the voice of crime victims has impacted a little on policy-making (Victim Support, 1995).

Crime and the fear of crime

Crime recorded by the police has increased inexorably since the turn of the century, markedly so in the post-war period, and spectacularly so since 1979, when a Conservative government under Margaret Thatcher came to power, committed to monetarist economics, neoliberal social policies and a tough stance on 'law-and-order'. In 1979 2.5 million crimes were recorded by the police, 5.2 million in 1994, testimony, in the main to the growth of unemployment, alienation and the pervasiveness of the acquisitive ethic during this period. Thereafter recorded crime began to fall, to 4.5 million in 1997, prompting claims by Conservative Home Secretary Michael Howard, that tough penal polices were working. Many observers were sceptical, both about the evidence and the explanation, because recorded crime is vulnerable both to increasing categories of criminal offences, changes in police recording practices and under-reporting by the public. It was only when the British Crime Survey (BCS) - a large-scale survey of victimisation begun by the Home Office in 1982, and undertaken thereafter at two yearly intervals - appeared to confirm this that a small degree of optimism set in, though the explanation remained contentious. The BCS had always shown that actual levels of crime were three times that of recorded crime; in 1998 that level had dropped.

Returning to recorded crime, 91 per cent is property crime, only 8 per cent is violent crime. Of the property crime a large proportion is burglary, theft of and from cars. Of the violence, minor wounding is by far the most common. Major wounding is rare, and in England and Wales, homicide accounts for approximately 700 offences per year. The trend in violent crime however, is against the general trend; it is rising, and as it is violent crime (whose prevalence, by dint of its drama and newsworthiness is magnified in press and television reporting) which creates public anxiety and fuels demands for ever tougher penalties, the sense of crime as a social problem cannot be said to be lessening. Fear of crime is high, even among old people who are statistically less likely to be victims of it; for this the media are largely responsible. Experience has shown that the mood of Britain can be profoundly altered by saturation reporting and analysis of quite atypical violent events, as happened in February 1993, when two ten year old boys murdered a two year old boy (James Bulger) in Liverpool. Killings of children by children are extremely rare, as are killings by strangers. 54 per cent male and 79 per cent female homicide victims are known to their assailants (as partner, spouse or friend) - and knives are by far the most common form of lethal weapon. Organised gangs, often involved in 'turf-wars' over drug dealing, are responsible for several murders per year.

Offenders in Britain are predominantly young men. Just over 40 per cent of all recorded offenders are under 21 years of age; one quarter are between 10 and 17. Over 83 per cent of crime is committed by men, and crimes committed by women of all ages are even more likely to be property crimes. Youth crime also correlates strongly with low family income, parental criminality, poor parental supervision, underachievement at school, lack of marketable skills, and, to a lesser extent, with the availability of drugs (about which there is growing concern in Britain). Explanations of the gender difference tend to centre on the greater informal social control exerted over young girls by their families, women's greater involvement with domestic tasks (giving them less opportunity for crime), and cultural norms which encourage aggression and assertiveness among males but not among females.

Statistics on race and crime are less comprehensive and harder to interpret. Some 5 per cent of Britain's population is non-white, and is concentrated predominantly in large urban areas. While there is clear evidence that African-Caribbean people are arrested, convicted and imprisoned on a scale disproportionate to their numbers in the population, it cannot be decisively inferred that they are more involved in crime. The belief that they are, rests on the fact that such 'black' communities tend to be more economically disadvantaged, younger, and denied legitimate opportunities for work and material advancement by the 'institutionalised racism' in the wider society. Alternatively, the racism of criminal justice agencies themselves, particularly the police and the courts, are blamed for the selective apprehension of black offenders. The race dimension is further complicated by evidence that crime, and involvement in the criminal justice system is *lower* among Asian people in Britain than among whites, yet they experience racism too. But unlike the black community, they are more integrated into commercial life, and traditionally at least, their children have done well at school (Home Office, 1997; Smith, 1997).

Justice for young offenders

Specialist residential provision for young offenders in England and Wales was created in the mid-nineteenth century, a specialist prison for 16-21 year olds (called 'borstal', but modelled on American reformatories) in 1907 and a specialist Juvenile Court in 1908. The ethos of these provisions was allegedly rehabilitative; in practice, particularly in residential care, the reality could sometimes be rather punitive. The national network of residential establishments for 8-17 year olds was called 'the approved school system' between 1933 and 1969, thereafter they became, and remain community homes, with or without education on the premises, administered by local government, sometimes in partnership with voluntary organisations. A succession of scandals in the 1980s and 1990s, created by adult ex-residents of these establishments, have revealed that far from being caring environments for difficult and disturbed children, many were places where systematic physical and sexual abuse occurred; it is perhaps unsurprising that a large number of adult offenders have histories of being 'in care'. Residential care is used much less for offenders than it used to be.

The Juvenile Court itself existed until 1991, thereafter it became the Youth Court and the once-dominant principle of commitment to the child's welfare, thinking in terms of meeting their underlying needs, rather than merely punishing their deeds, was weakened, if not eclipsed. The commitment to welfare had been legally at its strongest in the years after the passing of the Children and Young Persons Act 1969, but the impact was short-lived. Mounting research evidence questioned the effectiveness of welfare-based penalties and the moral worth of the rehabilitative ideal (for adults as well as for juveniles). This, combined with a revival of belief in the importance of punishment (especially after Thatcher's election in 1979), meant that the 1969 Act never fulfilled its promise. One measure within it, however, called at the time 'intermediate treatment', stimulated local authority Social Services Departments to develop imaginative community-based alternatives to residential care, and later custody, for young offenders, with the result, in the late 1980s, that the use of custody for offenders under 17 had fallen to less than 2000. Although, in the early 1990s, there was a police and media-based backlash against the allegedly lenient treatment of young offenders, causing numbers sentenced to custody to rise again. The administrative structures established to deliver 'intermediate treatment' have formed the basis of the most recent, and most elaborate initiative in youth crime, the multi-agency Youth Offending Teams (comprising local representatives from local authority social work, probation, police, health and education services) established by the New Labour government's Crime and Disorder Act 1998. These teams are intended to streamline and improve existing measures for young offenders, as well as tentatively introducing a new element of 'restorative justice' (allowing victims to challenge young offenders, and/or encouraging the latter to make amends).

Particularly unpleasant crimes, or perceived crime-waves by young people, periodically elicit calls, usually by politicians or press, for the reintroduction of whipping as a means of restoring order and respect for authority. Officialdom nowadays gives them no credence (Adams, 1998). Judicial whipping of young offenders was abolished in England and Wales and Scotland in 1948, and in Northern Ireland in 1968. It lingered on in the Isle of Man, a small island off north west England with the constitutional status of Crown Colony (akin to the Straits Settlements, once part of 'Malaya') until compelled to stop after the intervention of the European Commission on Human Rights, to which Britain was a signatory, in 1974. The original case against whipping - the absence of evidence for a deterrent effect, tinged with a sense that the infliction of pain on bare buttocks was excessively humiliating to the offender - was persuasively made by the Cadogan Committee (Home Office, 1938); only the Second World War and its aftermath delayed its implementation until 1948. The use of whipping, of both adults and juveniles in British colonies, declined even more slowly (see Killingray, 1994).

In England and Wales two punitive measures were substituted for corporal punishment. - attendance centres (which involved young offenders attending police-run gymnasia or sports halls for two hour periods on weekends, until a sentence of 12 or 24 hours had been served), and detention centres (short, up to six month custodial sentences, with military-style discipline). Attendance centres remain available to Youth Courts, but detention centres, despite attempts to revive them 'experimentally' in the early 1980s and again in the mid 1990s, lost their distinctiveness in the 1960s, and, like borstal, became absorbed into a single custodial sentence for young offenders, currently called a 'detention and training order' (although it has had a variety of different names in the past). Custodial sentences are administered by the Prison

Service, and although these institutions seem not to have hidden histories of sexual abuse on the same scale as residential care, they are, with honourable exceptions, periodically condemned by the Prison Inspector as insanitary and badly-run, incapable of delivering the education and training which young offenders need. At the time of writing, official consideration is being given to creating a system of youth custody separate from that of adult custody.

Most apprehended young offenders are not dealt with by residential or custodial measures. 60 per cent are cautioned (warned by the police) rather than prosecuted and of these approximately 50 per cent are never known to reoffend (Home Office, 1999). In the context of a caution, some are required to meet their victims, hopefully to feel ashamed and apologise, and/or to participate in voluntary recreational activities which may help them mature. If prosecuted, the courts have a range of community-based measures available to them, in particular a variety of educational and therapeutic programmes (whose precise details vary between localities) designed to challenge the attitudes that led to offending, set within the framework of a Supervision Order, or, for older youngsters, a Probation Order. Community Service Orders and Combination Orders (a mix of probation and community service) are also available for over 16 and 17 year olds. Fines and Compensation Orders (money paid to the victim) are available for all young offenders between 10 and 18, with parents being liable for punishment if their children don't pay, in order to increase their sense of responsibility for their offspring's behaviour.

A special set of measures exists for the small numbers of young people who commit grave crimes, e.g. murder or rape, dating from Section 53 of the Children and Young Persons Act 1933, which had abolished capital punishment for offenders under 18. These offenders, of whom the boys who killed James Bulger in 1993 are two of the most recent, are initially processed through a small network of specialised Youth Treatment Centres, and sometimes community homes with education, before passing into the young adult penal system at age 18, and the adult system at age 21. They are released only when psychiatric experts have deemed them safe, and when the Home Secretary believes it to be in the public interest. The European Commission on Human Rights has cast doubt on the Home Secretary's role in these matters, because of the unseemly political capital that was made out of the Bulger killers' trial. A further, equally ill-thought out consequence of the Bulger killing was a government proposal for persistent (as opposed to grave) young offenders in the

12-15 age range to be contained in five special custodial centres, run by private sector organisations. Three have been opened so far; the first was not well managed (Department of Health/Social Services Inspectorate, 1998).

Penal policy in disarray

As the Millennium turned, 65,298 people were imprisoned in England and Wales, with many commentators, both academic and official, fearful of further rises (Cavadino, Crow and Dignan, 2000)). Penal reform groups have long considered rates of custodial sentencing in England to be among the harshest in Europe, three to four times higher, proportionately, than penally liberal countries like Sweden and the Netherlands (though the crime rate is little different). Nonetheless, among the 135 establishments in the penal estate there are clearly some exemplary institutions. One particular prison, Grendon Underwood, run as a therapeutic community, has had commendable success in reducing reconvictions and there are others which are highly regarded. In many prisons, however, constructive work and education, let alone therapy for the mentally disordered offenders who find their way into prison for want of appropriate psychiatric resources, are in short supply, and the Prison Inspector, as well as penal reform groups, and reformed ex-offenders (e.g. Leech, 1993) frequently have occasion to find fault with their work, including, sometimes, instances of staff brutality towards inmates.

There is a tragic dimension to all this, for as recently as the late 1980s and early 1990s Home Office policies had been set fair to modernise the penal system, reduce the use of prison and boost the use of community penalties such as probation and community service - so long as they were designated 'punishment in the community', toughened-up and distanced from their benevolent association with social work (Dunbar and Langdon, 1998). The roots of this policy lay primarily in a recognition that imprisonment was not a cost-effective measure, the desire of the then Conservative government to reduce public expenditure. Entwined with it was acceptance, by Douglas Hurd, the relatively liberal Home Secretary at the time, that prison was often inhumane, and best used as a last resort with violent and dangerous offenders from whom society could gain protection in no other way. The coincidental occurrence of Britain's most serious prison riot, at Strangeways Prison, Manchester in 1990, focussed public debate on the limitations of imprisonment, and the Woolf Report

(Home Office, 1990), based on the enquiry into the riot and on the general state of the prison system at the time, produced a blueprint for a markedly more rational penal system. It was welcomed by all informed commentators.

The Criminal Justice Act 1991, on the other hand, created unease. The corollary of its emphasis on *'punishment* in the community', were tight restrictions on custodial sentencing, and significant voices among the magistrates and the judges claimed openly that this constituted political interference with the traditional independence of the judiciary. Police organisations felt the Act to be unduly lenient, tending never to believe that community penalties were adequate punishments for offenders whom they had devoted time and energy to apprehending. The Probation Service, on the other hand, argued that despite the Act's intention to reduce the prison population it was actually too punitive and resisted efforts to toughen their social work interventions (Worral, 1997). It particularly disliked the idea of the electronic monitoring of offenders, a measure imported from America, and welcomed the apparent failure of the Home Office's first localised experiments with it, as an alternative to custody for remand (pre-sentence) prisoners.

Under the influence of the 1991 Act, a pre-existing dip in the use of prison accelerated and the population fell to 42,000 in February 1993. Had Jamie Bulger not been murdered that month it may have fallen further. Such was the intensity of national and moral reappraisal after that event, a mood which sentencers felt called upon to reflect, that the sentencing not just of young offenders but also adult offenders was affected. Prison numbers began to rise. A new hardline Home Secretary, Michael Howard built ruthlessly on the new public mood, and set about reversing Douglas Hurd's key initiatives, largely in order to secure electoral advantage for the government over the opposition Labour Party, whose robust stance on law and order was, in his view, making the government look soft. Enamoured of American penal strategies, despite their manifest racism and brutality, Howard promoted a policy of 'prison works', (to incapacitate rather than reform), encouraging sentencers to use prison faster than places could be made available, offsetting the cost by inviting the private sector to build and run new prisons, and insisting publicly that increased use of imprisonment was the best means of public protection from crime. He also pressed the Probation Service to toughen-up, and established new experiments with electronic monitoring, this time with sentenced prisoners, but run, as before, by the private sector. By 1997, the prison population was 62,000. It was widely accepted by penal reform groups, the Prison Inspector and the Prison and Probation Services themselves, that 20,000 of these prisoners should not have been there, and would, if Howard had not undermined the principles behind the CJA 1991, have been subject to community penalties (Hicks, 1998).

Howard (a lawyer by background) has been the most punitive Home Secretary of recent times, but it is significant that even he never supported capital punishment. Hanging, the traditional method of execution in Britain, was abolished in Britain in 1969 and despite known public support for it, especially in the case of child murder and the murder of Britain's mostly unarmed police officers, Parliament has never voted to restore it. It was abolished, largely for thee reasons, after a campaign which stretched back into the nineteenth century. Firstly, there were statistical doubts about its supposed deterrent effect on potential murderers; secondly, it was inconsistent with the rehabilitative ethos of 1960s penal policy; and thirdly, it was not foolproof - clear evidence had emerged that certain individuals had been wrongly convicted and hanged (Block and Hostettler, 1997). Of the three reasons, the fallibility and prejudice of the criminal justice process remains powerful and the wrongful conviction and imprisonment of two groups of alleged Irish terrorists, one group of alleged child murderers, and an alleged sex offender, all exonerated in the 1990s after serving long sentences, has (quite apart from European directives on the matter), made it unlikely that capital punishment will ever be reintroduced in Britain.

Its abolition, however, has led to the accumulation of large numbers of 'lifers' in the prison system (an indeterminate 'life sentence', with release at the discretion of the Home Secretary, being the substitute for execution) and to heated public debate as to how much time in prison a life sentence should actually entail. It was not envisaged as, and has not traditionally been a *literal* life sentence, but during Howard's tenure of the Home Office approximately 25 lifers, guilty of particularly heinous killings, were informed that they will never be released (Newell and Cullen, 1999).

The Howard era left a depressing legacy for the New Labour government, elected to office in May 1997. New Labour gained power because it had reconciled itself to the market economy established under the Conservatives, and abandoned its historic but electorally unpopular 'socialist' commitment to the redistribution of wealth. It had used the law and order issue to win votes as astutely as the Conservatives had ever done, and whilst promising to be tough on the social and economic causes of crime, whose influence Conservatives had sought to deny, its promise to be tough on crime itself helped it to victory. New Labour were, to say the least, sanguine about the rising rate of imprisonment. While the new Home Secretary, Jack Straw, had never endorsed the crude principle of 'prison works' while in opposition, he was nonetheless powerless to impede the momentum behind custodial sentencing, hence its rise in 1999 to 65,298) (with a figure of 80,000 projected in the early years of the new century). Straw reneged spectacularly on an opposition promise to end prison privatisation, insisting that he now needed the space that only the private sector could provide quickly. He also continued Michael Howard's plans to develop electronic monitoring as a nationwide provision (from December 1999), both as a sentence and as a means of facilitating, and supervising, early release from prison (Whitfield, 1998). His plans for the Probation Service have proved even more drastic than Howard's - centralisng control of what had hitherto been a locally-based body and closer ideological and administrative alignment with the Prison Service, with which Probation had traditionally been in creative tension. Compared to the vision that existed at the time of the Woolf Report, these are not constructive developments. Other New Labour strategies, however, are more promising.

The emergence of crime prevention policy

The most important by-product from the early British Crime Surveys, which had merely been intended to map the real extent of crime, was the realisation that, in respect of crimes such as domestic violence, theft, burglary and criminal damage, only a very small proportion were ever processed by the criminal justice system. Formal criminal justice agencies did not prevent crime in the way that they were conventionally thought to do. They were mostly reactive. This 'discovery' coincided with the growing recognition in the police force that their effectiveness in reducing crime, which was increasingly being subject to the rigours of cost-benefit analysis, was most likely to be improved if they worked more closely with other statutory agencies. These developments, coupled with some strategic thinking in the Home Office and some good preliminary results from several 'Safer City' projects in large urban areas (Tilley, 1993) slowly shifted policy-maker's, and some professional's, attention from reaction to prevention.

Preventing crime entails action which either makes crime a) more difficult to commit, or b) less likely to occur. The former is largely effected by better security measures, locks, bolts and bars on commercial and domestic premises, car immobilisation devices, street lighting schemes, neighbourhood watch, private security guards, and above all Closed Circuit Television (CCTV) surveillance, whose use expanded massively in urban Britain after it was used to apprehend the killers of James Bulger, albeit too late to prevent his death. The latter involves more longer term initiatives, supporting families to bring up well-behaved children, asking schools to instil better discipline, recreational activities for energetic adolescents and the creation of employment opportunities for them. Throughout the 1990s, central government encouraged local agencies - particularly police, social services, probation health and relevant voluntary and private sector groups - to cooperate on preventing crime, based on combinations of the above measures and on detailed audits of crime in particular localities (Crawford, 1998). A particularly elaborate multi-agency structure for dealing with drug use and drug-related crime has been established, although some critics argue that too much attention is still given to prevention and enforcement, rather than to the treatment of known offenders (Parker, 1998). In general, it may be this multiplicity of local initiatives, rather than the increasing use of imprisonment that has caused the fall in the crime rate between 1994-1998. No-one knows for certain.

Although it has had to prioritise the management of a rising prison population and to maintain tough-sounding rhetoric on law and order, New Labour has attached particular importance to a long-term crime prevention agenda. Its Crime and Disorder Act 1998 put local multi-agency cooperation on a statutory footing (hitherto it had been voluntary, and therefore variable), and has required local government to draw up an annual 'community safety' plan for their area. These *might* include group curfews on youngsters under 10, out on the street after 8pm and thought to be at risk of crime by police and local authorities. The same Act has introduced a new set of measures to deal with anti-social neighbours, lax parents, the surveillance of known sex offenders and a variety of racially aggravated offences, such that if an assault, robbery or act of criminal damage can be shown in court to have a racial motivation, penalties will be greater. The murder of a black teenager, Stephen Lawrence in 1993, and the subsequent public enquiry into the incompetence of the police investigation into his death, has lent credence to such measures (Cathcart, 1999).

New Labour's specific policies on crime, unlike those of their Conservative predecessors, are set in the context of broader plans to reduce 'social exclusion' (poverty and political marginality) among young men and women, through welfare-to-work schemes and increased educational opportunity. Whether these plans are equal to the challenge is a moot point (Davies, 1997). There is certainly greater political acceptance that the social and economic context can have an effect on crime and that punitive measures, whilst necessary, are never likely to be effective on their own. In the interests of creating safer communities, effectiveness and its counterparts in managerial discourse, efficiency and economy, are now the watchwords of crime policy in Britain, and serious efforts are being made to ensure that all policy and practice, in prisons, probation and the crime prevention field are all research-based, and thereafter, evidence-led (Goldblatt and Lewis, 1998). While this attempt to put crime policy on a rational footing is to be welcomed, even the recent historical record suggests that it will remain vulnerable to the vicissitudes of the public mood, over-reaction to some events (James Bulger), under-reaction to others (Stephen Lawrence), and to the vagaries of political ambition.

References

Adams, R. (1998), *The Abuses of Punishment*, MacMillan, Basingstoke.
Block, B.P. and Hostettler, J. (1997), *Hanging in the Balance: A History of Capital Punishment in Britain*, Waterside Press, Winchester.
Blom-Cooper, L. (1997), *The Birmingham Six and other Cases: Victims of Circumstance*, Duckworth, London.
Cathcart, B. (1999), *The Murder of Stephen Lawrence*, Viking, London.
Cavadino, M., Crow, I. and Dignan, J. (2000), *Criminal Justice 2000: Strategies for a New Century*, Waterside Press, Winchester.
Crawford, A. (1998), *Crime Prevention and Community Safety: Politics, Policies and Practices*, Longman, Harlow.
Davies, N. (1997), *Dark Heart: The Shocking Truth about Hidden Britain*, Chatto and Windus, London.
Department of Health/Social Services Inspectorate (1998), *Inspection of Medway Secure Training Centre*, Department of Health, London.
Dunbar, I. and Langdon, A. (1998), *Tough Justice: Sentencing and Penal Policies in the 1990s*, Blackstones, London.
Goldblatt, P. and Lewis, C. (1998), *Reducing Offending: An Assessment of Research Evidence on Ways of Dealing with Offending Behaviour*. Home Office Research Study 187, Home Office, London.
Hicks, J. (1998), 'New Politics, New Probation, New Bind?' in D. Faulkner and A. Gibbs (eds), *New Politics, New Probation*, Proceedings of the Probation

Studies Unit Second Colloquium, University of Oxford Centre for Criminological Research, Oxford.
Home Office (1938), *Report of the Departmental Committee on Corporal Punishment (The Cadogan Report)*, Cmd. 2831, HMSO, London.
Home Office (1991), *Prison Disturbances April 1990: Report of an Inquiry*, (The Woolf Report), Cmd. 1456, HMSO, London.
Home Office (1997), *Race and the Criminal Justice System*, Home Office, London.
Home Office (1999), *Information on the Criminal Justice System in England and Wales - Digest 4*, Home Office, London.
Killingray, D. (1994), 'The "Rod of Empire" The Debate over Corporal Punishment in the British African Colonial Forces 1888- 1946', *Journal of African History*, vol. 35, pp.201-16.
Leech, M. (1993), *A Product of the System: My Life in and Out of Prison*, Gollancz, London.
Nelken, D. (1997), 'Understanding Criminal Justice Comparatively', in R. Maguire, R. Morgan and R. Reiner (eds), *The Oxford Handbook of Criminology*, Clarendon Press, Oxford.
Newell, T. and Cullen, E. (1999), *Murder and Life Imprisonment*, Waterside Press, Winchester.
Parker, H. (1999), 'What a Waste', *The Guardian* (Society), 26th May
Smith, D.J. (1997), 'Ethnic Origins, Crime and Criminal Justice', in R. Maguire, R. Morgan and R. Reiner (eds), *The Oxford Handbook of Criminology*, Clarendon Press, Oxford.
Tilley, N. (1993), 'Crime Prevention and the Safer Cities Story', *Howard Journal*, vol. 32, pp.40-57.
Victim Support (1995), *The Rights of Victims of Crime*, Victim Support, London.
Whitfield, D. (1998), *Tackling the Tag: The Electronic Monitoring of Offenders*, Waterside Press, Winchester.
Worral, A. (1997), *Punishment in the Community: The Future of Criminal Justice*, Longman, Harlow.

13 Imprisonment in Malaysia
ABDUL HADI ZAKARIAH

Introduction

In Malaysia, the manner in which offenders are dealt with by the criminal justice system is a legacy of the tradition introduced to the island of Penang by the British colonial masters about a hundred years ago. Twenty one years after Francis Light acquired Penang from the Sultan of Kedah in 1786, a Royal Charter of Justice of 1807 established the Court of Judicature of Prince of Wales' Island (as Penang was then known), thus marking the introduction of English law into this country (Wu, 1999). From then, British control and influence over the affairs of Malay States was exerted gradually until 1930 when the ruler of the last of those states to submit to British influence accepted a British advisor.

A major preoccupation of the British authorities during the years immediately following the introduction of English law into the country then was the maintenance of law and order. In achieving this objective, '...local customs and laws were allowed to continue but tempered by such portions of the English law as were considered just and expedient' (Wu, 1999, p.13). It is no coincidence then that the Royal Charter of 1807 also provided for the establishment of the forerunner of the Royal Malaysia Police force (Ibrahim, 1987). It was also in the island of Penang that the first prison in the country was built in 1849 (Yeoh, 1998). Later, as the British consolidated their control over the Malay States following the Anglo-Dutch Treaty of 1824, more prisons were built for the purpose of housing offenders. It is worth noting that these institutions were modelled after prisons in England and were administered according to the practice of Her Majesty's Prison Service.

Knowledge of the present-day crimes that are brought to the attention of, and dealt with by, this system is provided by the Royal Malaysia Police. In summarising the crime statistics for the period 1992-1994, Zakariah (2000) notes, of those crimes occurring sufficiently regularly that they are recorded, that the total number was fairly constant. This also applied to reported crimes against the person, accounting as they did for about 48 per cent of the total. Of offences against property, burglary, either during the day or the night, was most frequent, followed by theft of vehicles.

In considering sentences for those found guilty of offences, the courts have recourse to a number of options. The most commonly imposed are sentences of death, imprisonment, whipping and fines, with imprisonment being the most heavily used.

The following discussion focuses on the efficacy of imprisonment as a tool for the reduction of crime.

Imprisonment

Imprisonment may be divided into three categories, namely, imprisonment for life, imprisonment for a definite period, and imprisonment in default of payment of a fine.

According to section 3 of the Criminal Justice Act 1953, the general meaning accorded to the term imprisonment for life (or life imprisonment) is a prison sentence of twenty years. A similar view is expressed by section 57 of the Penal Code (of Malaysia). Specific statutes, however, have given a new meaning to the phrase imprisonment for life, namely, imprisonment for natural life, for example, the Firearms (Increased Penalties) Act 1971, the Arms Act 1960 and section 130A of the Penal Code. Offenders found guilty under these statutes will be subjected to that interpretation of the phrase. Mimi Kamariah Majid (1995) expresses surprise that the Internal Security Act 1960 and the Dangerous Drugs Act 1952 have not followed suit.

On the issue of imprisonment for a definite period, section 282(d) of the Criminal Procedure Code (of Malaysia) stipulates that every sentence of imprisonment takes effect from the date on which it was passed unless the court passing such sentence otherwise directs. The alternatives often resorted to by Malaysian courts include orders for imprisonment to commence from the date the offender was arrested or from the date of the offender's conviction. The first option is usually applied if the court is of the view that the offender has suffered enough punishment prior to the date of sentence, particularly if the offender was on remand prior to trial in court. The second option is normally applied if dates of conviction and sentence differ. This sometimes happens when probation reports or medical reports need to be prepared prior to sentence, but are not available on the day of conviction.

As regards imprisonment in default of a fine, section 283(1)(b)(4) of the Criminal Procedure Code stipulates that the court passing the sentence of a fine may direct that in default of payment of the fine, the offender shall suffer imprisonment for a certain term. Nonetheless, if time is allowed for the payment of such a fine, an order for imprisonment in default shall not be issued unless it appears to the court that such person has no property or insufficient property to satisfy the fine payable, or that the levy of distress will be more injurious to him or his family than imprisonment. Section 102, proviso (c) of the Subordinate Courts Act stipulates that when imprisonment is directed in default of payment of a fine or of costs or compensation ordered under the authority of any law in force, the imprisonment shall be consecutive to any other term or terms of imprisonment to which the offender may have been sentenced or to which he may be liable under a commutation of sentence.

A schedule is set which determines the quantum of imprisonment for cases where imprisonment in default of payment of a fine is imposed on an offender who has been convicted of an offence not punishable with imprisonment. Thus, where the fine does not exceed RM25, the period shall not exceed two months, where the fine exceeds RM25 but does not exceed RM50, the period shall not exceed four months, and where the fine exceeds RM50, the period shall not exceed six months (Majid, 1995). Although the provision is unclear, it appears that the amount of fines mentioned refer to the actual amount imposed by the court, not the maximum specified by statute. Besides, there are many offences punishable with fines where the amount is not specified by statute.

The imprisonment in default shall terminate whenever the fine is either paid or levied by process of law. If, before the expiration of the time of imprisonment fixed in default of payment, such a proportion of the fine be paid or levied that the time of imprisonment suffered in default of payment is not less than proportional to the part of the fine still unpaid, the imprisonment shall terminate. The fine, or any part thereof which remains unpaid, may be levied at any time within six years after the passing of the sentence. If under the sentence, the offender be liable to imprisonment for a longer period than six years, the fine may be levied at any time previous to the expiration of that period. In both these situations, the death of the offender does not discharge from the liability any property which would after his death be legally liable for his debts (Majid, 1995).

As is the case elsewhere, the sentence of imprisonment allegedly serves a multitude of purposes, the most frequently cited being retribution, reduction of crime, and as an expression society's abhorrence of crime. The retributive aim seeks to retaliate against the wrong doer for his offence which is viewed as an offence against society and the community, and in return society and the community through its agency, the courts, impose punishments or sentences. In modern times, and particularly with reference to Malaysia, the best example of this aim is entrenched in the legislation in the form of the mandatory death penalty for the offence of murder under section 302 of the Penal Code. The very existence of such punishments for their respective offences shows that society will not hesitate to retaliate for any infraction or infringement of its criminal laws. The reductive aim seeks to reduce the incidence of crime through any one or more of at least four means - deterring the offender from committing further offences in the future, deterring potential imitators from committing offences, providing offenders an opportunity for reformation and rehabilitation, and persuading the general public to take notice of the problem of crime in their community. The expressive aim suggests that the offender is punished not because he has committed something heinous, but merely to show that the offence in question is something to be abhorred by the community (Newman, 1978; Walker, 1980; Bean, 1981).

The prisons department of Malaysia

Offenders who are sentenced to imprisonment usually serve their sentences in one of the 27 prisons. As of 31st. August 1999, these institutions house about 22,000 adult prisoners, 45 per cent of whom are on remand. Females constitute about 4 per cent of the total. However, young adult offenders, that is, those between the ages of 18 and 21 years, usually, but not always, are committed to one of 4 advanced approved schools run by the Prisons Department. These institutions hold slightly less than 1000 inmates, 7 per cent of whom are females who are held in two of the institutions.

Generally, the responsibility of Malaysian prisons revolves around three main objectives. First is to ensure that prisoners are detained in custody until their release as ordered by the courts. This entails that effective measures are taken to ensure that all prisoners serve their respective sentences. Second is to ensure the safe custody of the prisoners throughout the duration of their detention through the maintenance of all rules, regulations and discipline to ensure a safe environment for all prisoners. Third is the rehabilitation of the prisoners.

It may be noted that the last objective has some resemblance to the reductive aim of imprisonment. So how does imprisonment reduce crime? We seek to answer this question through a discussion of three effects of imprisonment, namely, incapacitation, rehabilitation, and deterrence.

Incapacitation

Incapacitation is easily the most direct effect of imprisonment felt by offenders sentenced therein. It is not difficult to visualize imprisonment and other forms of incarceration as the most reliable means of preventing crime (Box-Grainger, 1986; Fox, 1952; Schrag, 1977). It does not require any modification of the custodial function to achieve the preventive objective. While the person is in custody, he/she is physically separated from factors which facilitate deviance, and cannot commit further deviance in the larger society: prevention is achieved for so long as custody lasts. While in custody, prisoners are denied the opportunity to acquire and utilize the factors necessary for any intended infraction (Matza, 1964; Hirschi, 1969; Lofland, 1969; Box, 1971; Clarke, 1980). These factors have been identified as facilitating places, hardware, others and actors (Lofland, 1969), and as skills, supply and social and symbolic support (Box, 1971).

A proper scrutiny of the argument above, however, shows that imprisonment is more likely to affect those individuals actually incarcerated than the actual incidence of crime in society. Thus it is reported that in England, imprisonment could reduce the incidence of crime by between 5 and 20 per cent (Brody and Tarling, 1980), whilst in the United States by between 10 and 20 per cent (Cohen, 1983). No similar studies have been conducted in Malaysia, but judging by the rate of recidivism in the country, rehabilitation in prisons seems to have some preventive effect. As at 31st. December 1995, only 48 per cent of all convicted prisoners were recidivists, the rest being first timers.

Rehabilitation

The view that criminal behaviour may be prevented through rehabilitation occurs regularly in theoretical expositions relating to such behaviour (Merton, 1957; Nye, 1958; Sutherland, 1973; Walker, 1985; Hollin, 1989). It is based on the notion that criminal behaviour and abnormality or some form of deficiency have some links and that human behaviour is the product of antecedent causes (Pursley, 1977; Palmer, 1984). It follows that if such abnormalities can be corrected, the criminal can be 'reinstated to his or her old dignity and privileges, before the fall' (Mathiesen, 1990, p.20). In the course of achieving this end, rehabilitation has been turned into a generic term which is capable of being ambiguous and vague. It has been variously described as a measure aimed at improving the quality of the offenders' lives by reshaping them into 'more effective, self-sufficient, self-actualized, socially aware, and socially involved individuals' (Irwin, 1974, p.140), or as a measure to enable offenders to return to society as independently functioning individuals (Wilmont, 1976), or as a measure to enable offenders to 're-enter society as contributing citizens, or, at least, not dangerous ones' (Fox, 1977, p.182), or as a measure for the improvement of offenders as husbands, workers and fathers (Walker, 1980). As a process, rehabilitation is multi-faceted and is based on social-scientific, and particularly psychological notions of adjustment. It is directed towards helping offenders by promoting law-abiding behaviour on their part so that they would be more acceptable to other members of society.

The Prisons Department of Malaysia adopted a similar notion of rehabilitation, namely, to facilitate prisoners to regain their self-respect and eventually return to the community as law-abiding and socially productive persons. In keeping with this notion, rehabilitation in prisons is implemented along three major routes. One, and the most established, is the provision of vocational training to all prisoners with a view to making them better equipped and more confident to compete in the labour market and to cope with the hardships of life.

Vocational training and prison work are an integral part of Malaysian prison life. Section 74 of the Prison Rules 1953 stipulates that every prisoner is to be engaged in useful work, preferably in groups outside their cells. Thus a typical prison in Malaysia would provide training in carpentry and woodwork, tailoring, laundry services, iron mongering, training in motor mechanics, printing and book-binding and copper tooling. Female prisoners focus on tailoring, hair dressing and knitting. It is felt that the skills they would eventually acquire would equip prisoners to obtain employment in non-deviant jobs and live on the wages accruing from such jobs without resorting to deviant behaviour to fulfil their needs.

The second is what Nigel Walker (1980) calls reformation, or what Schrag (1977) calls therapeutic or restorative functions of rehabilitation. This comprises of measures which seek to change the attitudes of the prisoners so that they would be less inclined to resort to unlawful behaviour to achieve their needs, even when they can do so without fear of the penalty (Bainbridge, 1989; Duffee and O'Leary, 1971; Wilson,

1978; Walker, 1980; Sloane and Potvin, 1986). In fact, Sloane and Potvin express full confidence that there was an association between religion and delinquency 'that is not confined to certain offenses or to certain subgroups or social contexts' (1986, p.104). All prisoners thus undergo a programme of religious training and guidance, and counselling all of which seek to induce the desired behavioural changes on the part of the offenders. All prisons also provide ample opportunities for prisoners to pursue their respective academic interests, if any. Members of different religious groups are allocated time and space for the observance of their respective religious obligations. By being reformed as such, they then would refrain from committing offences and cease to cause the community any more inconvenience, money or injury because of an inner conviction on their part that such behaviour is intrinsically undesirable to them.

The third route seeks to improve the prisoners' ability to relate to their significant others so that they (the prisoners) would be able to re-assimilate themselves socially after their release from the institutions. This requires the development of an offender's competence to promote a congenial relationship between them and their family in particular, and their community in general, with a view to strengthening their bonds to and promote their re-assimilation into their family and community. In this way, it is hoped that they can be re-assimilated into groups which emphasize values conducive to law-abiding behaviour, and, simultaneously, be alienated from groups emphasizing values conducive to criminality, and indirectly, pressures towards re-offending are reduced (Cressey, 1955; Hirschi, 1969; Price, 1969-1970; Box, 1971; Rogers, 1977). When ex-prisoners are assimilated into their communities, they are assumed to be bonded to the community, and control theories of criminal behaviour hold that people who are strongly bonded to the community are unlikely to commit offences (for example, Hirschi, 1969; West and Farrington, 1973; Campbell, 1981; West, 1982; Wilson, 1987; Lilly et al, 1989; Rosenbaum, 1989).

Malaysian prison authorities subscribe strongly to the idea of re-assimilation of prisoners. It is entrenched in Part 10 of the Prison Rules that all prisoners are allowed to receive visitors regularly, subject to certain conditions and regulations. They are also encouraged to write to their beloved persons and receive letters which are subject to censorship by the prison authorities. Additionally, time is allocated for all prisoners to engage in outdoor recreational activities.

Deterrence

Deterrence theory suggests that people do not dare commit crimes, even if they wanted or are able to, because they fear the negative consequences of violating the law (e.g. Bentham, 1948; Andenaes, 1966; Gibbs, 1968; Zimring and Hawkins, 1973; Walker, 1980; Walker, 1985). The notion of deterrence itself is somewhat slippery, but Walker's comprehensive definition is useful. To him, 'to deter someone from doing something is to influence him by a threat or threats so that he refrains from doing it, postpones doing it, does it somewhere else, gets someone else to do it, or finds other ways of achieving his aim' (1985, p.95). The threat is taken generally to mean the threat of some form of pain, or unpleasantness, or hardship resulting from the infliction of punishment (Zimring and Hawkins, 1973). In the context of this chapter, the threat is that of the possibility of one being sentenced to imprisonment. The fear generated by this threat supposedly inhibits potential offenders, or potential recidivists and society is therefore protected from harmful acts.

What are the effects?

Little can be said about the effectiveness of imprisonment as a mechanism for crime prevention in the country, for knowledge in this area is almost non-existent. The closest, albeit not the most reliable, indicator that we have is the finding that the recidivism rate hovers around 48 per cent. We interpret this figure into two opposite ways. One way is in support of the prison. An offender may have been fully rehabilitated, but yet, on being released, he faces extremely hostile social circumstances that eventually force him to commit offences and be committed into the prison. This possibility is real and has been discussed widely by critics of the prison. Imprisonment or the imposition of official measures on offenders have some undesirable side effects which need to be controlled because processing through the criminal justice system can result in a person suffering from certain inherent negative consequences, the most widely acknowledged of which is stigmatisation (Goffman, 1970; Walker, 1980; Spicker, 1984) which occurs because of the stigmatic propensity of both the process of custody (Walker 1980) and of custodial institutions themselves (Goffman, 1970; Spicker, 1984). An absence of measures or programmes to adequately negate these consequences may have two main effects, namely, the rejection of ex-inmates by the larger society, thereby reducing the effectiveness of preventive efforts, and the enhancement of the deviantising process experienced by the deviant actors thereby amplifying their deviance (Martin and Webster, 1971; Brodsky, 1975; Wilkins, 1964; Schur, 1980).

The second proposition is the direct opposite. Rehabilitation in prison is so ineffective that the reformation, vocational training and remedial training programmes therein have failed to change the criminal inclinations of the prisoners, to improve their marketability in the labour market and to help them develop congenial relationships with their significant others. Consequently, released prisoners find themselves unable to be re-assimilated into mainstream society, thus forcing them into committing further criminal acts which eventually lead them to be sent to the prison again.

Thus, both the possibility of uncontrolled stigmatisation of ex-prisoners and the ineffective training programmes in the prisons seem to render prison rehabilitation a futile exercise. A perusal of the characteristics of Malaysian prisoners and the conditions under which training is carried out may lend credence to this view. Almost 58 per cent of Malaysian prisoners are below 30 years old. Likewise 59 per cent either have never been to school or have received primary school education only. As regards income, 50 per cent were earning less than RM500 per month at the time of their conviction, whilst another 23 per cent were unemployed. All these characteristics point to their belonging to the lower social classes, and least likely to be amenable to training.

This brings us to the next line of criticism of rehabilitation in prison. Before embarking on the criticisms, it may worth mentioning that Malaysian prison subscribes to the philosophy of the Tudor times that 'idleness is the mother and root of all vices'. Similarly, some form of physical activity, of which vocational training is a type, would arrest the process of the deterioration of the personality, and help pass time more quickly. Despite its possible positive attributes, vocational training in Malaysian prison is not free from the general problems faced by all custodial institutions.

The first criticism pertains to the type of skills taught in the prisons. It is well known that the types of skills which can be taught depend on the availability of instructors who may be drawn from the prisoners themselves or from the staff. Prisoners come and go. Similarly, members of prison staff are subject to transfers. This suggests that the skills taught are those which are most conveniently available, and need not be determined by market demand, resulting in the possibility that on being released, prisoners may not be accepted for jobs for which they had been trained. Furthermore, as observed by Hall-William (1975) in England, prison workshops are not custom-built, most of the time resulting in overcrowding. This also hampers any attempt at introducing the economies of scale and full commercialisation.

More seriously, it is doubtful whether prison authorities would really desire large but economic workshop units, owing to the potential problems of custodial (rather than management) control that these units might give rise to. This touches on the issue of wholehearted commitment on the part of prison officers. Wholehearted commitment may encourage a process of accommodation between prison officers and prisoners which in turn may undermine an officer's authority.

Finally, there is the question of whether training is fully compatible with the rehabilitative aim. Whilst our data shows that at the time of conviction, 50 per cent of Malaysia prisoners were earning relatively low incomes, it does not indicate unemployment. This suggests that getting employment is not an issue amongst these persons. Rather, they need training which can facilitate the inculcation of the habit of regular and purposeful work at the tempo and in conditions as close as possible to those in open society.

References

Andeneas, J. (1966), 'The General Preventive Effects of Punishment', *Pennsylvania Law Review*, vol. 114, pp.949-983.

Bainbridge, W.S. (1989), 'The Religious Ecology of Deviance', *American Sociological Review*, vol. 54, pp.288-295.

Bentham, J. (1948), *An Introduction to the Principles of Morals and Legislation*, Basil Blackwell, Oxford.

Box, S. (1971), *Deviance, Reality and Society*, Macmillan, London.

Box, S. (1983), *Power, Crime, and Mystification*, Tavistock Publications, London.

Box-Grainger, J. (1986), 'Sentencing Rapists', in R. Matthews and J. Young (eds), *Confronting Crime*, Sage Publications, London.

Brodsky, S.L. (1975), *Families and Friends of Men in Prison*, Lexington Books, Lexington.

Brody, S.R. and Tarling, R. (1980), *Taking Offenders out of Circulation*, Home Office Research Study No.64, HMSO, London.

Campbell, A. (1981), *Girl Delinquents*, Basil Blackwell, Oxford.

Clarke, R. (1980), 'Situational Crime Prevention: Theory and Practice', *British Journal of Criminology*, vol. 20, pp.136-147.

Cohen, J. (1983), 'Incapacitation as a Strategy for Crime Control: Possibilities and Pitfalls', *Crime and Justice*, vol. 5, pp.1-84.
Cohen, L.E. and Kluegel, J.R. (1979), 'The Detention Decision: A Study of the Impact of Social Characteristics and Legal Factors in Two Metropolitan Juvenile Courts', *Social Forces*, vol. 58, pp.146-161.
Cressey, D. (1955), 'Changing Criminals: The Application of the Theory of Differential Association', *American Journal of Sociology*, vol. 16, pp.116-120.
Department of Prisons, Malaysia. (1995), *Prison Statistics*, Department of Prisons, Kuala Lumpur.
Duffee, D. and O'Leary, V. (1971), 'Models of Correction: An Entry In The Packer-Griffiths Debate', *Criminal Law Review*, vol. 7, pp.329-352.
Fox, L.W. (1952), *The English Prison and Borstal System*, Routledge and Kegan Paul, London.
Gibbs, J.P. (1968), 'Crime, Punishment and Deterrence', *Social Science Quarterly*, vol. 48, pp.515-530.
Goffman, I. (1970), *Assylums*, Pelican Books, Hammondsworth, England.
Hall-Williams, J.E. (1982), *Criminology and Criminal Justice*, Butterworths, London.
Hawkins, G. (1976), *The Prison: Policy and Practice*, University of Chicago Press, Chicago.
Hirschi, T. (1969), *Causes of Delinquency*, University of California Press, Berkerley.
Hollin, C.R. (1989), *Psychology and Crime*, Routledge, London.
Ibrahim, M.R. (1987), Polis Di Raja Malaysia - Sejarah Peranan dan Cabaran, Kuala Lumpur: Kumpulan Karangkraf.
Irwin, J. (1974), 'The Trouble With Rehabilitation', *Criminal Justice and Behaviour*, vol. 1, pp.139-149.
Lilly, J.R., Cullen, F.T. and Ball, R.A. (1989), *Criminological Theory: Context and Consequences, Newbury Park*, Sage Publications, California.
Lofland, J. (1969), *Deviance and Identity*, Prentice-Hall, Englewood Cliffs.
Martin, J.P. and Webster. D. (1971), *The Social Consequences of Conviction*, Heinemann, London.
Mathiesen, T. (1990). *Prison on Trial*, Sage, London.
Merton, R.K. (1957), *Social Theory and Social Structure*, The Free Press, New York.
Majid, M.K. (1995), *Criminal Procedure in Malaysia*, University of Malaya Press, Kuala Lumpur.
Nye, F.I. (1958), *Family Relationships and Delinquent Behavior*, John Wiley, New York.
Palmer, T. (1984), 'Treatment and the Role of Classification: A Review of Basics', *Crime and Delinquency*, vol. 30, pp.245-267.
Price, E.T. (1969-70), 'The Correction of Adult Offenders With Special Reference to South Australia', *Australian Journal of Social Issues*, pp.4-5.

Pursley, R.D. (1977), *Introduction to Criminal Justice*, Glencoe Press, California.
Rogers, J.W. (1977), *Why Are You Not A Criminal?*, Prentice-Hall, Englewood Cliffs.
Rosenbaum, J.L. (1987), 'Social Control, Gender and Delinquency: An Analysis of Drug Property and Violent Offending', *Justice Quarterly*, vol. 4, pp.117-132.
Schrag, C. (1977), 'Some Foundations for a Theory of Corrections', in R.M. Carter, D. Glaser and L.T. Wilkins (eds), *Correctional Institutions*, J.B. Lippincott, Philadelphia.
Schur, E.M. (1980), *The Politics of Deviance*, Prentice-Hall, Englewood Cliffs.
Sloane, D.M. and R.H. Potvin. (1986), 'Religion and Delinquency: Cutting Through the Maze', *Social Forces*, vol. 65, pp.87-105.
Spicker, P. (1984), *Stigma and Social Welfare*, Croom Helm, London.
Sutherland, E.H. (1973), 'Critique of the Theory', in K. Schuessler (ed), *Analyzing Crime*, University of Chicago Press, Chicago.
Walker, N. (1980), *Punishment, Danger and Stigma: The Morality of Criminal Justice*, Basil Blackwell, Oxford.
Walker, N. (1985), *Sentencing: Theory, Law and Practice*, Butterworths, London.
West, D.J. (1982), *Delinquency: Its Roots, Careers and Prospects*, Heinemann, London.
West, D J. and Farrington, D.P. (1973), *Who Becomes Delinquent?* Heinemann Educational Books, London.
Wilkins, L.T. (1964), *Social Deviance: Social Policy, Action and Research*, Tavistock Publications, London.
Wilmont, R. (1976), 'What is Rehabilitation?', *International Journal of Offender Therapy and Comparative Criminology*, vol. 20, pp.246-254.
Wilson, D. (1978), 'Sexual Codes and Conduct: A Study of Teenage Girls', in C. Smart and B. Smart (eds), *Women Sexuality and Social Control*, Routledge and Kegan Paul, London.
Wilson, H. (1980), 'Parental Supervision: A Neglected Aspect of Delinquency', *British Journal of Criminology*, vol. 20, pp.203-235.
Wilson, H. (1987), 'Parental Supervision Re-Examined', *British Journal of Criminology*, vol. 27, pp.275-301.
Wu, M.A. (1999), *The Malaysian Legal System*, Addison Wesley Longman Malaysia, Kuala Lumpur.
Yeoh, Y.H. (1998), *Penjara Sebagai Ejen Pemulihan Banduanita*, Graduation Exercise, Department of Anthropology and Sociology, University of Malaya, Kuala Lumpur.
Zakariah, A.H. (2000), 'Crime and Punishment in Malaysia', in R. Omar and J. Doling (eds), *Issues and Challenges of Social Policy East and West*, University of Malaysia Press, Kuala Lumpur.
Zimring, F. and Hawkins, G. (1973), *Deterrence: The Legal Threat in Crime Control*, University of Chicago Press, Chicago.